The Game Writing Guide

This comprehensive guide walks readers through the entire process of getting and keeping a writing job in the games industry. It outlines exactly what a beginner needs to know about education requirements, finding opportunities, applying for roles, and acing studio interviews. Professional writers will learn how to navigate studio hierarchies, transfer roles and companies, work overseas, and keep developing their careers.

Written by an experienced games writer with nearly two decades of industry knowledge, this book contains a wealth of interviews and perspectives with industry leaders, hiring managers, and developers from marginalized communities, all offering their tips and insights. Included are examples of materials such as job posts, writing samples, and portfolios, as well as chapter-end challenges for readers to directly apply the skills they have learnt.

This book will be of great interest to all beginner and aspiring games writers and narrative designers, as well as more experienced writers looking to hone their skills.

Anna Megill is an award-winning game writer and industry veteran with experience writing primarily for modern AAA games. In her nearly two decades of game development, Anna has worked for some of the top studios around the world, such as Ubisoft, Arkane, Remedy, and Square Enix. A longtime advocate for marginalized voices in games, she provides resources and advice to aspiring writers through her website. Anna currently works at Playground Games on their upcoming *Fable* game.

The Game Writing Guide
Get Your Dream Job and Keep It

Anna Megill

CRC Press
Taylor & Francis Group
Boca Raton London New York

CRC Press is an imprint of the
Taylor & Francis Group, an **informa** business

First edition published 2023
by CRC Press
6000 Broken Sound Parkway NW, Suite 300, Boca Raton, FL 33487-2742

and by CRC Press
4 Park Square, Milton Park, Abingdon, Oxon, OX14 4RN

CRC Press is an imprint of Taylor & Francis Group, LLC

© 2023 Anna Megill

The views and opinions expressed in this book are those of the author and do not necessarily reflect the views and opinions of Playground Games.

Library of Congress Cataloging-in-Publication Data
Names: Megill, Anna, author.
Title: The game writing guide : get your dream job and keep it / Anna Megill.
Description: First edition. | Boca Raton : CRC Press, 2023.
Identifiers: LCCN 2022055019 (print) | LCCN 2022055020 (ebook) | ISBN 9781032252384 (hardback) | ISBN 9781032252360 (paperback) | ISBN 9781003282235 (ebook)
Subjects: LCSH: Video games--Authorship--Vocational guidance.
Classification: LCC GV1469.34.A97 M44 2023 (print) | LCC GV1469.34.A97 (ebook) | DDC 794.8/3--dc23/eng/20220125
LC record available at https://lccn.loc.gov/2022055019
LC ebook record available at https://lccn.loc.gov/2022055020

ISBN: 978-1-032-25238-4 (hbk)
ISBN: 978-1-032-25236-0 (pbk)
ISBN: 978-1-003-28223-5 (ebk)

DOI: 10.1201/9781003282235

Typeset in Garamond
by MPS Limited, Dehradun

To Christopher Megill

The bestest big brother. You don't die in this one!

Contents

Acknowledgments

It took the strength of a thousand game writers to make this book, but I only have space to name a few. All my love and gratitude go to the following people (in no particular order) for contributing their wisdom and support.

Harvey Smith, Rhianna Pratchett, Greg Kasavin, Sam Lake, Kim Swift, Sam Maggs, Ann Lemay, Josh Scherr, Kim Belair, Whitney "Strix" Beltran, Clara Fernandez-Vara, Samantha Wallschlaeger, Richard Dansky, Mikko Rautalahti, Eevi Korhonen, Petteri Tuomimaa, Sandra "Sachka" Duval, Mary Kenney, Hazel Monforton, Son M, Tara J. Brannigan, Evan Higgins, Pete Lewin, Willow Morris, Christina Lassheikki, Ed Stern, Lisa Hunter, Natalie Concannon, Sahil Bajaj, Whitney Rowland, Osama Dorias, Jennifer Klasing, and James Phinney; all the devs and recruiters who shared their stories off the record; all the cool kids in The Mingle; my lovely colleagues at work; the ever-helpful Will Bateman at Taylor & Francis; and Toiya Kristen Finley, who kicked this whole thing off.

Mentor Interviews

- Ann Lemay, Narrative Director, WB Montreal. Interview, July 2022. Email and Slack discussions, 2021-2022.
- Clara Fernandez-Vara, Associate Arts Professor, NYU Game Center. Interview, December 2021. Email and Slack discussions, 2021- 2022.
- Ed Stern, Lead Writer, Splash Damage. Interview and email discussion, August 2022.
- Eevi Korhonen, Senior Narrative Designer, Housemarque. Interview and email discussions, June 2022.
- Evan Higgins, Senior Scriptwriter, Playground Games. Interview and email discussions, June 2022.
- Greg Kasavin, Creative Director, Supergiant Games. Interview and email discussions, June 2022.
- Harvey Smith, Studio Director, Arkane Austin. Twitter discussion, May 2022.
- Hazel Monforton, Senior Narrative Designer, Bungie. Interview and email discussions, June 2022.
- James Phinney, CEO & Co-Founder, Lost Lake Games. Interview, January 2022.
- Jennifer Klasing. Game Designer, Amazon Studios. Twitter discussions, 2022.
- Josh Scherr, Narrative Director, Crop Circle Games. Interview, February 2022. Email and Slack discussions, 2022.
- Kim Belair, CEO, Sweet Baby Inc. Interview and email discussions, July 2022.
- Kim Swift, Senior Director of Cloud Gaming, Xbox Game Studios Publishing. Twitter discussion, May 2022.
- Lisa Hunter, Narrative Director, Compulsion Games. Slack discussions, 2022.
- Mary Kenney, Senior Writer, Insomniac Games. Interview, Slack, and email discussions, 2022.

- Mikko "Mikki" Rautalahti, Narrative Director, Roleverse. Interview and email discussions, April 2022.
- Natalie Concannon, Director, Datascope Recruitment. Interview, July 2022.
- Osama Dorias, Lead Content Designer, Blizzard Entertainment. Interview, June 2022.
- Pete Lewin, Senior Associate, Wiggin LLP. Interview and email discussions, May 2022.
- Petteri Tuomimaa, Senior Recruiter, Noice, Inc. Interview and email discussions, 2022.
- Rhianna Pratchett, Freelance Writer. Interview, May 2022. Email and Slack discussions, 2022.
- Richard Dansky, Narrative Director and Central Clancy Writer, Red Storm/ Ubisoft. Email discussion, June, 2022.
- Sahil Bajaj, Freelance Writer. Interview, Twitter, and email discussions, 2022.
- Sam Lake, Creative Director, Remedy Entertainment. Email discussion, July 2022.
- Sam Maggs, Narrative Lead for Digital Publishing & Licensing, Wizards of the Coast. Twitter and email discussion, May 2022.
- Samantha Wallschlaeger, Lead Writer, Crystal Dynamics. Interview and email discussions, January 2022.
- Sandra "Sachka" Duval, Narrative Director, Hinterland Studios. Slack discussion, 2022.
- Sonia "Son M" Messar, Freelance Narrative Designer. Interview and email discussion, June 2022.
- Tara J. Brannigan, Head of Player Experience, Behaviour Interactive. Interview, July 2022. Email and Slack discussions, 2022.
- Toiya Kristen Finley, Freelance Writer and editor in general; game designer, narrative designer, game writer, editor, narrative and diversity consultant in games. Interview, July 2022. Email and Slack discussions, 2022.
- Whitney "Strix" Beltran, Narrative Director, Hidden Path Entertainment. Twitter and Slack discussions, 2022.
- Whitney Rowland, Scriptwriter, Ubisoft Quebec. Interview, July 2022. Email discussions, 2021-2022.
- Willow Morris, Level Designer, Playground Games. Interview and email discussions, July 2022.
- And many, many game devs who shared their wisdom anonymously or off the record.

Introduction

I wrote this book in fragments across a decade, although I didn't know I was writing it. It began its life as a short Frequently Asked Questions (FAQ) post on my personal website. I posted the FAQ out of desperation when I got buried by requests for information about game-writing: *What's the job like? How do I break into games? What skills do I need? Do I need a degree?* Emails pleading for advice arrived every few days, until I was overwhelmed trying to answer them all. I wanted to help, but there was no way I could respond to all the messages individually. So instead, I sat down and scribbled out some high-level advice. I covered the basics of the job and offered some general tips for breaking into the industry. I posted it and pointed hopefuls in its direction. They got help; I got my time back. Everyone was happy.

That basic FAQ served its purpose well, and I was delighted when it became a standard online reference for aspiring game writers. I added some information about pitching games and internships here and there, but otherwise the post remained unchanged for ten years. In those ten years, a lot happened. The games industry changed and grew, and my knowledge and experience grew along with it. I noticed gaps and flaws in the old FAQ, and I realized that many of my answers had become outdated. Students and new writers needed help with topics my basic post didn't cover. It became painfully clear that it wasn't serving its purpose anymore.

So, I decided to write a new, expanded post. I compiled the notes and reference materials I'd bookmarked for years. I planned sections for international work, applying for jobs, negotiating contracts, switching studios, and a wide range of other topics. The role of game writers had evolved, and I wanted to discuss what that evolution meant. Narrative design had gone from being another term for "game writer" to a complicated pastiche of interconnected roles. Companies were recruiting game writers for interactive movie series like *Bandersnatch*. There was so much happening in the world of game writing, so much new information to add,

DOI: 10.1201/9781003282235-1

but I could never find time to update the post. And as the days slipped past, I stopped trying.

But the pleas for advice kept coming. One message in particular touched me. It was from a young woman in Minneapolis who'd been cobbling together information about game writing from pages scattered all over the Internet. What little help she'd found was often vague and confusing to someone who barely knew the industry terminology. I was sad to learn that my ancient FAQ was still one of the best resources for aspiring game writers out there. Only a few other game-writing career references existed, and they were woefully incomplete. In her message, and the others I received, I felt a deep hunger for guidance that nobody was providing. I had to help, so I decided to update my FAQ. I thought I'd add a paragraph here, a short Q&A there, and give the entire post a brisk edit. But once I assembled my proposed changes into one giant, daunting list, I realized what I was actually looking at: a book. I was writing a book. To provide the level of help aspiring writers need, it had to be a book.

So, I talked to a publisher and here we are! This is the book.

There's a terrible, perhaps apocryphal, statistic that the average game developer's career lasts only five years. That timespan is even shorter for women and other marginalized devs. My goal with this book is to break that cycle and keep talented people doing what they love. It's not a book about game writing as a craft. Shelves of those books exist already, and I don't need to toss my thoughts on that pile. Instead, my book will talk you through the unspoken rules and expectations of life as a game writer. I'll offer practical advice in plain language. No unexplained jargon, no dry academic tone, and no insider knowledge required. Anyone who wants a career in games should be able to pick up this book and understand what it says—even complete beginners.

My book is designed to help working writers, too. Most game-writing advice I've seen is only useful up to a point. Books offer general, high-level information about the industry, but don't give the detailed breakdown that most new writers need. Or they'll offer help finding a job but not keeping it. This book won't leave you hanging. I'll walk you through the hiring process step by step, from finding job posts to acing onsite interviews. And I won't abandon you once you've secured work. I'll show you how to make a long-term career out of writing for games. I'll teach you the essentials for surviving as a game writer, how to work in a writing room, and how to put together a team as a narrative lead. I'll explain how game studios are organized, how to navigate hierarchies and negotiate role changes, and how to work your way up to your ultimate dream job. I also have advice about the specific obstacles that marginalized developers encounter—like what to do when you're the only person like you on the team. Where my own experience isn't sufficient, I'll provide insights from working professionals who know exactly what it takes to succeed in the games industry. I interviewed dozens of game developers, hiring managers, and recruiters for this guide. Every one of them was eager to share their wisdom and expertise. Collectively, we'll be your career mentor.

But before we get started, I'd like to introduce myself and explain why you should listen to what I have to say. If you bought this book, you might already know my work. If not, hello! I'm a game writer and narrative designer. I've been in the games industry for nearly two decades now, working for companies like Ubisoft, Arkane, Remedy, Square Enix, Nintendo, and ArenaNet. My projects have taken home many, many awards, including a few Game of the Year and Best Narrative wins. I've spoken at major game conventions around the world about everything from emergent narrative to crafting an interactive portfolio. I've moved all over the continental United States and Europe for jobs and uprooted my life several times—with two international moves in 2014 alone. Right now, I live in the English countryside, working as the narrative lead on *Fable* at Playground Games. I've been from one end of the games industry to the other, from small independent titles to huge, tentpole AAA[1] projects, so I have a holistic view of the game-development ecosystem. All this to say that I'm a working writer who knows the modern games industry. I know the challenges you're going to face. I know what studios want in a game writer. As an industry veteran and manager, I've been on both sides of the hiring process. I know how to land a job, and I know what studios look for in a hire.

But I'm more than my credentials. I'm someone who cares deeply about making the games industry a better, healthier place. I want more people to know the unique joy of writing games. To know how it feels to create a story, craft it with a team of talented colleagues, and then load into the world you built and *live* your story with players. There's no other feeling like it, and that joy should be accessible to everyone who wants it. Beyond that, I want to be the mentor I never had. I always wished for someone to show me the ropes, warn me about problems, and offer me advice. But while I met plenty of smart, caring people in the industry who helped me along my path, I never found the right fit for a mentor. Making the right connections is tough when you're starting out. And even if you find the perfect experienced dev to be your mentor, they might not be able—or willing—to take you on. The number of hopefuls reaching out for help these days is over-whelming. Who has the bandwidth to mentor thousands of new writers while keeping up with their own projects and goals? The honest answer is nobody. That's another reason I wrote this book: to reach writers that I don't have time to mentor individually.

This book offers advice for navigating the games industry *as it currently exists*, with its myriad flaws and deep-rooted problems. I absolutely believe that we can make games a better, safer, kinder, fairer environment for developers, but it's going to take time and work. I'm committed to making those changes from within, and I encourage others to improve what they can, where they can.

---

[1] Pronounced "triple A," these are large-scale games with massive budgets and high production values. They're the games equivalent of big blockbuster movies.

Hopefully, the games industry will be a utopia someday, and I can write a book that focuses solely on "How much is *too* much salary?" But until then, we have to face the realities of the industry and deal with the systems currently in place. Yes, it would be wonderful if every job offered remote and work-from-home options. And if neurodivergent devs didn't have to endure open office spaces. And if crunch and burnout didn't exist. But right now, that's part of the industry. If you're someone facing one of the many -isms, then this book can show you how to cope with those issues. I want to be clear, however, that this book is not a tell-all expose of the games industry. There's no "name and shame" in my advice, and I'm not interested in calling out any studios for bad practices. My advice isn't based on any one person's experiences at a specific studio. Also, to be very clear, nothing in this book is drawn from my experiences at Playground Games. All advice and anecdotes come from the shared knowledge of the people I interviewed. I won't pull my punches when it comes to the problems in this industry, but my focus is on how to solve them and thrive.

The developers I interviewed spoke on the record when they were comfortable, but to get the honest advice and insight that will really help you, I offered the protection of anonymity in certain cases. It's hard to talk honestly about problems at a studio if you're worried about backlash or violating your NDA.[2] Happily, there were few occasions when people felt they couldn't speak openly. But when you see language like "an anonymous game dev says" or "one recruiter noted," understand that it's there to get at the truth.

This book focuses on the AAA games industry in North America and Europe. Mostly because that's my area of expertise and because those regions are a dominant force in AAA development and publishing. The games industry is not a monolith, however, and Japan, Mexico, India, and South Africa, among others, have different business cultures than the United States and Europe. I recognize that some of my advice won't apply globally. And, of course, there are places in the world where industry opportunities are almost nonexistent. Wherever feasible, I sought out voices from those regions to hear their perspectives and understand their needs. Studios might be scarce there, but people still dream of making AAA games. I want this book to help them, too.

I wrote this book in the third year of a global pandemic with fascism on the rise and human rights endangered around the globe. It often felt like I was writing in quicksilver, the words sliding off the page into obsolescence as fast as I could dash them off. The world I'm describing in this book might not exist soon. And the people I'm writing this book for might soon lose access to the opportunities I'm describing, as they fight for survival. Sometimes, I wondered why I was giving career advice when the world's burning down. But every act of creation means

---

[2] NDA means non-disclosure agreement. It's a legal document that binds developers to secrecy about their work.

something. It's a shout of defiance into darkness and a hand stretched across the abyss. It's an offer of hope.

My original goal was to help the widest possible audience become game writers. I wanted to make my advice accessible, practical, and personal so it could open doors for nontraditional hopefuls. But now, I'll be happy to help even one person catch their dream. As game writers, we create new worlds for people to escape into. We write dreams into reality. Maybe it's all code in a machine, but it lives inside people's hearts and minds. The letters I've received over the years telling me how much my stories mean to someone—that's real. And that connection to players has fed my soul and kept me in the games industry.

To get the most from this book, we need to work together. I'll be honest about how tough it is to break into the industry, how many obstacles remain once you're in, how tedious the work can get—and how it's still absolutely worth it. In return, you need to be honest about what you want and how hard you're willing to work for it. I'll show you how to pick a role and prepare for it, find ways to shine, and fight any dragons you encounter, but you're the one who has to do the work. This isn't a standard school textbook with exercises and a quiz at the end of every chapter. Instead, I'll challenge you to take concrete steps toward your goal. You'll come out of the resume chapter with a solid document to submit to studios. You'll come out of the networking chapter with new game-writing contacts. And you'll come out of this book with a clear path to your dream job. But only if you put in the work. Are you ready for that? If you are, let's get started.

Chapter 1

Definitions

There is a challenge for writers who work in video games: to eschew the writer's customary godlike power to shape and sequence all events, to instead "tell" as much of the story as possible through things that might happen or not, might be seen or skipped, perhaps not even noticed; to instead tell as much of the story as possible with the environmental set dressing through which players wander at their own pace, through dynamic events that cue player-character response, and—the game writer's holy grail—through the player's exploitation of game mechanics. When the player acts, the game system responds dramatically, and in the same second the player's mind is hit with a rush of narrative realization—the pleasure of epiphany—that is when the video game writer has served the project well.

—Harvey Smith, Studio Director at Arkane Austin

Do you remember the exact moment you decided to write video games? Remember that flash of epiphany? I remember mine. It was a sweltering summer night in 2001 and I was at home, sweating my way through a video game with Bad Writing. The heat made me cranky, so the stiff dialogue jarred me harder than it normally would. I winced at a clunky line and thought, "I could write better crap than this." A lightbulb flickered on in my mind. "I really *could* write better crap than this!" I figured I could write at least that badly. And that was that. My dream was born.

But a dream is only the first step. My vague ambition remained just that; I had no plans to turn it into reality. I was happily bartending, a job that felt a world removed from the fantastical video games I loved playing in my off hours. But time passed and tending bar lost its thrill. I grew restless. I wanted more for my future

DOI: 10.1201/9781003282235-2

than slinging drinks until I was old and bitter. I tried to imagine what else would make me happy. What work could I stand to do every day for the next forty years or so? And making games popped to mind. I didn't even know for sure that "game writer" was a real job. When I told people I wanted to write video games, they condescendingly said, "I think you mean *design* them." Which was a fair point back then, but not exactly encouraging. Game writing opportunities have surged in the past two decades as the industry has recognized the value of narrative and looked beyond game designers to write story, but in the early Noughties, pure game writers were rare. I searched for job openings but came up empty-handed. I didn't even know where to look. The few resources I had, gaming magazines and a handful of websites, had nothing. Tumbleweeds rolled through my hopes. But a lack of opportunity couldn't stop me. Determined to write games, I went back to school to get the right education for my goal.

I took some community college courses to get started and then transferred to a small, traditional liberal arts college in New England. My big break came the first week at my new school. I met the QA[1] lead at the only video game studio in town when he was *in the act* of advertising for testers. Pure serendipity! I told him I was interested in video games, and he connected me to his studio. I applied for a testing job, landed the gig, and there it was: my first toehold on the industry ladder. My video game career had begun.

I put myself through college working as a tester, first for that studio, then as a contractor for small game companies. I volunteered to write any game text I could at every studio I worked at, until I finally joined the *Guild Wars 2* narrative team as an official writer. From there, it was a steady progression of industry roles until I ended up leading my own team. Now, I can't imagine doing any other kind of work. I love it.

Defining Terms

But I'm getting ahead of myself. You have to know what your goal is to achieve it, so let's define some terms! I won't split hairs with these definitions, I promise. Outside of academia, people aren't as finicky about distinguishing terms, and you'll sometimes hear words like "story" and "narrative," used interchangeably in AAA. There are occasions when precise definitions matter, but for now you only need to learn broad-stroke concepts. That said, I won't start at square one. I'll assume you already have some fundamental knowledge of writing, whether that's traditional writing such as novels or interactive writing such as website content. I expect that you know what video games are and that you've played some. And I hope you understand that writing for games has come a long way in the last few decades. Modern video game stories can be as rich and profound as any other art form. Creating them isn't, as some of my

---

[1] QA = Quality Assurance. These are the testers who find and report bugs in the game.

friends like to joke, just writing "the beeps and boops" of sound effects. It's a craft practiced by professionals who care deeply for interactive media. It's also an absolute bloody mess when it comes to standardization. I'll lay out the basics here, but keep in mind that there is *no universal definition* for many of these terms and practices.

The Basics

First things first: What exactly is a game writer? What do they do? These are trickier questions than you might realize because every studio has its own requirements and they overlap with other disciplines like narrative design. A narrative designer (ND for short) and game writer can perform the exact same work but go by different names, depending on the studio. On my path to senior roles, I was a writer at ArenaNet, a narrative designer at Airtight Games/Square Enix, and then a scriptwriter for Ubisoft. The work involved was largely the same, regardless of my title. So, does that mean that a writer and narrative designer are the same thing? No, not at all! Well, sometimes. Let's just say it's complicated. That's true for many narrative roles. A director at one studio might have the same responsibilities as a lead at another. A senior at an indie might do the same tasks as a mid-level writer at a bigger studio. The best way to explain this snarl of titles is to walk you through what each narrative role on a AAA project does.

The Hierarchy

The video game hierarchy is structured like your standard pyramid. Entry-level roles are concentrated at the base and creative directors, game directors, and studio heads are at the tippy top. But one role stands above them all:

■ **Idea Guy:** This is the person whose sole job is to come up with interesting story ideas for video games. They spend all day dreaming up badass characters and explaining plot details to the team. Sometimes they draw pictures. No game could be made without—okay, okay, I'll stop. I'm just kidding. There's no such job. There's no role that "only" involves dreaming up ideas. In games, ideas are cheap. Every creative role involves an element of ideation. What matters is your ability to realize those ideas. Even creative directors—the people steering the game—need more than a strong vision. They need to know how to align everyone with that vision to make a viable game. That's why you'll see game developers' eyes glaze over when you say, "I've got a great idea for a video game!" Oh yeah? You and everybody else, pal. It takes vision *plus* knowledge *plus* resources *plus* hard work *plus* time to make a game.

So, now that I've dispelled the Idea Guy myth, let's talk about what the video game hierarchy really looks like.

The AAA game-writing pyramid generally goes (in descending order): directors, leads/principals, seniors, mid-level roles, juniors, and interns. If you mapped out those tiers, they'd look something like this:

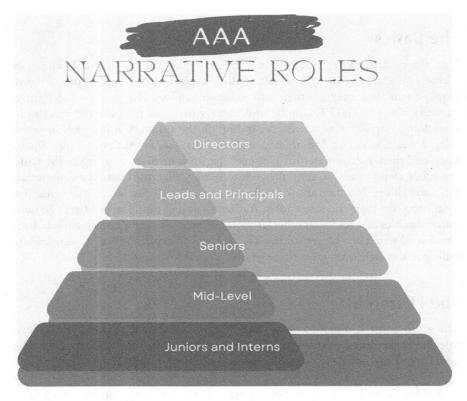

The narrative pyramid.

It's important to understand these tiers when you're applying for jobs. I'll discuss this more in later chapters, but for now all you need is a sense of the structure and how roles align with it.

■ **Creative Directors:** At the top of our project pyramid is the creative director, the vision-holder for the entire game. They oversee the project and keep all the disciplines pointed toward the same goal. They often have business responsibilities, like adhering to a budget and presenting to shareholders, and promotional duties like meeting with publishers and the press. They're also likely to be the big names on a project and have the final say on everything in the game. Some famous CDs are Hideo Kojima, Tim Schafer, Kim Swift, and Cory Barlog.

■ **Narrative Directors and Narrative Leads**: This role is top of the food chain for all things narrative. They're usually the conduit to the creative director and own the narrative vision of the game. It's important to note that "narrative" in video games doesn't just mean dialogue, characters, plot, and all the other elements of a story. Narrative is also how that story is delivered through the various systems and design elements of the game. Narrative designers, dialogue designers, editors, and many other non-writing roles may fall under this umbrella. Director roles also involve casting actors, negotiating with recording studios and directors, and evangelizing the story to publishers and the wider team. Some narrative directors are Richard Dansky, Sachka Duval, Novera King, and Ann Lemay.

■ **Worldbuilders and Lore Masters**: I put this role near the top of the hierarchy to reflect its responsibility and influence, but it's usually either combined with another role like Lead Writer or Principal, or it sits outside the hierarchy entirely as an editorial force. The roles are fairly self-explanatory. Worldbuilders create the broad strokes of the universe: the culture, beliefs, regions, trades, etc. of the game world. Lore masters are tasked with enforcing worldbuilding specifics in day-to-day decisions. Would a magician believe in the gods? How sentient are lava monsters? Would the people in this desert region have a water festival? All the nitpicky details that keep the world consistent and believable. Nowadays, these roles have largely fallen out of use as a stand-alone job. There was a staff "lore-brarian" at Ubisoft Massive, but her work revolved more around intellectual property (IP) needs and lore was one of many responsibilities on her plate.

■ **"Story By" or Story Lead**: Another title that often exists more as a credit than an actual role. If the game is written by an established author (like *Clive Barker's Undying* or *Tom Clancy's Splinter Cell*) or if an outside writer is brought in to write the story treatment, then this title is usually created to capture that contribution. Just to make things confusing, however, Story Lead is occasionally the same role as a Narrative Lead.

■ **Lead Writer or Lead Narrative Designer**: This role answers to the Narrative Director and is responsible for *realizing* the narrative vision of the game. That means they work with other disciplines on the characters, dialogue, worldbuilding, and other elements to tell the story of the game. The lead writer is responsible for guiding the team, nurturing their writing, and making sure all narrative elements are tonally correct and up to standard. They often write the so-called story bible for the game. Narrative design leads oversee the design and implementation[2] work of

---

[2] In its most basic form, "implementing" a design means taking the design plan or words on the page and entering them into the game engine (software like Unreal or Unity) so they become playable.

their team and keep it aligned with quality standards. There may also be a strong administrative element to the role with assigning tasks, setting deadlines, and creating schedules and workflows. Leads are also line managers: They have one-on-one meetings with the team, give annual assessments, relay HR information, and are usually the ones responsible for hiring. Sometimes the production or management part of the job is split out into a separate role: "Story Manager." You probably know a lot of lead writers: Lauren Mee, Darby McDevitt, and Samantha Wallschlaeger, to name just a few.

■ **Principal Writer and Principal Narrative Designer**: This path is for very experienced narrative devs who don't want to lead a team; they prefer to develop their craft instead. Their expertise is respected, and they will usually "own" a significant portion of the story. While they might mentor less experienced writers, there is no built-in obligation to do so like there is with lead roles. Their job is to write. Principals often act as the lore masters for the game. This title isn't widely understood outside the studio environment, but some writers who qualify are Clay Murphy, Colin Harvey, and Craig Owens.

■ **All Senior and Advanced Roles**: I created a catch-all category for senior roles because there are too many to list out. Senior is more an indicator of increased responsibility and authority than it is a discrete job. If you've been doing good work in your discipline as a mid-level writer or narrative designer, you'll eventually get promoted to senior. This allows you to have more say in the game story, to write major characters and substantial pieces of the story, and to participate in external processes, like recording sessions and storyboarding. Advanced Writer is a more liminal role. Mary Kenney was an advanced writer at Insomniac Games before her promotion to senior, and she describes the role this way: "It's essentially a mid-level writer who has a touch more responsibility than a 'writer.' This usually means they 'own' more content from start to finish and with less oversight. Advanced writers aren't typically expected to participate in meetings with directors or external partners, and they aren't expected to mentor other writers." So you might become an advanced writer on your path to a senior role, just like she did. Senior writers and NDs are often well-known figures on social media, such as Mary or Hazel Monforton.

■ **Writer and Narrative Designer:** This is where things start to get dicey. When I asked online what the difference is between a game writer and narrative designer, nobody could give a clear answer. Here are some of the responses:

• Is it bad that I've done both and I still don't know …? —Emma Kidwell
• You really woke up and chose violence this Monday. —Sophie Mallinson

- I don't know and at this point I'm too afraid to ask.—Jacob Mills
- Game writers cry. Narrative designers cry systemically. —Bertine van Hövell[3]

All of these "I have no idea" answers came from professional game writers and NDs. While they're clearly jokes, they surface a longstanding lack of clarity about the roles. If the people doing the job aren't sure of the distinction, then how can anyone know? I wish I could leave this topic at "it depends on the studio so read the job description carefully" and move on to the next chapter, but as your mentor I'm obligated to at least distinguish the most important elements of each role.

Veteran writer James B. Jones offered this explanation: "Personally, 'game writers' do the actual wordsmithing while narrative designers approach the story from a structural, mechanical, and design angle. Some folks do both."[4] That definition roughly matches my understanding of the two roles: Writing is *what.* Narrative design is *how.* And both roles do a little of each, no matter what. Let's dig into the specifics, starting with the writing side of narrative first.

- ■ **Writer:** Also known as scriptwriter. Or screenwriter. Or content writer. Or … yeah. You get the idea. It's the person who writes story and dialogue. The old-school combo role of designer/writer still exists at some game studios in the form of quest design or narrative design, but these days most studios bring in dedicated writers to craft a story and punch up dialogue.
  What game writers *do* depends on the studio. The overlap between writers and NDs can make the roles hard to untangle. If you have to draw a distinction, here's a good metric: only one role *has* to write, by definition. They type out the actual word-by-word writing of the game. Writers put those snappy one-liners in the mouths of characters. They write the villain's gloating monologue. They write the voiceover (VO) lines for that memory montage that makes you cry. Their day-to-day work breaks down into tasks that focus primarily on story as content—the lines of dialogue, the descriptions of items and weapons, the complex characters that inhabit the world, and the overarching plot. All the surface material of narrative that players see and experience.

So, if that's writing, what does a narrative design role look like? Well, if you ask NDs, it looks like this:

---

[3] @EmmaKidwell, @sophmallinson, @JacobWMills, and @lostagainb, Twitter, 2022.
[4] @TheJamesBJones, Twitter, 2022.

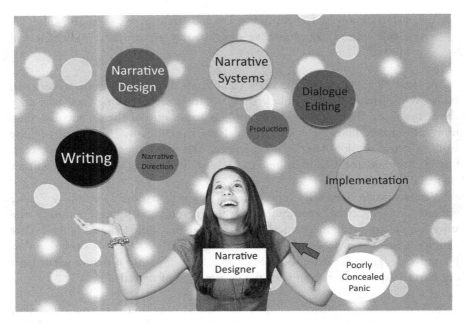

Narrative design in action.

It can definitely be like that at smaller (or understaffed) studios. But if all is going well, narrative designers focus on the *delivery* of storytelling. They create all the hidden design work that underlies the surface writing. Think of story as a circus big-top tent. Narrative design provides the big tentpoles, the web of ropes and pulleys, and the elaborate scaffolding that define and support the structure. Writing is the colorful, fun fabric draped over that framework that makes it recognizably a circus tent. This is a drastically simplified explanation, of course, but you get the idea. Keeping this circus-tent metaphor in mind, let's look at the story "scaffolding."

Narrative Design Roles

To me, narrative design is a branch of game design, and maybe even of system design. An ND designs, prototypes, tests, and implements game systems—the systems that handle not only dialogue, but anything that is "manifesting" the story.

—Sachka Duval, Narrative Director at Hinterland Studios

Narrative design is one of the most varied and least understood roles in games. It's also a relatively new role, in terms of a distinct position at a studio. As the old designer-writer combo roles split into specializations of design/implementation and pure writing, communication problems arose between those two departments. It turned out that when you have design working along one track and writing working along another, their work gets disconnected. It creates the notorious "ludonarrative dissonance," that disconnect between what the story tells you to do and what the gameplay allows you to do. A classic example of this is when the story tells you to "hurry, hurry, the world's about to end! You have to save it!" But the gameplay lets you chop wood or chase chickens for several hours as if there's no life-threatening event happening at all. Another famous example is Nathan Drake in the *Uncharted* games. He's charming, funny, likeable, a good guy—and an unstoppable serial killer. His character *must* kill to progress the game. So how do you fix disconnects like this? How do you bridge the gap between story and gameplay? The answer is narrative design.

There are many types of narrative design: narrative systems design, narrative design implementation, technical narrative design, and good old standard narrative designer, to name a few. Let's break those down.

■ **Narrative Systems Designer:** This role works on the delivery systems for narrative. This includes conversation & dialogue systems (how characters talk to you), UI[5] elements (how you buy items, save your game, etc.), procedural elements (dungeons that have different floorplans and enemies every time you enter them), and much more. As Sachka said, this role is design-centric. This book doesn't focus on design paths, so I'll give you the details right here, and then that'll be it for this role. Here's a great breakdown from Whitney "Strix" Beltran, the narrative director at Hidden Path Entertainment.

Narrative systems and content design require the ability to work with scripting. Whether it's Unity's visual scripting, UE5 blueprints, or independent scripting languages like Lua or Python, those technical skills are a must. Design thinking for narrative systems: How does the localization pipeline for dialogue actually work in implementation? What are best practices for structuring conversation systems? How do we work world-state tagging into character personality? Procedural narrative, how do?

---

[5] UI = User Interface. That's what we call all those menus in games: your inventory, storefronts, pop-up windows with information about loading or saving, everything with text in it that exists outside the context of the game fiction. To get fancy, UI writing is often called "non-diegetic text."

In the pre-production phase, technical narrative designers make features. Like, say, a dialogue tool or a romance system. They will plan, prototype, script, and implement this feature. They will keep careful technical documentation (hopefully). Technical narrative designers do not generally do world-building, character development, story development, or writing. It's desirable to have good affinity and overlap in a pinch, but that is left to other roles on the team. Sometimes this job is done by people with "gameplay designer" or "level designer" as a title.

If Strix's terminology isn't familiar to you, don't worry! It'll all make sense by the end of this book. The main point for now is that this role can be highly technical and often doesn't fall under the Narrative umbrella at all. But it's critical for providing the game's storytelling framework.

■ **Narrative Design Implementer:** This is a less technical role than systems designer, but it requires importing narrative elements into the game. Implementers enter lines of dialogue into game tools. They might set up a "tripwire" around an NPC[6] that triggers a line of dialogue when players get within a certain distance. Or they might place a note on an in-game table for players to read as they're passing through the room. They follow the blueprint of narrative design to build the story inside the game engine (software). Implementers often work with other disciplines such as Level Design and Environment Art to set up the quest flow through a map. When they're done, you can play through the story as a game!

■ **Narrative Designers:** Narrative designers use gameplay systems to construct the circus-tent framework that writers will cover with their story. They may also structure the flow of quests—how the story is delivered moment by moment. The overarching plot, key characters, and story themes (the what) are decided higher up, but NDs decide *how* to relay that story information. Say the story calls for a big, dramatic moment where a dragon swoops down and snatches away your true love. Epic action scenes like that are usually cinematics.[7] A character wants you to make a choice? That's likely a conversation that branches into options at the end. The narrative designer decides which method of storytelling—cinematic, conversation systems, etc.—works best for the needs of that scene. Their goal is to deliver the greatest, most efficient narrative impact from each story beat. This role overlaps with pure writing the most and is often viewed

---

[6] NPC = non-player character. This is any character in the game that isn't controlled by players.
[7] Cinematics are the movie parts of video games. They're also known as cutscenes or cines.

through the lens of narrative features. Eevi Korhonen, the senior narrative designer at Housemarque, explains what that means.

I design narrative features, so any feature that is used primarily to convey the story of the game, such as Xenoglyphs or Databank entries in *Returnal*. I also do a lot of worldbuilding in collaboration with the rest of the narrative team and the output of that is usually various documents (or just informal chats) to be provided to art, cinematic and audio teams.

Narrative features are the building blocks of the game story and create spaces for writers to fill. This can be literal, when a narrative designer stubs in placeholder text for a note that says something like "[information about alien attack HERE]." The writers go through and craft the text of that note line by line and implementers place the note in the game world. Sometimes one person does all three tasks. That's how interwoven narrative roles are.

I could keep going and define every variation of narrative designer out there, but I think you get the idea. Writers and narrative designers both work on story-related elements, and it's tough to draw a clear line of demarcation between the roles. But, in general, writers own text and story, while NDs own structure and systems. Whew! Now that we've cleared that up, let's move to the next step in our hierarchy.

■ **Narrative Editor:** Here's a little-known fact: Many writers are terrible editors. We can't spell, our grammar is atrocious, we overuse em dashes, get emotionally attached to commas, and guess our way through hyphenation. No AAA game could make it out the door without an editor. A good editor doesn't just correct the textual elements of your writing; they also provide notes on the content. When I was an editor at ArenaNet, I wrote long notes of feedback on the story structure, like "You just opened the gates to a beautiful city, and I want to explore it! Why are you sending me back out into the countryside on my next mission?" Good editorial feedback can turn decent writing into fantastic writing. It catches those sneaky typos and makes dialogue shine. (Yes, I'm sucking up to the editor of this book. Learn from me!) Editors are also liaisons to Loc[8] and lore, keeping tone, diction, and style in line. Most smaller studios hire outside agencies to edit their work or trust QA testers to catch mistakes, but big studios like Riot Games and Blizzard Entertainment have dedicated editors working in-house.

---

[8] Loc = localization. Pronounced "loke." This team translates games into other languages and cultures.

■ **Junior Writer and Intern:** I lumped these two roles together because they represent that first step into the industry. Both roles allow inexperienced writers to learn on the job for a modest wage. Entry-level positions like this are rare in AAA now, which is a shame. When you're fresh out of school and just starting in the industry, a junior role can be a great springboard to full-fledged writing work. Or if a hiring manager sees raw talent in your samples, but you have no professional writing experience at all, they might agree to take you on as a paid intern and give you that needed foot in the door. As a junior, you follow a more senior writer and participate in their daily tasks. You write barks[9] and notes, item descriptions, and help process audio files and scripts for recording sessions. The purpose of this role is to learn, so you should get a chance to try a little bit of everything.

■ **Contractors:** If you've looked at the career pages of major studios and wondered where all the entry-level jobs have gone, here's your answer. Contractors have largely replaced the junior writer and intern roles that used to provide a foothold in AAA. As a project grows, studios will often bulk up their workforce by hiring devs on contract. This arrangement is great for freelancers, who can join a team for a defined period of time, do their job, and then move on to another gig when the contract ends. But if you're looking for a permanent, in-house position, it's tough to make the leap from contractor to full-time employment (FTE). I'll talk about contract roles more later on, but think of them as cyclical, time-limited, or external staff at all levels of experience.

If you put all these roles together into something like the organization charts you find at studios, it looks like figure on the next page.

■ **Other Disciplines:** One key point that my handy-dandy diagram fails to show is how the narrative hierarchy intersects with other disciplines. Departments such as Audio, Art, Level Design, Loc, and QA work so intimately with narrative that they intersect at every level and every role. I've mentioned the close collaboration with Level Design and Art before. Audio and Cinematics will help you realize the story through motion-capture performance (aka mocap), music, and glossy cutscenes. Animation will bring your characters to life. QA will catch your mistakes before they go humiliatingly public, and Localization will make your wisecracks funny in other languages. Production keeps the game on schedule so that it actually ships. At every step of the process, you'll have to take the needs of these disciplines into account, and they'll work with you to realize the grand vision of the game.

---

[9] Barks are short lines of one-off dialogue, like "I'm out of ammo!" and "Watch your back!"

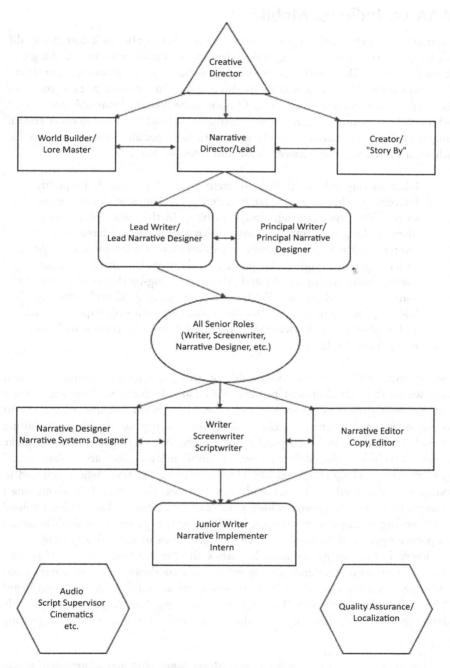

The narrative hierarchy as an organizational chart.

AAA vs. Indie vs. Mobile

Narrative hierarchy varies from studio to studio. It can also look completely different when you're in the independent (indie) or mobile branches of the games industry. Most folks in indie games wear many hats because teams are smaller and less specialized. It's a great way to try out a bunch of different roles at once and have greater control over your work. On one indie project, I was QA lead, writer, editor, ND, community manager, and marketer. Whew! But I got to experience all angles of the story that way. Many game writers, especially freelance writers like Rhianna Pratchett, float between indie and AAA. In her words:

> I like mixing things up with different styles of project. It keeps life interesting. There are completely different challenges with every game so you're always adapting; always learning. In the indie space, you're often working with smaller teams, so that means you can have more of a voice. And as writers in games that's something we can often struggle to truly get. But you're also usually working with a smaller budget, maybe doing multiple jobs and it's more flying-by-the-seat-of-your-pants style development. With AAA you get the "shiny"—the big budgets, the big names etc. But those also come with big expectations and multiple stakeholders. Situations like "story by committee" are more commonplace.

Beyond AAA and indie, the mobile side of games can have an entirely different cadence to their development process, with more frequent updates and shorter development cycles. Many mobile games rely heavily on in-game advertisement or monetization[10] elements—like asking you to pay to avoid long waiting periods—and that can be off-putting for writers. But every game needs to make money somehow, right? Mobile games are simply more upfront about that need. I got my start working on games like Hasbro's *Littlest Pet Shop,* where you had to buy a stuffed animal in the real world just to access the game. Talk about smart monetization! My *LPS* game is long gone, but I still use the knowledge I gained from writing its in-game newspaper. It's all valuable experience, so don't be afraid to pursue opportunities outside of AAA to get a foot in the industry door.

Every branch of games secretly thinks they're the best branch. However, there's a distressing tendency among writers to look down on other wings of our industry. I've seen prominent indie writers sneer at "safe" AAA work and heard AAA writers mock "clumsy" low-budget indie titles. Mobile games inexplicably draw the most disdain, despite their incredible popularity and staggering

---

[10] Monetization = how a game makes money. Mobile games often have a "freemium" model: free to buy and play, but with ads, in-game purchases, and progression barriers to encourage spending.

financial returns. These are not rational biases, so don't get sucked into them. Every type of game-making has its pros and cons. I like the deep dive into story that AAA in-house work lets you have, but I know many writers who prefer the faster pace of indie titles or the modularity of mobile games. It's entirely a matter of personal taste and values. My advice is to try them all on for size (if possible) and see which one suits you best.

The Flow of Writing

Now that you have a better understanding of all the narrative roles, let's talk about how they fit together. How do writers take a story from an idea to a game you can play? What does the flow of work through this hierarchy look like? In most AAA studios, it looks like this:

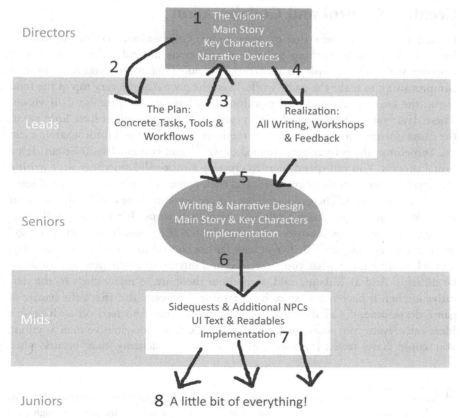

Story flow through the hierarchy.

As you might expect, it usually starts with a concept at the top. The narrative director and lead writer create the story. They propose or "pitch" story ideas until one gets approved, then they plan out the high-level story beats, major themes, and key characters. They might divide the story into chapters or substories. They work with the narrative design lead and worldbuilders (among many, many others) to determine the path of that story through the world. The principals and seniors write the major characters' biographies, map out their story arcs, and work with narrative designers to "break" it into cinematics, conversations, and readable elements like notes, signs, and so forth. Then the writers come along and flesh out the scenes with characterful dialogue. The final steps involve edits for clarity and continuity, working with localization to translate text into other languages, and checking for errors with QA. Along the way, writers will collaborate with every other team on the project to achieve their storytelling aims. It takes an entire team to ship a game, so good communication between disciplines is critical.

Creative Control and Collaboration

It should be clear by now that game writing is collaboration. Period. Games are huge. Unless you're working on a tiny project as an indie developer, you're working with other people to realize the world. That means you're constantly compromising to make the game work. Even the people at the very top of the food chain, the creative directors and worldbuilders, have to compromise their vision. These days you're likely to work on an existing IP, so you might have little say in the game universe or character arcs. Sometimes technology will limit what you can do. Sometimes the project gets "scoped down"[11] and content has to be cut. It's a brutal process. You can spend months creating a rock-solid storyline, with writing that sparkles and characters you love, and then come in to work one day and learn it's all been scrapped. The game concept has changed, or there's no budget for your missions, or it simply doesn't resonate with higher-ups. It's not just "kill your darlings" in the games industry, it's often "watch the genocide of your darlings" when entire regions get slashed. You have far less control than you'd have with, say, a novel. Letting go of what you've created and buying in to the new direction can be difficult. And as Rhianna said, sometimes there are so many chefs in the narrative kitchen it becomes a "story by committee" process. But that's the nature of game development! Collaborating with creative people who feed off each other's ideas can elevate your work, making it better and more imaginative than anything you could have realized alone. There's a strange alchemy that occurs when

---

[11] Scope = the scale of the project, measured in resources like game features (co-op play, boss fights, journals, etc.) and staff. "Downscoping" reduces the scale of the game through cuts—usually to features.

disciplines combine their creative power. They produce work that transcends the sum of its parts. Work that is inspired, moving, and magical. But to achieve that brilliance, you have to relinquish control and embrace a communal process.

The Right Path

With all of these role possibilities, how do you decide which path to pick? The good news is that you don't have to decide right away. There's no "one true path" into games and no set journey through it. There's a great deal of crossover in the roles and you'll have plenty of time to try on different hats and see which one fits best. To translate my personal credo into general advice, I'd say that you should always remember why you got into the industry and make that your north star. If you got into the industry to make games and you don't care what game you work on, then your path is easy. You can work in any branch of the industry on any project. You'll have abundant choice—even it means working on games that you'd never personally play. If you got into the industry to tell your *own* stories, then you might work for indies where you have more control. Or learn to code so you can create a game from scratch. Or launch a Kickstarter. Do what it takes to own your game stories. If you're like me, however, your goal is to work on narrative-focused AAA games with stories you love. Games that you'd want to play yourself. A goal this specific takes strategy, hard work, and brutal self-honesty. You'll have to prepare well and be ready for anything the industry throws at you. You might have to move at the end of every project and start over at new studios. You might have to learn skills outside your comfort zone. Following your star will take you places you can't even imagine right now. But no matter your dream, no matter your north star, all paths start with those first, small steps. So, choose your role. Define your goal. And turn to the next chapter.

Chapter 2

Education

Broaden your horizons! Don't just play games for inspiration—read widely, go to the theatre, listen to radio plays. Be interested in people and the world. Be a sponge for stories in all their forms. You never know what might inspire you so give yourself a deep well to draw from.

—Rhianna Pratchett, Freelance Writer

This year, more than 85 students will graduate from New York University's Game Center and start looking for jobs.[1] Those students will join thousands of other game-program graduates around the world to compete for jobs. Add to that number all the graduates from previous years and game-writing professionals who are switching roles for better opportunities. The result is that the number of applicants vastly outstrips the number of open roles. Finding an entry-level job in AAA is hard with such fierce competition. I'll say that again for those of you dealing with rejections: it's *hard*. The odds are even more daunting when you consider how few game-writing jobs exist in the first place. If you have your heart set on writing for a top studio on one of their flagship games or for your favorite, popular IP, you're looking at maybe 5–10 narrative spots on the entire team. I conducted an informal internet poll a few years back that concluded there are fewer than 1000 prestige game-writing jobs in AAA *globally*. Competition for these roles is intense, and it takes the right combination of talent, skill, and plain luck to land one. So how can you compete in this overcrowded arena?

---

[1] Thanks to Clara Fernandez-Vara for her program statistics.

DOI: 10.1201/9781003282235-3

The Good News

The statistics for entry-level roles on prestige projects are as bleak as it gets—but even those jobs aren't impossible to get. And, if you look outside that narrow slice of the industry, you'll find plenty of opportunities for junior and mid-level writers in games. All you need are the right skills and experience. The AAA hiring managers and recruiters I interviewed expect candidates to have *some* industry knowledge already. They don't hire applicants with no games experience at all. That's the hard truth. Here's where you groan and say, "Thanks a lot, Anna! I already know that." I get that it feels like a locked door, but there are ways past it, I promise. I'll explain how to get the experience you need to … get the experience you need, but first let's talk about getting the right training. What essential skills do you need to succeed?

The Right Skills

Here's the big question: "Is writing enough?" Is being a good writer enough to secure one of those rare pie-in-the-sky roles? The answer is yes! You can get a job as a writer, especially a contract writer for barks and UI text, with writing skills alone. Some junior roles don't ask much beyond an interest in games and a way with words. I once worked with a senior writer whose tech knowledge was so limited that he scribbled everything longhand and had a designer type it into the tool for him. (A headache for everyone involved.) I've known brilliant writers who can barely turn on a computer. They were all strong writers—they had to be—to offset missing skills in other areas. So, yes, you can make a career in game narrative with writing skills alone if you're damn good at it.

But let's be honest here: good writing skills are the baseline requirement for game writers. If you want to be the best candidate for a role, you need to be better than basic. You should pick up additional skills that offer you an advantage in the industry and give a leg up on your competition. Here are some useful "extra" skills for narrative jobs:

- screenwriting
- storyboarding
- film or theater experience
- content writing
- production
- editing
- implementation
- dialogue scripting
- language (translation)
- specialization (ex: military experience)
- narrative design
- game design
- systems design
- level design
- tools expertise
- QA knowledge

This is a small selection of abilities that will improve your chances. The most obvious "adds" are from disciplines that intersect with Narrative. I studied computer science in college, and I have an editing and testing background, so I have an advantage over people who "only" write. First-person shooter (FPS) games often hire writers with military backgrounds so the soldiers' dialogue and characterization feel authentic. And it's common for people to enter game writing from related disciplines, like level design or cinematics. At Naughty Dog, writer Josh Scherr started out as an animator before becoming a writer. He began offering feedback on cinematics scripts, which led to helping out with script contributions. From there, he was made part of the story development process on the *Uncharted* series—although his full-time focus was still leading the cinematics team.

> Eventually, Neil approached me and asked if I wanted to move on to writing full time. It was obviously a big transition, and I was terrified at the prospect of leaving behind my field of expertise to do something that I had never done professionally. But I also figured, when am I ever going to get another chance like this? So, I said yes. And much to my delight, it ended up working out. So that's the roundabout way that I got into a writing position. I didn't specifically go to school for it. I didn't specifically apply for those jobs. I didn't explicitly work my way up through any of those things. I got in partially through the back door and my own pushing for it.

Josh was able to switch to game writing because he demonstrated a deep understanding of character and dialogue that translated well to narrative work. His skill set transcended his own discipline and became broadly applicable.

Most in-house AAA writers who've reached senior level in the industry have a Swiss-army-knife skillset. You'll be on a team which also has a mixed bag of talents, so you'll need to fill in gaps with your skills or complement a colleague's weakness with your strength. The more experience you have with every element of game writing, the better. Can you write a story treatment, character biography, cinematic, branching conversation, marketing and trailer copy, pitch, story "bible," and design document on top of standard barks, scenes, and UI text? Fantastic! Versatility is a plus. By the time you wrestle a project over the finish line, you'll likely write every single narrative item in that list and then some. When employers know you can write a story from soup to nuts, they'll hire you before writers who are only familiar with item descriptions or barks. And any talent or knowledge you can bring *in addition to your writing skill* will give you an edge.

Game Writing vs. Traditional Writing

Maybe you're already a writer and you're considering a move from your field into game writing. I see that a lot these days, with writers entering games from media like TV, film, and theater. If that's you, then writer Toiya Kristen Finley[2] has some good news for you: "Writing is writing, and storytelling skills are storytelling skills. If you have a solid foundation in narrative, your storytelling skills are going to translate to any medium." And if you know how to write for an audience, you're most of the way there. All that's left is to adjust your usual writing technique to the needs of this highly interactive medium. Game writing has some specific constraints:

- **Nonlinearity:** This can be a real challenge in open-world games! Players can progress through your story out of its intended order (the "golden line" of the game), so you have to plan for their whims and check in before critical dramatic points. Checkpoints and hidden conditionals[3] ensure players know what they're supposed to know so your plot will still make sense and hit the right emotional beats. It also helps to think of game narrative in a modular way, with self-contained scenes or segments of dialogue that players string together like beads on a necklace to tell a story.
- **Interactivity:** Games aren't the only interactive medium, of course. Theater has audience participation or collaboration, like Punchdrunk's immersive "Sleep No More." Art installations such as teamLab's "Graffiti Nature: Lost, Immersed, and Reborn" incorporate drawings from viewers. Kpop has rousing fan chants that turn live shows into call-and-response routines. I'm not going to wade into The Discourse[4] around this topic. It's a pointless debate. We can all agree that interaction is fundamental to the game experience without trashing other media. But what does it mean to center interaction in a story? You'll hear game devs talk about "player agency" in reverent tones. For writers, that simply means allowing players to drive the story and actively contribute to its unfolding—or at least letting them think they can. This means making space for players to affect the world and characters through their actions and decisions.
- **Synergy:** Or harmony, or "ludonarrative consonance," or whatever you want to call it. It's those moments when story and gameplay align perfectly to

---

[2] Toiya's full title is freelance writer and editor in general; game designer, narrative designer, game writer, editor, narrative and diversity consultant in games.

[3] Very simply, tags and conditionals help the game react to what players do. For example, IF a player has met the character Poppy in the game (the condition), THEN a line of dialogue about Poppy plays (the reaction).

[4] You'll sometimes see discussion around certain topics become fevered, industry-wide debates. That's the current discourse. My least-favorite discourse topic is "Are games Art?" because come on. Of course they are.

produce an emotional response. It's when, as Strix says, the "game feels good, bro." The "show don't tell" rule in traditional writing becomes "play not words" when translated to games. It's more than avoiding walls of text or empty dialogue or adding "press X to cry" interactions. It means investing gameplay actions with feeling. Here's what I mean: when your older brother dies in *Brothers: A Tale of Two Sons*, the first thing you have to do is bury him. You have to drag his body across the ground, push it into a grave, and spread dirt over it. This could be comical, except that the game leans into the mechanics of the moment. The player has controlled both brothers up to this point. The older brother was on one joystick; "you" were on the other. You've built up muscle memory in your hands as you built up experiential memories with your brother through story moments. When you work the controls without him for the first time, you feel his loss *physically*. You have to learn how to function without him—to physically work the controls without him—because you can't progress in the game if you don't. But learning to move without him means accepting he's gone. It means letting him go. Every awkward move you make to bury him reminds you that he's not there moving the controls with you. It's a gut punch. That visceral connection between the story loss (your brother dies) and mechanical loss (your brother is missing from the controls) combine in gameplay action (burying his body) to create a devastating moment of grief. I cried my eyes out. That's what I mean by synergy. And as Harvey noted earlier, it's game narrative's holy grail.

So, there you have it. Those are the biggest differences between games and traditional forms of writing. There are more, of course, but that's enough to get you started.

All media have unique restraints, but you'd be surprised how much they have in common, especially games, theater, and film. I once worked with a Hollywood screenwriter who had just moved to games. He said the transition was easy except for how informational game writing is. Screenplays and movie scripts need only entertain, he said, but game writing has to instruct too, so it can progress. The trick is to entertain players while telling them what to do next.

But let's say you already understand the demands of interactive writing. What other skills should you add to your repertoire?

Tech Skills

Most of the big studios use their own in-house programs, which are often more sophisticated than publicly available software. This is great news for two reasons: it makes narrative work easier, and they won't expect you to be familiar with it before you start. In fact, there's no industry tech standard for game-writing jobs that

I'm aware of, beyond being able to use email, documents, spreadsheets, and production software like Jira or ADO.[5] I never worked for a studio that required any previous design or programming experience for their writers, but narrative designers should be familiar with Perforce and game engines such as Unreal or Unity in addition to their narrative skills. I learned Python, Javascript, and Actionscript (remember Flash?) at university, but I haven't used them for work. Never. Not even once. They help me understand the behavior of the game and its systemic limitations, but that's about it. Familiarity with screenwriting software is also an advantage, because in-house software functions in similar ways. Check out Final Draft or Scrivener and conditional storytelling software such as Twine or Articy to get started. At one studio, we actually wrote cinematics in Final Draft and then imported the files into the studio's proprietary game engine, so it's useful to know standard commercial programs.

Generally, the usefulness of tech skills depends on whether or not you need to implement the story yourself. At companies without dedicated writers, you'll be expected to do light design work and implementation, so having that knowledge would be a distinct advantage. But still not a requirement!

Programming Skills

"Do writers need to know how to program?" I asked a group of game writers this question, and they unanimously agreed that programming knowledge is helpful, but not necessary. The more you understand the underlying systems of whatever game you're working on, the better. They are the tools in your kit as much as cinematics or diction are. But understanding how to write a good story is much more important. Pacing, character development, plot—it's the writer's responsibility to make sure these elements are in place so the story is sound. However, NDs should "know some scripting software," says narrative designer Son M. "You don't need to know *all of them* but having some in your pocket will only help you! Especially when you're in a small team and need some sort of standardization (everyone does scripts differently)." The better you understand your game's mechanics and structures, the better you can use them to tell your story. This is especially true in procedurally generated games (games with randomized content) and branching narratives that offer players a choice of paths. But no writing role in AAA requires programming to craft a meaningful story. So, the short answer is that you don't need it, but some knowledge might be helpful.

---

[5] These programs track features, tasks, and schedules and serve as a database of bug reports and fixes.

Basic Education

So, how do you get these skills? What kind of education do you need? Where do you even start?

First off, finish high school (or its equivalent) if that's possible for you. Remember my statistic about the five-year career average? You might want that diploma for something else if you decide to leave the games industry. There's no need to study game design or game narrative at this stage. Take classes that provide foundational knowledge in a wide range of subjects—the classic liberal arts education. It's safer to follow your interests at this stage and study what you love. You can always specialize later.

When I was in high school, making games never crossed my mind as a possible career. I played video games, but it was just one of many hobbies. I was far more passionate about reading, writing, and drawing back then. I knew I'd be something creative and impractical—like a writer or an artist—but I didn't imagine a career in games. I simply wanted to get paid for doing something I loved. Like reading. Oh, how I dreamed of reading books! Forever! For money! So when my school required that we follow someone around at their job for Career Day, I chose to shadow an editor at a big publishing house. She was kind, but confused. "This is your dream job?" she asked, over and over again, as she showed me how to mark up manuscripts. Shy, fifteen-year-old Anna nodded. "Yes." Well, it was my dream job until I saw how tedious it was. No dream could survive the fifth reading of a dense text about flywheels and machined cogs.

And that's how I became a bartender.

In all seriousness, writers draw on their entire life experience to create stories. They are sponges for information and weird little facts. What they don't already know, they research. There's a joke that if you saw a writer's internet search history, you'd toss them in jail, because it's stuff like "how to crack a safe" and "most painful way to die?" Important to know! And easy knowledge to obtain. But you'll need formal education on top of googling skills. Obviously, English literature classes were critical for me as a writer. But I've also drawn on my studies of history, politics, science, and, yes, even bartending to make convincing, well-rounded characters. Maybe someday I'll use my extensive flywheel knowledge in a game. You never know! That's the beauty of writing. To get this breadth and depth of information, I advise you to read as much as you can. Study great literature. Learn the foundations of telling a good story. Mary Kenney lays it out for you:

> Know the basics of storytelling. Self-taught is fine! I came to fiction after college (I didn't take a single creative writing class in college, egad).

I had to read up on all ye olde jargons of fiction writing—Save the Cat, the Hero's Journey, and so forth—by myself.

But in graduate school and even during my first years in the industry, I caught a ton of shade for wanting to focus on storytelling and writing in games. "Mechanics! Learn mechanics! It's all about mechanics!" Well, sure, mechanics are great, but so are characters, dialogue, arcs, and themes. In my first couple of years, I could write dialogue decently well, and I had a spot of coding experience, but I had absolutely no clue how to plot a story or track character arcs. Focus on learning those basics, too, and it'll make you a stronger designer and writer.

That's the kind of education you should get as a budding game writer. Basic writing knowledge. If you can't string together a compelling sentence, you shouldn't aim for game-writing jobs. That should go without saying, but believe me, it doesn't. The harsh truth is that you can't get a job as a writer unless you can write. No, scratch that! You can't *keep* a job as a writer unless you can write. Some people lie their way past all the recruiting safeguards or get crony-ed into positions they're not qualified for (yes, it happens on rare occasions), but sooner or later they have to do the work. And that's when skill and knowledge matter.

University

I was in school for seven years at three colleges, and I'll be paying off those student loans until the sun goes supernova. My college career is not typical, so I won't hold it up as an example. I especially don't want to encourage other Americans to take that path when you don't need a fancy degree to get a game-writing job. Don't believe me? Here's what recruiter Petteri Tuomimaa has to say about educational requirements:

> In the roles that I've hired for, education is not that big of a deal. There are exceptions to this rule, based on things like being able to move into the European Union. You need to have higher education or a certain salary level to move to, say, Finland, which might be difficult to attain from a gaming company. So, in that case, education matters. But when you're already in the target country, it's not that important. When you have the skills from formal education, that also definitely helps, especially when you're a junior. But if you're further along in your career, then I don't think education makes that much of a difference.

Don't believe Petteri? A recent analysis of narrative job postings across the industry showed that only one third of them asked for a degree, most commonly a BA. And even then, it was fine to have comparable work experience instead.[6] So for education, you should finish high school and get some kind of continuing education *if possible*. There are some cases of entirely self-taught (no higher education) individuals doing well as writers in the game industry, but it's a harder path and some doors might be closed to you. Most successful game writers have completed college and have some real-world writing experience. If you decide to go with a traditional college education like I did, I recommend a focus on English literature and language, comparative literature, or creative writing. But you don't have to stick that close to writing! I know writers with degrees in all sorts of majors—from theatre to engineering to psychology. It's more important that you learn to communicate your ideas well, manage your time, and explore a wide range of media.

Advanced Degrees

It's not necessary to get your master's degree, but it's helpful. Evan, a senior writer, credits graduate school for jumpstarting his career. He went to undergrad for English literature, and then MIT for his masters in comparative media studies. He wrote his thesis on storytelling, "specifically in video games and speculative fiction," he said.

> Going to grad school was useful because I reset my career and got a lot of training in writing. The most important thing that came from it is that I got an internship at Bioware and that was my foot in the door of the industry.

Okay, you're thinking, if a college degree is good and a master's leads directly to a job, then I should go for the highest degree possible, right? No. Nope. Definitely not. One point that I heard over and over is that there's absolutely no need to go for a PhD. Take it from someone who knows, senior narrative designer Dr. Hazel Monforton:

> I would not recommend any aspiring game writer pursue a PhD, unless they are really passionate about doing so. I can only speak to English Literature PhDs, though I know people who are studying video games

---

[6] Lassheikki, Christina. "Game Writers and Narrative Designers. The evolving role of story-telling professionals in game development." 2022, Master's Thesis, Aalto University School of Art, Design, and Architecture.

at the doctoral level. But it is not necessary professionally and will take up a lot of time and energy, and the assumed thing is that you will go on to teach and do research rather than leave academia. I don't think a PhD gives anyone an advantage in applying for game writing jobs, at least not on the CV level.

In Evan and Hazel's cases, the skills they learned were valuable and opened doors to the games industry, rather than the degrees themselves. Hazel notes that people believe higher education teaches you how to communicate clearly and concisely, but that's not true. She said her degree mostly taught her to recognize patterns.

> This might seem very simple but it is a skill that does take years to develop (and not something that only PhDs can do, of course.) Being able to pick out literary techniques, their uses, their effect, and how they connect with other elements of the story is something that I honed while doing my doctorate.

You could learn those skills through self-education if the degree isn't important to you. However, if you think you might leave games someday and move into academia—which is a popular exit ramp from the industry for late-career game writers—then a doctorate *might* be an advantage. That one, particular case aside, you're better off getting into the industry as soon as you can.

Game Programs

Schools like Digipen and American University's Game Lab offer game design courses and creative writing and game-writing classes, so that's also a good educational route. I spoke with NYU Game Center Associate Arts Professor, Clara Fernandez-Vara about her program. She explained that students learn more than just using the tools for making games, they learn game design and game development too, with classes in management and scrum[7] to prepare them for the real world of game production. Clara heads up the games studies area, where students analyze games and learn how to think and talk about them critically. If that sounds elementary to you, keep in mind that I've just spent two chapters discussing basic industry terminology. As Clara observed, her students likely won't become academics afterwards, but "at least if they go to GDC, they can understand their practice and explain it to others. That way they don't look

---

[7] Scrum is the production framework of games. It breaks down projects into short sections of time called "sprints" and relies on iteration and frequent adjustments to stay on target for goals. Producers run this process.

like idiots. It's a skill, right?" On top of that, NYU's program explores "labor practices of the industry" to prepare their students for real-world game development. Internships and practicums are also an integral part of modern game programs and give students practical, hands-on training in the exact skills they need for the industry.

It's important to find the right program for you as a potential game writer. Not all game design programs treat narrative as a separate discipline worthy of respect. During my research, I stumbled across a few "narrative" classes that only taught barks and item descriptions. Clara notes scathingly that they include "writing because they're thinking about it as 'flavor text.' And I'm like, 'No, it's not flavor text. This is the core of the game.' We have to build more interesting worlds." She's right. You won't learn the skills you need from programs that view narrative as a "wrapper" for mechanics. Research game programs carefully to make sure they offer the right classes and training for the role you want. Many game programs offer a generalist curriculum for game-writing degrees. They teach you a little bit about every aspect of game-making. But what's the point of going for a degree in a specific discipline if it's not your focus? You know the saying about "jack of all trades, master of none." That time and money is better spent on a more tailored curriculum that gives you the specialized skills you need. If you don't learn game-narrative skills in school, you'll have to learn them on your own. Be aware of that fact. Also, be wary of any game program that "guarantees" a job at graduation. The games industry is incredibly competitive and even the top-tier design schools can't make that promise. It takes networking and sweat to land a games job, even with a degree. Many grads go years before landing their first industry gig, so go into games programs with your eyes open and have a backup plan to stay afloat during your job search.

Alternatives to College

All this talk of education is great, but the reality is that many people can't afford college and can't easily access specialized games programs. Game writer Sahil Bajaj went all the way to the US for his education because "there is practically no game-writing scene in Dubai," but even that avenue is closed for many people. What do you do then? Is it possible to enter the games industry with no formal education at all? Good news! It is. You'll face some challenges, but it can be done.

Online Education

If you don't live near any game schools or if you live in a country or culture where those opportunities aren't available to you, then online classes are your friends. Many schools have moved online, so you can take classes and get certificates as long as you have computer access. Did you know you can get a Harvard education from the comfort of your own home? Their online school offers classes in literature and screenwriting and computer programming—if you want to go the traditional college route, that is. If the Ivy League's not for you, check out Udemy, Coursera, or your preferred college's continuing education annex. If you want more specialized skills, many game programs offer their curricula online too. Full Sail and the Academy of Art have popular online programs. Some studios sponsor programs such as Ubisoft's Pixelles Montreal Game Incubator, a two-month game workshop for women and BIPOC. Susan Connor's game-writing hub, The Narrative Department, has moved fully online, so you can take everything from Gamewriting 101 to more advanced screen-writing classes from an established storyteller.

Many of the schools I listed have scholarships and funding available, so it's worth investigating the possibilities to see if you qualify.

Writer Beware!

This is the first of several warnings I'll give you about predatory services. There are many game programs, articles, courses, and online workshops for writers that are terrible. They aren't just inaccurate, they're outright harmful. They'll give you "insider tips and tricks" that lead to stiff or formulaic writing. They promote tools and structures that professional writers would never use. I came across an article that, with every appearance of seriousness, said you should outline your entire story before deciding what genre your game will be or what the world is like. If you've never written a game, you might have no idea why that advice leads to problems. Be careful! You could end up learning a slew of bad habits you'll have to unlearn.

So how do you avoid harmful advice? Check credentials! Before signing up for a class, see if it's accredited. Research the program and instructor. There's a reason I listed my bona fides in the introduction to this book. I want you to see what work I've done and decide for yourself if I'm qualified to advise you. Make sure you do the same with any potential instructor. Ask yourself these questions:

- "Have they worked in the games industry?" If they've never worked pro-fessionally as a game writer, all they're teaching is theory. They don't know what it's like to apply that theory in a development cycle, with all its con-straints and crises. What works on paper doesn't always work in practice.
- "How long did they work in games?" If they've worked in games fewer than three years, take what they say with a grain of salt. They haven't seen enough of the industry to assess how widely applicable their knowledge is.
- "How long ago did they work in games?" This isn't always a red flag because many seasoned game writers leave the industry to teach. An experienced

veteran can teach you a lot—but not necessarily about the modern games industry. Add another salt grain here.

■ "Have they done the job they're teaching?" This is a pet peeve of mine. I see devs teaching narrative classes who've never held positions in narrative. Sometimes they're designers, sometimes producers, sometimes even engineers. Imagine the outcry if I tried to teach a class in their disciplines! In your day-to-day job, these are the people who come to your team with "suggestions" for making your story "better." They're usually wrong, and they don't know what they don't know. They straight-faced say things like "Have you ever heard of the Hero's Journey?" and force you to Reset the Sign.[8] As instructors, they often promote hackneyed storytelling techniques. Chug an entire shaker of salt for this one.

I'm not suggesting that credentials are everything. A class can still be terrible even if the instructor knows their stuff. But it's safer to stick to reputable institutions and courses. Ask your friends and established writers online for recommendations. Look through the syllabus and course materials if they're available. Check out review sites such as Rate My Professors to see what the experience was like for other students. But take reviews with a dash of salt too! (Now you understand why game writers are so salty.)

What if you don't need a diploma or certificate and simply want the knowledge? Well, then it's even easier to educate yourself. Industry events such as The Game Developer's Convention (GDC) and Develop: Brighton host talks from the top game devs in the industry and make those presentations available online for free. (Okay, *most* of them are free.) You can learn about everything from basic game design and writing to the latest advances in interactive storytelling and technology. Many devs post tips on their blogs (Emily Short's blog is a gem), and some of us write actual books about game writing. Check out your library to see what's available or pick up a copy online. Some textbooks can be a bit pricey, so consider pooling your money with other writers to create a small, shared library.

Internships

If you want to skip the college step completely and learn practical skills, then an internship is a great way to get your foot in the door. What better way to learn the job than by doing the job? The days when untrained interns fetched fresh Monsters and snacks for devs are long gone. Interns are no longer glorified gophers who don't learn new skills. Nowadays, they perform tasks related to the career they

---

[8] The overuse of the Hero's Journey is a running industry joke. I'll explain it in detail later, along with The Sign.

want and earn wages for their work. The bad news is that internships still don't pay much and they don't guarantee future employment. You could bust your butt and do an excellent job but still be let go when your internship ends. However, if you are, you'll at least have that coveted industry knowledge and experience that recruiters are looking for and can apply for fulltime work. So, it's worth it for that foot in the door. But be warned! Internships can be as hard to land as entry-level game jobs. When indie company Die Gute Fabrik offered an internship, they received over 3000 applications.[9] The competition for AAA internships can be even more intense.

Most major game companies offer internship programs. Electronic Arts (EA) and Ubisoft have robust programs to provide professional training for interns while they're still in school. "Feeder" programs like Ubisoft's are designed to spot and train talent early and hire them into the studio. I doubt I need to explain the advantages of getting trained for the exact job you want. Other major studios such as Bioware offer onboarding tracks for recent graduates, and ArenaNet has a targeted Narrative Mentorship Program. MassDigi's Summer Internship Program comes highly recommended for its focus on team-based game creation. If you're interested in working for one particular studio, ransack their website for internships and workshops.

A WORD OF CAUTION FOR INTERNS

Reputable companies like the ones I listed have excellent programs for interns, and I encourage you to check them out. However, beware of any program that isn't crystal clear about your pay and responsibilities. Unfortunately, sometimes the inexperience of interns gets abused, and they're asked to do menial work that isn't part of their job. Sorting controller cords, running errands, and photocopying should not be major responsibilities. If you're an intern or junior, remember: you're there to learn game writing, not be a flunky. On the flip side, if you're asked to do more challenging work such as writing screenplays by yourself or owning a part of the story, you should be promoted to full writer and paid accordingly. Read your job description carefully and know what your duties are. Push back in a diplomatic way if you think you're being asked to do more than you should. But hopefully that won't happen and you'll have a happy foothold in the industry. Onward and upward!

---

[9] "2021 Game Writing Internship – What We Did and What We Learned." Die Gute Fabrik. Last modified April 5, 2021. https://gutefabrik.com/what-we-did-and-what-we-learned/

Grants

Sometimes you can receive government arts grants that will cover the cost of your wages. Film Victoria in Australia offers lump-sum grants that, with some budgeting, can cover several months' worth of wages. Free labor is an enticing proposition for studios! They don't have to pay you, worry about coming up with a program for you, or vet an army of applicants. They get a worker for a decent length of time with little fuss. What's not to like about that? The easier and cheaper it is for a studio to bring you on, the more likely it is to happen. Look outside of games to make opportunities happen inside games. You'll have to research and apply for grants yourself, which is no small amount of work, but getting a foot in the door is a tremendous payoff.

Summary

So there you have it. There's more than one educational path into the games industry. You can pick the route that best fits your unique circumstances. You'll likely need a BA or an MA if you want to work internationally, but it's not a requirement otherwise. Education is critical for learning skills, but a college degree isn't a magic wand to zap away all obstacles. There are other ways to get the knowledge you need. Read. Write. Get your work out on the web where people can see it and give you feedback. This step is essential for developing your skills and growing as a writer. Join writers' circles and table-read forums. And for eff sake, do more than just play video games. I heard this advice over and over when I was interviewing people for this book. Writers will call on their entire lived experience to create games. You need a wide range of knowledge about all imaginable topics. Linguistics are useful for puzzles. Historical knowledge always comes in handy—look at the *Assassin's Creed* games. Even weird interests you think are professionally worthless can turn out to have value. In my case, I've been fascinated my whole life with the strange and arcane. Stuff the internet calls "the unexplained." I'm a storehouse of trivia about eerie phenomena like the Bélmez faces and the Cuban Sonic Weapon Conspiracy. I never dreamed that knowledge would come in handy until I interviewed for a game called *P7*. Once I saw the game pitch, I realized I'd inadvertently researched source material for that game my entire life. My esoteric knowledge had a purpose! I poured it all into the project, every obsession and oddity, until it became the shifting box of weirdness you know as *CONTROL*. Everything you learn is useful, especially when it exercises your imagination. As Rhianna said, give yourself a deep well of inspiration to draw from.

CHALLENGE

Assess your writing skills and determine how they align with the specific needs of game-writing. Identify any weak spots. For example, if you've written mostly novels, you should strengthen your screenplay or interactive writing skills. Make a list of what skills you need to work on.

- Find three educational opportunities such as online classes, internships, game incubators, and other similar programs that teach the skills you need and are attainable for you.
- Contact all three programs to express interest and find out what financial aid they offer.
- Apply to your top two picks.

OR

- Read any five books on game writing or narrative design. Here's my writer's shelf:

My craft library.

- Complete any exercises within the books.
- Hang on to your work, because we'll revisit it later when creating samples for your portfolio.

Chapter 3

Finding Work

Remember that game writing is its own discipline, with challenges and benefits unique to active-consumption storytelling. Only get into it if you're willing to learn (and learn to love!) the discipline for what it is.

—Sam Maggs, Narrative Lead for Digital Publishing & Licensing at Wizards of the Coast

When I started out as a writer, I had no clue how to find work. If there was a central resource for game jobs, I didn't know about it. The ads on Gamasutra (now Game Developer) and in the back of industry publications didn't offer much in the way of writing gigs. So when I looked for work, I pulled up a list of the studios in my region from GameDevMap and cold emailed them all to ask if they were hiring writers. Most companies never responded. The few that answered had no writing jobs. I couldn't find an open narrative role anywhere. It was a depressing time to be a new game writer. The industry has changed since then, thank goodness. There are more narrative jobs than ever, and now there are centralized databases for finding them. Devs share industry tips and FAQs (how this book started), jobs at their studio, and sometimes they'll even collate big Google docs of job openings and resources, like the one Jan David Hassel maintains.[1] There are Twitter hashtags and writers' groups and recruiters that bring jobs to you on a silver platter. So why the heck is it still so hard to break into the games industry?

---

[1] "JD's Game Jobs List." Jan David Hassel. Last accessed August 8, 2022. https://docs.google.com/document/d/1CU1H-8ZQWUPIBrT3VaUjjSMpOrarfpfhI86q8Bkpr_8/edit

DOI: 10.1201/9781003282235-4

The game industry has a senior shortage and a junior oversupply.

—Sonia "Son M" Messar, Freelance Narrative Designer

Part of the answer lies in the statistics we discussed last chapter. There are more jobs, but there are also more writers applying to them. Many roles never get advertised because they're filled by in-house promotions or word of mouth. (Everybody at a studio knows a dev friend who "would be perfect for the job.") Yet, despite all those factors, writers still find work. How do they do it? How do they get that first step inside the door? I asked a group of game devs:

- While in school I went to GDC and realized I was terrifyingly unprepared for a job in game dev, but met a lot of devs in the conference associate (CA) program. In 2011: Applied to Bioware Austin for a junior cinematic design contract, on the referral of a friend I'd made at GDC. —Ashley Ruhl
- I got a job as a game programmer/designer working on an online card game system. But it wasn't until 2009 that I got my first freelance writing gig. I got that and other gigs through friends in the industry that I met through meetups, game jams, and conventions. —Chris Tihor
- I had made a lot of small games and written a lot of stuff and had done a fair amount of web dev throughout high school/college. EA came to recruit engineering interns on campus and I went to hear one of their engineers speak; he worked on *The Sims*! (I love *The Sims*.) I talked with him for a while after his talk and he asked me what I would change in the sims if I could. I had an answer for him, was asked to interview for a design internship, and became an EA intern a few months later. —Katie Chironis
- I had planned to go into animation/film as a storyboard artist, but then tagged along with some friends to GDC 2011 on a whim (mostly as an excuse to travel with them.) A few companies actually liked my storyboard portfolio and I got a couple offers, one of them Telltale! —Jolie Menzel
- Went to game art school (4y). The first year I started navigating Twitter to follow and network with game devs and artists. I started posting my art and was reached out by a studio to do some work in my summer vacation going to my second year. Then internship > freelance > Mojang. —Jasper Boerstra
- I started in games journo knowing beforehand that I wanted to transition into games writing and made twines to pad my portfolio until I started getting contracts. But a lot of my work has come from luck, people taking chances on me, and more luck. —Emma Kidwell

See the pattern? Over and over, what works is a combination of networking and pure luck. Let's talk about luck first.

Fortune Favors the Bold

You're probably wondering how on earth you make good luck happen. Do you roll in a big pile of four-leaf clovers? Nail horseshoes to your forehead? (Don't do that.) Can you *really* channel good fortune into your job search? Honestly? No. But here's the thing: some of it isn't really luck. Opportunity rarely comes as a bolt from the blue; most of the time, "luck" is the natural result of hard work. It takes effort to position yourself so lightning can strike. Writers who succeed have built an arsenal of skills, trumpeted their goals, and connected with working devs to land that first role. Remember my origin story about meeting the QA lead for the only game studio in town? I called my big break "serendipity," but I worked my butt off to be at that exact place in that exact moment. I made a plan to return to school for game writing, earned funding for it, packed up my whole life to move to a new town, played games so I was knowledgeable, connected with friends who knew people at the only studio in town, had them introduce me to that QA lead, mentioned I was looking for game work, and *that's* when lightning struck. Not entirely luck when you think about it that way, huh? If you're following the advice in this book, you're already making your own luck.

Making your own luck also means putting your intent out there. I don't mean this in a mystical, manifest-energy-into-the-universe way. I mean actively spreading the word. Let people know you want to write games. Share work online so it will appear in web searches. Write thoughtful, game-related blog posts. Create some Twine or inklewriter games. Showcase your public portfolio. Get your work out there where people can see it. It's good practice, in every sense. You could even write an article for a prominent industry site like Game Developer or RPS. Hazel Monforton got "discovered" as a writer when her article about *Dishonored's* Outsider caught the creative director's eye—after she'd become involved in the game's community and networked with its creator. Another example of a "lucky" break. It doesn't matter if you write game reviews, industry articles, twine games, or start a blog. The main point is to put yourself out there and keep reminding people that you can write and you want to work. Position yourself well, so opportunity can come knocking.[2]

Networking

At this point, you've set your goal, built up your skills through education—formal or not—and you've broadcast your ambition. Your next step is meeting people in the industry. Networking is the single most useful thing you can do to break into games. Your connections will know what projects are in

---

[2] There's a genuine element of luck to job-hunting, and I won't pretend there isn't. You can do everything right and still not succeed. Some parts are beyond your control. Just make sure you're on top of the things you *can* control.

development at each studio. They'll teach you industry vernacular. And, most importantly, they'll help you apply to roles at their studios. You need someone on the inside who can vouch for you—or least pass along your resume. But don't just befriend established devs! Your peers are just as important. You will rise together through the ranks and be industry leaders together in future. Make friends with them now. It warms my heart when I see new writers sharing advice and cheering each other on. You need support like that in any industry, but it's especially useful when you're bashing your face against the glass wall around the industry. Sahil puts it beautifully:

> A group of peers is crucial. I'm telling you now, they will be the biggest help to you in your career and it's always nice to have someone to talk to on your own level to learn from on a communal level.

So how do you build this network of devs and peers?

Social Media

I bet you already know the drill for making connections: put yourself out there and network like wild on social media. Pick your platform of choice! Recruiters love LinkedIn. Discord and Slack are great for in-depth conversations. You can even look for work on Instagram if you want, although one recruiter said that approaches there are "questionable." But devs and hopefuls alike said Twitter is the place to be for games industry networking. It advanced my career, without a doubt, by introducing me to a community of people I'd never have met otherwise. It helped me find people who care about games and story, and it led me to some enduring friendships. Scriptwriter Whitney Rowland points out that "it takes a lot of work to dig through the chatter. And you've got to take everything with a grain of salt—not everyone's advice is helpful." Twitter can also be a toxic cesspool, especially for marginalized devs. (As I write this, many devs are moving to platforms like cohost or into industry-focused discords like The DIN or GIG.) So how do you navigate these treacherous waters to reach your goal?

Networking Strategies

Every game industry hopeful should be networking their nibs off long before they start looking for work. Students should start while they're still in school. Follow people whose work you admire and chat with them about games. Your smartest networking strategy is—wait for it—to be yourself. Yeah, yeah. I know it sounds corny, but it's the best way to make connections that will last and lead to long-term work. Sahil's Twitter strategy was "just being myself and friendly" and trying to meet people. His natural behavior eventually led him to make game dev connections, which then led to work.

> In 2021, a peer level friend who was working with Sweet Baby recommended me for a job, and I spent two months working on an escape room with them. Since then, I got one of my current jobs as a referral from my boss at Sweet Baby and another from a fellow peer. All my work so far has come from being recommended internally.

What Sahil discovered is critical. One recommendation leads to another and another and so on. That chain of connections adds up to steady work through word of mouth alone. And you get that by being sincere and open about your goals. Networking as a performance is rarely as effective.

When I started as writer, I thought networking was gross and fake. Why should I have to suck up to people I don't like just to get work? And if that's how you're approaching networking, then yeah, it *is* gross and fake. People can sense when you're feigning interest. Believe me, we can tell when someone is being nice to us because they want something. I've had messages asking for favors that turned nasty when I said no. One dev received long emails that gushed about his "god-tier" writing and asked for help—but got his name and key projects wrong. Whoops! But when you approach networking with an attitude of "Hey, I'm just trying to meet people and you seem cool," then you end up making authentic connections.

Asking for Help

Every year, game programs send students out to ask professionals for help with projects. When I first started getting these requests, it involved answering a few questions about what it's like being a game writer. I was always happy to donate an hour or two to the task—some of my advice echoes through this book. But the demands have increased over time, and this year I received a request for twenty weeks of mentoring and project feedback. That's five months of work, unpaid. I respect the hustle, I sincerely do, but come on now! That's not a reasonable request.[3] Writers will usually ignore absurd emails like that, but you're okay to ask simple questions or request advice. Many writers have FAQs on their websites. Make sure you read those before contacting the dev with questions. They might have already provided the answers you need. But if you approach a dev with respect, they'll answer with respect. Whitney's message resulted in my writing this book, so maybe follow her advice about discernment:

---

[3] If your instructor tells you to ask a professional writer for five months of free work, send them to me. I'd love to have a little chat with them.

I was careful who I went to directly. I only reached out to people when it was clear from social media they were kind, smart, experienced, and mentorship-minded. So my queries were humble and highly specific, and in return their responses were encouraging and super helpful.

One final note on contacting devs: Do not send them story ideas or scripts unless they ask for them. First of all, stop giving your work away for free. Second, remember what I said about the Idea Guy. Third, we cannot look at them for legal reasons around intellectual property rights. When fans send 200-page documents stuffed with invented lore and story ideas and their own wild imaginings for games I'm actively working on, I treat those messages like they're radioactive. I don't even open them. So send fan mail instead. I love fan mail!

Networking Etiquette

Speaking of dos and don'ts, let's talk networking etiquette. Nobody articulates it beyond vague phrases like "show respect," but we all know when the code is broken. A lot of well-known devs, the ones you're likely to follow at first, deal with some eccentric and abusive behavior on social media and are wary of people they don't know. They can't tell if you're joking around or if you're a dangerous person who's going to show up at the studio with an axe. (Yes, that happened.) I've watched fans get blocked by the creators they love on Twitter because they treat it like a chan or WhatsApp chat. It's not. I want you to understand that the games industry—especially the game-writing corner of it—is tiny. If you're rude or abusive to one game writer on social media, a thousand eyes are watching you. Everyone knows everyone, and word spreads fast. Be smart from the start so you don't spend your career running from your past.

HOW TO TALK TO DEVS

- **Good:** Can you recommend any good Twine games?
- **Bad:** Can you help me make my Twine game?
- **NO!:** I sent you my Twine game. Can I get some feedback? I need it by Tuesday.

- **Good:** I saw you tweet about playing *Hades*. How did you like it?
- **Bad:** I was digging through your tweet history & saw you mentioned *Hades* two years ago ...
- **NO!:** I can see you playing *Hades* right now. I like that color on you.

Okay, I'm obviously being a bit tongue in cheek with the phrasing, but I'm dead serious about the advice.

You Are a Brand

Recruiters warned me that they google potential candidates and can be influenced by what they find. Curate your search results so that you're projecting the image you want. You don't want the first hit on a Google search to be your drunken TikTok rendition of a sea shanty. Or maybe you do! I'm not here to tell you what your brand should be. I'm merely advising you to look at it closely with the eye of a prospective employer so you're sure it's what you want them to see. Of course, you can always separate your accounts. Have your private locked account and your public account. It's up to you if the work account is private or your main, but don't cross those streams if you can help it.

Freelancers rely on brand more than in-house writers, because they *are* their company. Toiya has this advice for standing out as a brand.

> To simplify what "brand" means, it's what one is known for, how they present themselves, and how others see them. What about you is memorable? For example, I know a writer who paints their nails before every conference they attend. When I and others see them, we'll ask them about their nails. While that might seem kind of silly, it keeps people from forgetting who that writer is. There are thousands of writers and narrative designers in the industry, and it's ridiculously competitive. Anything that gets you remembered (you know, beyond being an awful human being) is helpful. Considering that developers fill the vast majority of jobs through referrals, you're not getting referred if people don't remember you.

Your brand goes beyond your signature look or quirk. It's also the content you put out into the world. Pick a few key interests and develop those into the public face of your work. For example, my social media brand consists of about five key topics: games, writing, cats, activism, and weird stuff. That's it. (Kpop fell off the list three years ago, alas.) But there's so much to talk about with just those topics! The most important thing, and this is critical, is that those are genuine interests. Focus on things you care about. Tweet from a place of passion, and it will speak to people who share that passion. If networking means talking to people, you might as well talk about stuff you love.

So, that was a lot of information about networking through social media! I spent this much time on it because it's the quickest and easiest way to meet game devs when you're just starting out. But it's far from the only way.

Game Dev Organizations

A more traditional way to make connections is joining a professional organization like the International Game Developer's Association (IGDA), Writer's Guild of

Great Britain (WGGB), Women in Games International (WIGI), or the Game Devs of Color (GDOC) community. Folks in the Seattle area probably know about East and West Side Industry Nights, where game company folks gather and network. It's a good place to start. There are similar networking nights in any town with a major development house. Join IGDA and get involved with their game-writing special interest group (SIG). Join an online game writers' group like the ones on Twitter or Discord. Online social meetups for devs have exploded since covid hit. See if you can connect to one of them. Contact designers and writers at companies where you want to work and politely ask them for a short chat. They might say yes! Also, look for connections outside Narrative's tiny corner of the game world. Toiya emphasizes that you can learn a lot from non-writers about what they do and how to work with them. She notes that "the vast majority of writers you know are not going to get you work. The more people you know, the more opportunities you have."

Conventions

Game conventions are essentially gigantic networking events. Devs come there with a networking mindset, so they're usually quite open for a chat. Follow accounts for meetups like the Game Developer's Convention (GDC), Game Developers of Color (GDOC) convention, or smaller cons like NarraCon or the East Coast Games Conference (ECGC). Most countries have regional gatherings. Everything from the Nordic Games Conference in Sweden, to GStar in South Korea, to Africa Games Week in South Africa, and Gaming Istanbul in Turkey. It's important to note that I didn't mention cons like PAX or gamescom, and that's because they're more for fans than developers. They're a lot of fun, but for serious networking and the chance to learn something at industry panels, try to attend the developer-focused gatherings. Passes can be prohibitively expensive, so see if you qualify for grants. Failing that, volunteer to work the con or arrange meetups outside the convention center if you live in town. Many conventions offer a virtual component these days so you can watch livestreams of speakers and panels and mingle in chat rooms and lobbies. Not quite the same as going to the con in person, but hey, you save money on hotel rooms.

Applying from the Middle of Nowhere

Some of you are reading my advice about networking and quivering with frustration. It's all well and good to make contacts on Twitter or join game-writing organizations, but how does that help you when you live nowhere near a tech hub? When your local IGDA chapter is a two-hour drive away? When there are no studios nearby and no way you can move to work at one? Is a gamedev career even possible? Great news: *yes*, it is. In fact, the pandemic has made working from the middle of nowhere easier than ever.

- **Remote Work:** Increasingly, even the biggest studios are offering remote work. Bioware, Bungie, and EA all offer remote writing work. Many mobile studios and midlevel prestige studios like Failbetter Games have offered remote work for years. Whitney made her big jump into games during the pandemic, "partly because the online/work from home pivot for studios opened up a lot more remote work options around the country (and the world)." Her advice for people outside the big industry hubs is to get "comfortable with talking about yourself, your goals, and your work ... over the phone or on video." Competition for remote roles is fierce, because of the wider candidate pool, but some chance is better than no chance.
- **Indies:** If there's no AAA studio in your neck of the woods, there might be an indie team or two. Samantha Wallschlaeger started out in a "small Midwestern town with no connections, so it was a long process of volunteering online for indie projects and modding teams, and sending in application after application to bigger studios." After two years and "a lot of stubbornness" she landed a junior role. Now she's the lead writer at Crystal Dynamics.
- **Personal Projects:** If there's no game dev scene at all, you can start one. Pitch a game idea and see if anyone online is interested. Crowdfund it through Kickstarter or Indiegogo (easy to say, hard to do, I know), and work on it as a side project to your main job. Start a local game night or find collaborators for a game jam. Online collaboration is your best bet when the local scene is dead.
- **Game Jams:** These are a fantastic way to "find your people" and start making valuable connections. It also gets you hands-on practice with your craft and concrete work for your portfolio. To get started, check out Global Game Jam or any of the jams on itch.io's jam page.[4]

Find Open Positions

While you're out there building your power network, you should also actively look for job openings. This requires work, but not as much as you might think. Unlike the dark ages when I was breaking in, you don't need to search every individual company's website for job listings. (Although, you can still do that if you want.) Behold the miracle of centralized job databases! As I'm writing this book, the best place to find game-writing roles is GrackleHQ. It's free, searchable, and there's no registration required. Other large job databases are GameDevJobs, GameJobsDirect,

---

[4] "Game Jams on itch.io." Itch.io. Last accessed August 8, 2022. https://itch.io/jams

Indeed.com, and Indiedb.com. Work with Indies has a job board chock full of opportunities. Here are some other boards and sites:

Job boards

■ GIBiz's Job Board	■ HitmarkerJobs
■ RemoteGameJobs	■ @gamejobhunter
■ @xpgamejobs	■ @GameJobsCoFeed

Tara J. Branigan runs a job board for all game disciplines, and established writers often share opportunities through their professional accounts. It's hard to believe now, but there used to be a weird sort of competition around job posts. If you saw a post and other writers didn't, then it sucks to be them! That was the attitude I encountered when I started, anyway, which I found repulsive. I want to win a job because I'm the best writer for the job, not because I beat other candidates to the listing. I can't take full credit for this recent trend of sharing job ads, but I've always aggressively shared any opportunities that came my way. Now, it's the norm, hallelujah, so definitely follow people at your preferred studio to catch openings they share.

Studio Career Pages

If you want to work for a specific studio, the best place to look for work is on their website's career page. Companies will usually post the job there first, and they'll have information about the studio culture and benefits packages. If you use GrackleHQ, visit the studio's career site for more information before applying. Check out how the studio represents itself. Do their games interest you? Does it look like a place you'd like to work? If you're a marginalized writer, do you see yourself represented there? Veteran designer Willow recommends "looking through the company's social media for posts referencing events such as Black History Month or Pride." The studio should appear to care about events like these, by posting photos of the studio or staff participating in them. "Rainbow filtered logos are cheap and easy, but the hurdles required to have an in-studio event and to subsequently post that to social media" suggest base-level support. Affirming posts from company leadership also say a lot about the studio's culture.

Recruiters and Agents

Recruiters often get a bad reputation, which isn't nice, but in most cases it's actually a great job where everybody wins. Sometimes a short message is the beginning of a process that can change the course of someone's life.

—Natalie Concannon, Director at Datascope Recruitment

Most AAA studios have recruiters who are dedicated to finding talent for the company. Unlike smaller studios or indies where a dev might do recruitment work on top of their regular duties, larger studios have staff whose primary responsibility is finding the right candidate for each role. They message potential candidates about job roles and actively try to match the right role with the right person—and that person might be you! Make sure your LinkedIn profile is up to date and that you have the "I'm looking" light turned on, and you'll start showing up in recruitment searches. Embarrassing story: When I first started out, I thought recruiters were like agents. I thought they were there to help me, personally, find work. But they're absolutely not. Oh boy, are they not. I learned that lesson the hard way. Think of them more as matchmakers. They have a good-looking job and they'd love to find a charming dev who's a perfect fit for it.

Agents exist in games, though, and are helpful in certain circumstances. When writers I spoke to had agents, it was usually from their work outside of games. Son M has several agents.

I have an agent for my prose work, an agent for my comic work, and an agent for my TV work. None of them represent me in games. It's actually incredibly uncommon to have an agent represent a game writer.

She notes that things might change in the future because she sees more agents representing entire indie studios. Because those agents represent studios and not individual writers' work, "getting an agent (who makes money off the commission) seems difficult. Nevertheless, having someone there to negotiate your salary is always a wonderful thing." I heard similar sentiments from Rhianna Pratchett, who got her agent through film work and "transitioned them into representing me for games as well as there are very few specific game-writer agencies out there." She recommends getting an agent if you can, and calls out Linx as a possibility in the UK.

Contract Jobs and Staffing Agencies

We don't talk about contractors. Every AAA studio I've worked at has narrative contract roles, from QA editors to seasoned senior freelance writers who get contracted per project. I was a contractor. I work with contractors right now. Yet, contract roles are weirdly absent from conversations about working in the games industry. I'm not sure why this is, because these limited-term roles have largely replaced junior and entry-level roles in the industry and are an excellent way to break into games. Smaller narrative subcontractors such as Talespinners and Sweet Baby Inc. can help you build your skills and fill out your resumes with credits. I strongly recommend pursuing opportunities with them if you get the chance. Sahil got some of his first work by reaching out to Sweet Baby, and credits them for helping him grow.

However, I won't pretend that contract jobs are all sunshine and roses. If you contract with a studio through a large third-party agency such as Aquent, Aerotek, or Parker, they take a big chunk out of your pay. This means contract wages may be quite low. It also means you *technically* don't work for the studio; you work for the agency. This matters when it comes to things like references, benefits, perks, health insurance (in the United States), and even attending company events. The leap from contract to FTE can be extremely difficult if you're not embedded in a studio, and your role on any project is precarious. Many contract jobs have legally mandated "breaks" where you can't work at the studio for a short stint. During those breaks, contractors must find another job or go on unemployment. I encourage you to research contract work so you understand all their pros and cons. Contractor jobs are abundant and far easier to get than rare in-house junior roles. They're often the reason you see entry-level positions that require three years of experience or more. It's not as paradoxical as it seems from the outside, because the studio may be trying to "convert"[5] a contractor who's been doing the job for several years already. If you're unable to break into the industry through traditional routes, contracting work can smash through that wall and get your foot on the ladder. But enter any contracting work with realistic expectations; there's no guarantee it will lead to anything except more contract work. My advice here is to do your research, talk to people who work for staffing agencies, and see what your options are.

How to Use Resources

Now that you know what to look for and where to look, start your job hunt! Sites like GrackleHQ collate information gleaned from trawling job pages and list them chronologically. Enter your role keywords and you'll get a list of available industry jobs with the amount of time since they've been published. It's a useful tool to help you decide whether or not to apply. If you see a position has been listed for 225 days, it's likely either filled already or the studio is having trouble filling it. Useful information, either way! Sites like Indeed or Glassdoor require registration and tend to have more commercial writing jobs—roles such as content writer or communications

---

[5] Convert = hire as an FTE. When this happens, the contractor stops working for the third party and signs a permanent contract with the studio itself.

editor. But Glassdoor has useful information about the company, including feedback from candidates, information about their hiring processes, and critically, salary ranges for roles. Keep in mind that companies curate these sites to keep them generally positive. Sometimes rejected candidates and unhappy employees go there to retaliate. Bring out your salt-shaker again!

The search keywords you enter will vary by role, but I get good results from the following terms: game writer, narrative, interactive writing, content writer, narrative editor, story designer, and worldbuilding.

Red Flags

In this age of headlines about game industry scandals and abuses, it's hard to know which studios have welcoming environments. Maybe you decided to become a game writer because you love Textbox Studio's[6] games, but now you're heartbroken to read the headlines about its toxic atmosphere and aren't sure it's for you anymore. Or perhaps it's made you wonder if other studios are terrible places to work and their scandals haven't been made public yet. It's a fair question to ask. If I'm not familiar with the studio, I'll check Glassdoor and ask around in writing groups to see what people think about it. Follow some people from that studio on Twitter—not just the high-profile folks, but people doing the job you want to do. How do they talk about their day to day? Are they always tired and drained? Do you see them posting about work on weekends or after hours? Do they all seem to have financial woes when the company is doing well?[7] These are signs that you should look deeper into the studio's culture. There are many studios with great reputations that are not so great behind the scenes. Or they may be wonderful places to work for some people, but not so great for others. You won't know for *sure* if it's right for you until you work there.

Inside Job

Companies often prefer to hire from within because they know what they're getting. If a candidate is already familiar with the game and development pipeline, they can hit the ground running. As we saw with contract work, many writing jobs are never advertised because it's so easy to find qualified candidates already in-house. Or writers tell their friends who are also writers. At this very moment, I know of four writing jobs that aren't advertised on the game companies' websites.

---

[6] Textbox Studios is fictitious. I created it for the sole purpose of illustrating points in this book. You'll see it again!

[7] Companies release annual financial reports and representation data for their investors. Read them. That's who you're working for.

They'll be filled without the general gaming public ever knowing the slots were open. That's why networking is so critical. You need someone on the inside.

Some studios have employees "do the job before they do the job," which means they're doing the work of one role while still officially occupying another role. For example, a mid-level writer might take on senior work to show they can handle it before the promotion goes through. That's what you're competing with. Your rivals aren't just other hopefuls or industry writers looking to change gigs. You're competing with someone who might already be doing the job. That's how I got my first pure narrative role.

When I started at ArenaNet as a contract QA editor, I used every opportunity to remind my employers that I had game-writing experience. I introduced myself to the writers and made sure they knew I was interested in joining their team. I volunteered to write the story bible for *Guild Wars 2* so they wouldn't have to hire an extra contractor for that. Every time they needed anything involving writing, I raised my hand. When they needed to staff up, I was an obvious choice. The whole hiring-from-within thing worked in my favor there. (Although, somewhere a contractor was cursing my name.) Another time, the writing team went into crunch and needed some temporary workers. We had a tight schedule so there was no time to go through a formal job search—a process that can take months. So instead of listing the job openings on our website, we looked through the pile of resumes we already had from previous searches. They included some speculative applications writers had submitted on the off-chance that something would turn up someday. One writer also turned in a friend's resume with a personal recommendation. We ended up hiring two junior writers from that pile of existing applications. Their resumes were in the right place at the right time. Like I said, it all comes down to luck and networking. Get those lined up and the rest falls into place.

CHALLENGE: GROW YOUR NETWORK

- Choose a social media site—Twitter, Discord, LinkedIn, whatever you want—and connect with three professionals who currently have the job you want.
- Read everything they post for three weeks and see what information they share. Don't contact them! Just observe their posts. At the end of that time, ping them with your most burning question related to their expertise. For example, if a writer has been posting about screenplays all week, you might ask them if they can recommend good sites for reading game screenplays. At worst, they'll ignore you. At best, they'll point you toward a valuable resource and you'll have established a small connection.
- Repeat until you have a large enough network that you see job posts go by daily.

Chapter 4

Applications

Continuing your writing will make you a better writer, especially if you're getting feedback from people. Even when I was underemployed or unemployed, constantly writing on my own projects really helped me focus on what was important. It kept me going and understanding that even if I don't get everything I'm applying for, I can still keep working on my own projects and keep progressing. I definitely recommend always having a side project going when you're trying to break into the industry.

—Evan Higgins, Senior Scriptwriter

So, you've done your homework, networked your sass off, checked all the job sites, and followed up every opportunity. Finally, you see a job post that sounds perfect. It's your dream job! You're ready to go for it! Now, all you have to do is convince the studio to hire you.

The Job Post

You are looking for a certain kind of writer. You're not just looking for somebody who can write. You're looking for somebody who is a good match.

—Mikko "Mikki" Rautalahti, Narrative Director, Roleverse

Every word in a job listing gets scrutinized ten times over before it goes live. Recruiters assemble job posts, but they consult with hiring managers and producers to make sure they understand what's needed for the role. What work will

DOI: 10.1201/9781003282235-5

candidates do? What are the must-have skills? How much wiggle room is there for non-games experience? Once the recruiter and team align on the role needs, the recruiter writes the post. Narrative teams often write up their own posts and hand them off for recruiters to adjust with necessary studio and legal information. This includes steps to apply, instructions for submitting samples, information about the studio and job benefits, and all those required legal disclaimers. Many companies run posts through language checkers to avoid biased terminology. Once the ad has been written, analyzed, checked, and approved by various departments, it's posted online and recruiters start spreading the word. They post ads on the studio page, LinkedIn, third-party career sites, and job boards—any site that might reach their target audience. The job post is engineered to focus on a core set of skills while attracting the widest possible pool of candidates. The ad found you, so hurrah! You're part of the intended audience! But do you have a shot? How do you know if you're the writer they're looking for? Let's look at one of those ads.

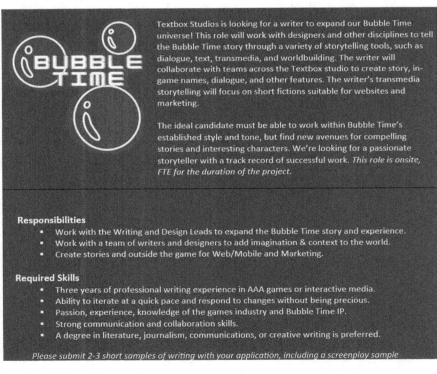

Textbox Studios is looking for a writer to expand our Bubble Time universe! This role will work with designers and other disciplines to tell the Bubble Time story through a variety of storytelling tools, such as dialogue, text, transmedia, and worldbuilding. The writer will collaborate with teams across the Textbox studio to create story, in-game names, dialogue, and other features. The writer's transmedia storytelling will focus on short fictions suitable for websites and marketing.

The ideal candidate must be able to work within Bubble Time's established style and tone, but find new avenues for compelling stories and interesting characters. We're looking for a passionate storyteller with a track record of successful work. *This role is onsite, FTE for the duration of the project.*

Responsibilities
- Work with the Writing and Design Leads to expand the Bubble Time story and experience.
- Work with a team of writers and designers to add imagination & context to the world.
- Create stories and outside the game for Web/Mobile and Marketing.

Required Skills
- Three years of professional writing experience in AAA games or interactive media.
- Ability to iterate at a quick pace and respond to changes without being precious.
- Passion, experience, knowledge of the games industry and Bubble Time IP.
- Strong communication and collaboration skills.
- A degree in literature, journalism, communications, or creative writing is preferred.

Please submit 2-3 short samples of writing with your application, including a screenplay sample

A writing job post.

Read through the ad carefully. It can be hard to read between the lines of job posts, so here's what it all means, in plain English:

- Hey, we're making a sequel to our game. It helps if you're familiar with it.
- We need a writer who can work with our team on stories for the game and various ads and websites, so be versatile.
- We want you to work fulltime in the studio.
- Someone must like your writing enough to have paid you for it. For years.
- This is a creative role.
- Must be able to kill your darlings and keep creating.
- Must like video games and writing.
- Must play well with others.
- A college degree would be nice.

Pretty simple, right? It's not so intimidating when you strip away the jargon. If it still seems daunting to you, keep in mind that the ad describes the *ideal* candidate. All of those bullet points are negotiable, so don't be afraid to apply even if you don't tick every box. But maybe you match their ideal candidate better than you think. Let's dig into the details of these requirements. If you look closer at the criteria, you'll see they fall into three distinct categories:

- Experience
- Skills
- Job requirements.

Let's talk about what's expected for each of these categories.

Experience

You might know the job title, but how do you know if you have enough experience for it? That's tricky to gauge, especially if you're trying to translate your title as an indie dev into AAA terms. I know an experienced writer for indie games who recently tried to make the leap into AAA. She applied for a narrative director spot at a major US studio. She knew a role like that was a long shot, but was still shocked by how fast the rejection came. She didn't realize how great a leap that director role was from her current senior role. For an intensely anticipated game like that one, her competition was the best narrative talent the industry can offer. And, sure enough, when the studio announced their pick for director, it was someone with decades of experience leading similarly high-profile projects.

Sometimes studios have a specific person in mind for high-profile roles like that and write the job description to attract them. There's no way a writer can know that from outside though, so they have to take a chance. Recruiters are generally sympathetic to the situation but said that applicants frequently try for roles that are simply beyond their reach. I heard about college students applying for senior roles and people with absolutely no writing, design, or industry experience shooting for coveted director roles. I chalk up many of these ambitious applications to honest mistakes. People simply don't know the studio hierarchy. It's hard enough to parse when you're working in AAA, but it must seem opaque and random to people outside the industry. And, let's be honest here, some of those long-shot applications are from writers who know they're rolling the dice. No guts, no glory, right? But it's best to go for a role you can actually land. So how can you know if you're aiming too high? How do you look at a job post and determine if you have enough experience for the job? The key section is "what we expect from you." These are the core requirements for the role. Let's take another peek at that ad.

One thing jumps out right away: there's no "senior" or "junior" modifier on the job title. Look back at the hierarchy in chapter one, and you'll see this is a mid-level position. Mid-level means you don't need the know-how of a senior writer, but you shouldn't be a blank slate. I see a lot of film, indie, and mobile game writers make the switch to AAA at the mid-level. It's the sweet spot for crossover. If you've shipped an indie game or worked on a TV series, simply explain how your experience translates to AAA game development. It's that easy.

You'll hear people say looking for work is a "numbers game" and there's some truth to that. The more applications you send out, the better your odds of finding the right job. Be smart about it though, and don't carpet bomb the industry with your resume. I encourage you to apply for any job you think you can handle, but be realistic. The chart of ad requirements on the next page says it all.[1]

As you can see, you're unlikely to get writing roles without some sort of similar experience. The more responsibility a role has, like lead and director, the harder it is to sell a lack of industry experience. No studio's going to look at your Twine game, say, "This kid's a star!" and hand you the keys to a multimillion-dollar project. It's too risky. The brutal truth is that AAA projects attract so many applicants that they're spoiled for choice. When you're looking at thousands of resumes per role, you can reject all but the top 5% of candidates and still have an excellent selection to hire from. To secure a game-writing position in AAA you need experience as a writer in some field: games, film, TV, *something*. Even if you're an amazing writer, you'll be competing with other amazing writers who *also* have experience. I get how frustrating that news is, but I won't sugarcoat it. "But, Anna," you say, "How am I supposed to get experience? All the jobs I see expect you to have it already!" It's true. Welcome to the AAA experience paradox.

---

[1] Lassheikki, Christina. "Game Writers and Narrative Designers. The evolving role of story-telling professionals in game development." 2022, Master's Thesis, Aalto University School of Art, Design, and Architecture.

Experience

Prior experience was a key requirement for most of the jobs in the sample. As already discussed in the section on seniority, prior work experience was listed as a requirement for a vast majority of the positions regardless of level. But, what does experience mean?

Experience type	Short description	Count
Similar position	Working experience in a similar position	82
Years	A minimum amount of experience	71
Shipped projects	Released game projects the person worked on for a significant part of the development process	64
Game writer work	Experience working as a game writer	47
AAA	Experience working in AAA game development	35
Writing	Writing experience in general	34
Narrative designer work	Experience working as a narrative designer	30
Similar projects	Experience working on a similar game to the project hiring	27
Other media	Experience working in other mediums than games	23
Game industry	Experience working in the game industry in some capacity (not necessarily narrative)	21

Table 10: Most requested experience.

The most common desired specific experience was working experience in a similar position to the advertised one (count: 82); often expressed in years (count: 71). This meant experience in game writing or narrative design for game writing and narrative design positions, copywriting for copywriting, project management for producers and managers, localization for localization, and so on. Even in the junior positions, working

Key requirements in job posts.

The Experience Paradox

As Son M explains:

> I knew I wouldn't be able to step into games myself without some sort of work history. Introducing the cycle of needing experience to get more experience.

Ahhh, there it is in a nutshell. You can't get a job without experience, but you can't get experience without a job. So how you do break free of this catch-22? We discussed some strategies for that in the last chapter, like QA or contract work. You can transfer internally from technical writing or level design or any narrative-adjacent discipline that might be less competitive than game writing at the entry level. But internal jumps require you to have a foot in the industry already, and, uh, that's the hard part.

Another strategy is to have comparable experience outside of AAA, preferably work that uses a similar skillset. Let's go back and take a closer look at the job description to see what sort of work you'd be doing. Are you already able to do this kind of work? Have you done this kind of work in another form, perhaps in another medium? Maybe you never wrote a screenplay for a AAA game, but you wrote an entire feature-length script for a competition. Or you wrote a play in college. Or you wrote a smaller-scale version of the exact type of game the studio is making. Then you have experience! If you combine that with work on an indie team or in AAA in another discipline, you can craft a compelling case that you're able to handle the job. "To beat that experience hurdle, I did what any indie inevitably does," Son M said. "I decided to make my own game and studio." Her indie work was fulfilling and made her "genuinely happy," but it also put skills and experience on her resume that could directly translate to AAA work when she was ready for that transition. That's how you do it!

Onsite vs. Remote

Now, let's look at what the role requires besides experience. As you can see, this is not a remote position. I know, I know. It would be great if every company offered remote work, but currently they don't. Things are starting to get better though! I used to be very discouraging in this section of my FAQ, but now I don't need to be. As terrible as the coronavirus pandemic has been, it's forced many companies to reexamine onsite requirements and acknowledge that remote work is a feasible solution. So why doesn't every studio just go remote? There are reasons for it, ranging from legal issues to tax agreements to simple time differences. When I was working in Finland, we had a contract writer based in Seattle. It was difficult to coordinate meetings and writers' room sessions because of the vast time difference. That poor writer went nocturnal to keep up with our development cycle. Senior staff is often expected to be at the studio leading meetings, driving schedules, and coordinating with other teams. Some companies have tax incentives and government requirements that force them to hire within the country first. (An obstacle to keep in mind if you're looking at international roles.) I know there are rebuttals to every point I raised and maybe more companies will listen and go remote in the future. But the raw truth is that if a studio insists upon an onsite writer—whatever their reasons—and you can only be remote, you'll likely lose the job. But you won't know unless you ask, so at least talk to the studio and find out if remote work is possible. Be clear about your needs from the start. If the job clearly states the role is "onsite only" and you need to be remote, don't wait until you get an offer to say that. They might be able to accommodate you for a short period, but they'll eventually want you in the studio. If not you, they'll go with another candidate who's willing to relocate. Established writers have some bargaining power in this situation. I know two US writers who successfully negotiated hybrid and remote work arrangements for jobs that were meant to be onsite. So, it can happen. But if you're a new writer, you're better off not wasting everyone's time. And hey! Maybe you enjoy travel and experiencing new cultures. In that case, onsite work is no barrier for you and more opportunities are available.

Communication and Collaboration

Let's go back to that job listing. What are some other requirements? It says communication and teamwork are important. That means being a team player, rolling with development changes, and being able to handle constructive criticism are non-negotiable parts of this job. Making games is a collaborative process. Narrative—especially in story-driven games—unites all departments, from programming to PR. You have to communicate your ideas clearly, accept feedback with grace, and make needed changes without getting huffy or hurt. I'm not saying you'll have group hugs with your team all day, but you need to get along with them and not be precious about your writing. If you don't like working with other people, then AAA games aren't a good fit for you. Collaboration and communication are a part of this, as writers must evangelize the story to other teams and prevent what I call "narrative drift." That's where communication breaks down and people end up working on material that uses an outdated version of the story as its source. This can mean wasted work for them and wasted time for everyone if it has to be redone. In a worst-case scenario, there's no time for redoes and narrative has to find a way to use the work, even though it no longer fits into the story. If you've ever played a game and encountered a scene or a section of dialogue that felt tonally off from the rest of the story, that's most likely narrative drift. The only cure for it is constant communication. It's no surprise then that "the most important single skill, mentioned in 51% of job ads" is communication. "Outstanding, excellent, exceptionally strong, enthusiastic, clear, continuous, collaborative, effective"[2] communication is the glue that holds projects together. It's a bedrock requirement.

---

[2] Lassheikki, Christina. "Game Writers and Narrative Designers. The evolving role of storytelling professionals in game development." 2022, Master's Thesis, Aalto University School of Art, Design, and Architecture.

Writing Skills

Back to the job ad! Another requirement is that you "write well." I know this seems painfully obvious, but this is where most applicants fall down. Yet, it's the most critical part of the job. You must write well, in English (or whatever the primary game language is), and be able to prove it. Maybe you've done a lot of design work, or you're a master at production scheduling, or you've memorized every line from *Disco Elysium*. Cool, cool. How's your writing? You must be able to demonstrate, through samples and a writing test, that you can write a compelling game story. Some ads won't explicitly call out this requirement because they assume you wouldn't apply for the role if you can't write. But I know from personal experience that some candidates will apply with no writing ability. None. I'm not talking about the ability to write interactive stories either. It's not screenwriters who are moving from TV or film into games or indie writers moving into AAA. Those are people who are skilled at writing in their own media and are interested in expanding their repertoire. If that's you, don't hesitate to apply! But if you've never written professionally, if you have no work to show, or if you've never received feedback on your work to know if it's any good, then please. Think hard before applying. Amateur writers make the process harder for everyone. They slow the process down, as Petteri notes.

> A lot of people want to work in the industry and that's the problem. It's easy to write. Pretty much everyone in the world writes something. And that makes you feel that, okay, because I can write, it means that I can be a writer. That's not the case. But not everyone knows it, and it means that there's a huge amount of applications for writing jobs.

He explains that having to plow through so many unqualified applicants jams up the process and forces recruiters to prescreen applicants with requirements like industry experience and game writing skills. "And then it's impossible for you to break into the industry."

This is why it's so important to get objective feedback on your work. If you've only scribbled your thoughts into a notebook and never shared them, you can't know how good or bad your work is. You have to put it out there and find out where you need to improve. That's the only way to become a good writer. Learning to accept critique also helps with that "don't be precious" requirement. It's scary, but it's the critical first step. If you haven't done this yet, stop right now and do it. Go. Get some feedback. Come back to this section when you're ready.

As the sign says.

Hey, you're back! Great. Now that you're confident you have what it takes to write professionally and have work to share, let's continue.

Where were we? Oh, right. You've looked over the requirements and they're a good fit for you. You have the necessary skills and experience and you're ready to apply. What's next?

Online Forms

Mikko "Mikki" Rautalahti lays out the challenge:

> The first hurdle is that you have to make a first impression that says "I have my act together enough that I can do a simple thing and follow the instructions that are given." And if you can't do that, it's kind of horrible, but it's a sign of something. It's not an absolute judgment of you as a person, but it means that there are criteria. And you didn't meet the criteria.

Keep reading the ad to find out what you should you do next. Most ads will direct you to an application process. Even if you apply through a studio's website, you might find yourself using third-party software—something like Taleo or Jobvite. There it's just a matter of filling out an electronic form and submitting a resume and cover letter. That's easy enough, right? If you're going through an agency recruiter, it's even easier. Natalie Concannon explains that they contact the studio for you and "often pitch your application over the phone or write a little paragraph themselves." They sometimes have information about the project genre and timeframe that isn't on public-facing posts, and that's a real advantage for unannounced projects. But if you're applying on your own, here's how you do it.

Step 1: Instructions

Go ahead and set up an account if it's for a service like Taleo. Save your account information, because a lot of different studios use the same services and you can reuse your login credentials. Quickly click through the application to see what materials they're asking for. You'll usually need the following:

- Resume
- Cover letter
- Samples.

You should have a template for these ready to go when you start applying for work, but don't worry if you don't. You're not submitting them yet. Page through the application form and make a note of any critical information like deadlines or unusual requirements like work visa documentation. Then *read the application instructions one more time*. Know what's expected of you and follow the instructions carefully. Don't give recruiters an easy reason to bin your application. If you're unsure of any instructions, ask for help. Your network will know what to do, so lean on them.

Now, close the form and get ready to do some homework.

Step 2: Research

If you're lobbing the same application materials at every studio without doing any research, then you're already at a disadvantage. You should find out everything you can about the project and studio and tailor your application to match what they're looking for. Jump on your favorite search engine and start digging up information. Here's what you should find out about:

- **Project:** What game is the role for? If the ad doesn't say then check the studio website to see if they've announced the project. If they have, then watch the trailer, and click through the press materials. You're looking for genre, tone, and release date. This information will come in handy when you're tailoring your resume and choosing your writing samples. The release date might tell you where the game is in production and what sort of work you'll be doing. The game is slated for release in late 2022 but they're hiring writers in January 2022? Odds are the game is in full production and the cinematic writing is done. They likely need help with barks and UI text to get it over the finish line. But if you see no release date or announced project? Potentially, you could be entering during pre-production and have a chance to build the world and create a story from the ground up. Of course, this is speculation. Every project is different and there's no way to know for sure until you talk to the studio, but timeframe can give you an idea of what skills to emphasize in your application.

- **Studio Culture:** You should have done a background check on the studio already to know if it's the kind of place you want to work. Now you should be doing research to see who the big names are at the studio. Are they people you're excited to work with? What are their past projects like? Look through their website and see how they're representing themselves. Look at the pictures of the devs on the site. Remember that these images are carefully curated to present a specific image. What is that image? Do they have a group photo on the "About Us" page that is all white men? Then you might not feel comfortable there as a woman or a Black man. Read through all the text. Blogs are a goldmine for discovering what's important to a company. What values are they emphasizing? What is the studio's vision? What are they putting out there into the world? Note any key words or ideas they use. "Innovation." "Collaboration." "Groundbreaking." "Traditional." "Global." Keep those concepts in mind for when you write your cover letter.

- **Salary and Benefits:** Sadly, very few job posts state the salary range for the role. But use your resources: Glassdoor and the gamedev Google docs are good places to see what that role pays. We'll discuss salary negotiations in a later chapter; here, you're just checking to see if the role pays enough to interest you. The last thing you want is to go through the entire hiring process only to learn that their offer is far below what you need to survive. Get a sense of it now before applying. Salary information is rare, but companies usually post benefits and perks on their websites. It says a lot about a company if they offer generous PTO or mental health days or shares in company stock. If the job is onsite in another country, you'll definitely want to see mention of a relocation package. Again, you're not looking for specifics now—those can all be negotiated later on—but you do want to get a feel for what working at this studio would be like.

Once you've done your research, you should have a good sense of what the company cares about and what they want from this role. You're ready to apply!

Step 3: Custom Fit

Recruiters are your primary audience so tailor your application materials for them. Only a small percentage of applications get sent on to hiring managers. Writers have asked me what I thought of their application, and I've had to admit that I never saw it. So don't worry about managers yet! At this first step, you're trying to impress the recruiter. You're trying to show them that you have what it takes to get this job—and you don't have much time to do it. Several recruiters mentioned a "thirty-second rule." What does that mean? It means they should be able to grasp the essentials of your application at a glance. You have thirty seconds to convince them you have the right skills or your app goes in the bin. Petteri recommends that you "spend a lot of time on the application, not a lot of time on a cover letter, and a lot of time making sure that all the documents that you include are the best possible." Forget the advice about stuffing your application with keywords to pass some sort of software scanner.[3] Focus on convincing a very real, very human recruiter looking at your application that you're worth hiring. I'll walk through how to do exactly that in the next few chapters. For now, make sure you've filled out every form, provided every bit of requested information, and met the deadline. Hit send and *whoosh*! You're on your way. Good luck!

Timing

People often ask if there's a best time to apply for game-writing jobs. The answer is no, because every project is different. However, there are some bad times to apply for work. Several recruiters said you shouldn't apply during the April-May rush. That's when a fresh crop of graduates flood the market with resumes. You might get lost in the crowd. And don't apply right before the winter holidays (Christmas, Hanukkah, New Year's, etc.) because many studios are closed and devs are on vacation. Your application might sit there for weeks or hang at a crucial step. Also, if you're applying to European studios, many of them semi-close during July when everyone goes on summer vacation. You probably don't want to apply at the end of June. . This isn't a hard "don't." I've applied during all those windows and had no problems. But be aware that the application process might move slower at those times, and be patient.

Ghosting

But let's say you didn't read my book in time and sent in your application to a Swedish studio in July. Or you got an encouraging response from a recruiter and then they disappeared on you. What then? Across the board, recruiters said it wasn't deliberate and didn't reflect anything the candidate did. "It's not a malicious thing," Natalie said. "Recruiters are often just very pushed for time."

---

[3] You can do the trick where you put a block of keywords at the bottom of your resume in white text so they're invisible, if you absolutely must. But a successful resume will have human eyes on it, so keep that in mind.

Another recruiter explained that sometimes technology fails and emails get lost. Sometimes your assigned recruiter goes on medical leave or vacation and your application simply slips through the cracks. Petteri once found a request for feedback that got filtered incorrectly and lost for three months. He still answered it, but ruefully said that "this person probably hates me and thinks I wear an evil mustache. You know, like I want to torment them. Just give the benefit of the doubt." I've heard stories of candidates receiving rejection emails years after submission. Unfortunately, it happens. A decade ago, I applied for a writing job at Irrational Games, and I didn't hear back from them for months. I'd long given up by the time I received a rejection email from them that began, "Hi Matt! Thank you for your interest ...."[4]

Those are extreme cases, but mistakes happen. Here's how you handle those situations.

- ■ **Application with no response:** If you sent in a general application and never heard back from the studio, there's not much you can do. Some studios don't send rejection notices for the big slush pile of applications. My strategy (defense mechanism?) for this reality is to assume every application is a no. Send in the form, hope for the best, but keep moving and submitting to other studios. The old "fire and forget" strategy. If it's a yes, you'll get a pleasant surprise when you hear from them. If it's a no, then you haven't wasted any time on a dead end. Either way, there's no need for communication beyond the application.
- ■ **Application with response:** If you're waiting for a response from a recruiter who contacted you about your application, it's fine to ping them if they go silent. Don't assume the studio is trying to send you a negative message. It's probably just an oversight. Wait until it's been no less than a week, ideally two weeks, and then email to nudge them. If you still don't hear back, nudge them again after one more week. If you haven't heard back after two reminders, let it go. It's awful when it happens, and it's not a great way to have your hopes end, but you don't have a choice. Pushing the issue will make you look bad. One recruiter describes "daily spamming" from angry candidates, and another received threatening messages. Terrorizing recruiters is not going to get you a job. Don't do it. Just let it go and move on to other possibilities.
- ■ **In the Hiring Process:** If you're fairly deep into the hiring process when you get ghosted, it's safe to ping the studio with reminders. It's also okay at this stage to gently remind the studio that you have other opportunities. Don't hesitate to ask questions or nudge recruiters, as it's rare to ghost candidates at this stage. But mistakes can happen! I had one studio disappear for two

---

[4] I maintain that they never rejected me, and they'll write to offer me a job any day now. Any day ... .

months after (what I believed was) a good interview. I was disheartened, but after a few reminders with no response, I gave up. Out of the blue, they got back to me, and I learned that the old recruiter had left without handing off my information to the new recruiter. We resumed the interview process, and I got the job. Petteri says slips like this aren't uncommon, but still unfortunate. "I'm sorry for everyone I've ghosted in my life," he said. "But it happens."

Reapplying

What if you're turned down for one job, and then the studio posts another job that seems like a better fit? Should you apply? Yes! If you were rejected for a senior role and they post a mid-level job, go for it! But *don't do the reverse.* Unless the studio specifically said that you were overqualified for the mid-level and asked you to apply for the more senior role, you won't get hired for a more senior role than the one you were rejected for.

What if it's been a few months and you see that the company is still hiring for the job you got rejected for? Should you reapply? Wellll … maybe. Petteri suggests contacting the recruiter instead of reapplying. "Say, 'Hey, I applied for this job four months back, but it seems like it's still open. What's the situation?' And then they'll probably tell you that 'Okay, I didn't find the right kind of person yet.'" In those cases, it's up the recruiter to decide how to proceed. The job description might have changed or the role needs might be different. Maybe you'll look more appealing than you did before they interviewed fifty less-qualified candidates with no success. There's absolutely no harm in asking.

It's also fine to apply for the *same* role if your situation has changed substantially. If you were rejected for not having any interactive writing experience and you worked on a successful indie game since then, reapply. If your samples were underwhelming before, but now an NDA has been lifted and you have much better work to show, reapply. Any significant change to your skills or experience that aligns you more closely with the requirements is a good reason to reapply. But outside of substantial changes to your skillset, recruiters recommend waiting six months to a year before applying for the same role again.

Speculative Applications

What about the method I used when I was a baby writer? Sending unsolicited emails to every company in the region to see if they have any openings that aren't listed. Seems like a good plan, right? You can let them know you're interested, maybe include a link to your website or resume, and see what happens. I know many people who got jobs that way. I got jobs that way. Petteri doesn't discourage it, but he suggests being selective. "Instead of doing the shotgun approach where you're just applying to everything, pick your battles. Maybe start with one or two companies that really speak to you. That's something that helps breaking in."

Unlike job posts where you know there's a role to be filled, speculative applications are a shot in the dark. You might never hear back. You might hear back months later. You might hear, "We've got nothing now, but we'll keep your resume on file." All you need is one studio to say yes, and you're on your way. Petteri agrees that it's worth trying spec apps but says breaking in is "tough, and I'm sorry for everyone that needs to make that jump. It's a kind of brutal industry in that way."

Rejection

Listen, my friend. You're going to hear a lot of nos in your career. You're going to meet a lot of people who don't like your work. You're going to have more doors slam in your face than will open. You're going to know that job you applied for is *perfect* for you—but nobody else will see it, and you'll get rejected. It's terrible. It's painful. It's easy to get angry or feel like giving up. I know. I *know*. And I know it sounds weird, but you'll learn to roll with it. You'll learn from it without letting it destroy you. It will still hurt, so let yourself hurt. Curl up in a fetal position. Scream from a mountaintop. Eat a tub of ice cream. Be kind to yourself and do what you need to feel better. Then pick yourself up, and come back fighting. Ask yourself, "What can this teach me? How can this rejection make me better?" Find ways to take what you've learned and apply them to your next attempt. Do what Whitney did. She looked for patterns in her rejections.

> I started tracking my application progress (meaning: immediate form rejection vs. personalized rejection vs. 'we'll hold on to your application' vs. interview request). I was constantly updating and improving my application materials based on these successes/failures. An incremental education.

Eventually, her efforts paid off and she landed a scriptwriting job at Ubisoft. That can be you.

Rejections aren't personal. Only one writer can get that job you applied for. One writer out of thousands. For whatever reason, you weren't the one this time. It doesn't mean you're a bad writer or a bad person. A lot happens behind the scenes during hiring. Schedules change. Hiring priorities shift. One dev told me that he was emailing an offer to a senior candidate when the role got axed. I was in the final interview stage with one studio when their entire project got cancelled. You might be unlucky and end up competing with an industry rockstar for the role. Or it could come down to simple bad timing. Sweet Baby Inc CEO Kim Belair points out that when companies get 700 applications and find the right candidate early, that means your work "didn't even get read because you were number 650. It's so demoralizing." There are a million factors outside your control. Don't take it personally and keep looking.

Feedback

You might be asking, "How the heck will I know why I was rejected? I just got a form email thanking me for my interest." Rejections early in the hiring process don't often come with feedback, it's true. But that doesn't mean you can't ask for any. Don't be afraid to ask the recruiter (politely!) what you can do to improve your chances. There's no guarantee they'll respond. Some do, some don't. In some cases, your application might get rejected before it was seen by anyone qualified to assess it. But no one will hold it against you for asking for feedback. The further you get in the process, the more feedback you'll get. I always write up brief feedback for initial screenings, more detailed feedback for writing tests, and a personal email for long "onsite" interviews. It's my understanding that this feedback doesn't always get to applicants in the rejection email, but it's there if you ask about it. Not every hiring manager writes feedback, and I want to be clear that you shouldn't expect or demand it. It's incredibly time consuming to write up that much feedback and most leads simply don't have the time. We're also cautious not to say too much for legal reasons and because some candidates want to … argue about it. But you won't know unless you ask.

Sometimes, a company will tell you to apply for a more junior role or wait until another project starts hiring if it's a better fit. Sometimes, they'll give good, detailed critique that lays out exactly what parts of your application or writing need work. And sometimes, you'll get feedback like this rejection note one writer shared with me:

> Thank you for your patience. I shared your sample with our lead writer, but I return with disappointing news. He's appreciative of your effort but doesn't see your skills or level as a good fit for the team's current needs.
>
> Now I must add insult to injury and say that I don't have detailed feedback for you. We're moving at a fast pace to finalize the game right now and unfortunately can't spare time for individual evaluations. However, the lead writer mentioned issues like a lack of dramatic development and exposure, lack of tension, loose pacing and plot progression, poor

characterization, stylistic issues, on-the-nose dialog, show vs. tell, and failure to evoke emotion as his reasons for declining your application. If I get more specific feedback from him in the future, I'll send it along.

I know this isn't the outcome you hoped for, but I appreciate your willingness to attempt this challenge. I'm sure your future holds many more opportunities, and you will continue to grow throughout your career. Perhaps our paths will cross again in the future. Let's stay in touch![5]

This is shameful feedback. Shameful for the studio that sent it. The critique is too vague and high level to be constructive, it doesn't help you grow, and it's inexcusably cruel. Bizarrely, I hear that it's the studio's standard rejection response. Your only takeaway from a rejection like this should be "whew, I dodged a bullet!" Be glad you found out early what they were like and avoided mental scarring.

After Submitting

But enough about rejection. You're just getting started! You've found a promising role, checked out the company, and learned the ins and outs of applying to studios. Of course, you can't send an application off by itself. You'll need to send a resume and cover letter too. Let's talk about those next.

CHALLENGE

- Find three jobs you're interested in and break down the ads to answer the following questions:
  - What level is the role?
  - How much experience is needed? Do I have that or *comparable* experience?
  - What are the essential skills? Do I have any skills that match or are similar?
  - Where does the job take place?
  - If remote, what is the time difference? If onsite, do they offer a relocation budget?
  - What materials are they asking for? Do I have them? Can I get them?
  - What are the salary and benefits for the role? Is that enough to live on?

---

[5] Some details have been changed to protect the candidate's identity.

■ Research three studios and answer the following questions:
  • What type of games do they make? (genre, tone, etc.)
  • What is their studio culture like? Are people like me there?
  • What are the studio's values? How do they align with mine? (Ex: They incorporate NFTs into their games, and I'm opposed to them.)
  • Is there a deadline for the application?
  • How do I apply?

Keep this information handy for the next few chapters.

Chapter 5

Resumes

Is your narrative in tune with the player fantasy or is it in opposition? Does your narrative match the gameplay? Does your cutscene have anything do with what the player has done? Context is everything.

—Kim Swift, Senior Director of Cloud Gaming,
Xbox Game Studios Publishing

Time to write a new resume! Most writers don't sit down and craft an amazing resume from sheer willpower alone. They go online for some tips first. A quick search yields hundreds of sites and services that promise to craft a "competitive," "polished," "job-winning," and "PERFECT" resume. The advice is clear: Stick to the facts. Sell yourself! Have a bold mission statement. Mission statements are old-fashioned. Include your hobbies. Don't include non-work information. Focus on skills, not experience. Recruiters only care about experience.

Okaaay, maybe it's not so clear. I see more conflicting and just plain bad advice about resumes than I do about anything besides game writing itself. When every site claims to have the secret formula to success, whose guidelines do you follow?

If you're looking for a magic bullet, then I'm sorry. There isn't one. You can follow every rule on those resume sites, use their custom templates, spend a fortune on custom content, have epiphanies with their career counselors, and still not get a job. Why? Because it all comes down to individuality. Your individual experience as a writer; the individual requirements of the role; and the individual assessment of the recruiter. One recruiter might prefer a short, spare list of jobs in chronological order. Another recruiter might want details on your so-called soft skills. What recruiters want may be different from what hiring managers are looking for. It all depends on who's looking at your resume for each job. You have no way to know in advance what they want, so what the heck

DOI: 10.1201/9781003282235-6

are you supposed to do? It's a confusing process. To get answers, I interviewed hiring managers from every corner of the games industry and recruiters from some of the top AAA companies in the world. And I drew on my two decades of experience on both sides of the hiring process. I found conflicting advice, yes, but I also found clear patterns. (And strong opinions!) There's a core of information that everyone wants and then there are nice-to-haves. I'll break it all down step by step, so you can craft a resume that gives essential information but still lets your unique qualities shine through.

Essentials

Resumes are simple when you get right down to it. They say who you are and what you've done and give enough accomplishments to extrapolate what you might do in the future. They're lists of basic information presented in a way that says "Hey! I'm perfect for this role. Hire me!" It's the presentation of this simple information that gets tricky. If you're applying for a game-writing or narrative design role, your resume should tell the story of who you are. If it's a garbled mess and difficult to parse, then you've failed to communicate your story. It doesn't speak well to your talent as a writer. Writers are communicators. This is your area of expertise. Show that in your application materials! Now, before you go and turn your resume into a short story or start fictionalizing your work history, let's talk function and format.

Function

When a recruiter is examining your resume, they're trying to answer a simple question: Can this person do this job? Petteri can see if a programmer is qualified by simply looking for keywords. "If I'm looking for someone experienced in Python, for example, and they don't list Python, and the cover letter doesn't say anything about Python—that's instant rejection. I'm not looking for a senior who doesn't have that." But for writing jobs, it's more difficult to quantify skills. Software proficiencies don't cut it. "'Yeah, I know how to use Google docs and a keyboard so hire me.' No. It's not that simple." What he's looking for is evidence you've utilized your writing skills in previous jobs, and that might look different for every candidate. That's great news for you, because it means you have room to make a case for yourself. No keywords or specific programs needed. As long you include enough information for recruiters to assess your qualifications, you're golden. Here's the essential information your resume should contain:

- Your name (I'm not kidding. People forget.).
- Contact information (important!).

- Relevant job history.
- Relevant skills *and their context.*
- Education, certification, or professional membership if relevant.
- A link to your website if you have one.
- A link to your online portfolio if you have one.

That's it. That's all recruiters need. Simple, right? Yet it's so easy get confused when you're assembling this information into a document.

Format

It bears repeating that resumes are there to show your suitability for a role, ideally through a track record of doing similar work at similar jobs. Your brief for this assignment is to tell studios why they should hire you in succinct terms. That means fitting a persuasive history into a condensed format that showcases your strengths. If you need to explain or clarify a detail of your experience, do it in your cover letter. That's what cover letters are for: explanation. Resumes are for facts. The ugly truth is that recruiters and hiring managers don't have much time to spend on your resume. It would be wonderful if we could kick back with each application and read through the materials at leisure to understand the candidates. But that's almost never the case. Most hiring managers are lucky to grab a few minutes here and there to look through applications. They need to read as many as they can in that time, so your resume should lay out critical information as cleanly and clearly as possible. If they scan your resume and don't see the necessary skills coupled with relevant experience, they'll move on. It sounds harsh, but you have to understand that they look at hundreds of applications for each job and can't spend a lot of time deciphering a messy resume. To get a sense of the scale, think about this: one big West Coast studio posted a writer role and got over a thousand applications *every day* for it. For one listing! Imagine what it's like to wrangle dozens of roles at once. When they're under pressure to get promising candidates to the hiring manager as quickly as possible, they have to get through those resumes fast. That's how you get the thirty-second rule. I know it's discouraging to hear that, but you should know what you're up against.

Your resume must make a good impression to get past this first hurdle. It must lay out essential information in a clear and convincing way. The good news is that there's no "correct" format for resumes. The bad news is that some formats are more effective than others, and it's easy to go horribly astray. So, with the time constraints in mind, let's look at formatting possibilities.

Here's how a traditional resume lays out that essential information.

The Classic

Nona Magley

TinyTown Norway
+00 0000000
www.NonaMagley.com

Writer, Indie Darling Games 2020-Present
- Wrote and edited text in "house style" for award-winning indie titles
- Collaborated with other teams to advance the game narrative
- Provided narrative support for all departments: design, art, marketing, etc.
- Wrote and edited copy for promotional materials
- Achieved high levels of client satisfaction

Writer, Cats Are Awesome!, 2019-2020
- Wrote and edited interactive text for popular cat website
- Collaborated with designers and marketers to meet weekly deadlines
- Wrote and edited copy for promotional materials
- Drove production and coordinated deliverables schedules for partner company

Blogger, Global Adventures, 2017-2018
- Conceived, wrote, and edited text for Global Adventures website
- Edited and implemented weekly interactive content to deadline
- Collaborated with designers to realize compelling travel "missions"
- Coordinated timed handoffs of multimedia assets internationally

SKILLS
Twine, Trello, Adobe Suite, Office Suite, TikTok/YouTube,

A classic resume.

You can see that this snippet covers all the basics in a simple, bulleted format. Your most recent role at the top followed by your previous roles in reverse chronological order. You can include a summary at the top and sections for education and additional skills, but those are optional. So what are the pros and cons of the classic format?

Pros

- It's easy to read. The format is widely recognized, so recruiters can scan it quickly and get the info they need. It won't get binned for being hard to understand. It's also easy to cut and paste into online application forms and job sites like LinkedIn.
- It shows career development. If your first job was junior writer and your most recent role is lead writer, then recruiters know that you've grown in ability and responsibility. It shows a clear career trajectory and suggests that you've earned the role you currently have through your performance at previous work.
- All the critical information can go into the bullet points: your work experience, your skills, promotions, accomplishments, and proficiencies. It's simple and easy.

- It provides context for your skill set. Hiring managers don't need to extrapolate how you'd perform in a writing role from a skill you listed. They know you're a good fit for the role because you've previously used that skill in a work context. Other studios trusted you to do that type of work, so they probably can too. It's a form of endorsement.

Cons

- It's common. Basic. There's nothing eye-catching or engaging about the format. You're forced to rely on the content to stand out. This works great if you have an impressive work history to put on display, but it spotlights a lack of experience for industry beginners.
- The chronological order exposes career gaps that you'll have to explain away. This can be especially hard on parents and anyone with chronic medical issues.
- It amplifies discrimination. If you worked at a studio with issues like cronyism, sexism, racism, or other discriminatory practices, you might have been unfairly denied opportunities, promotions, and titles. This can translate to a less impressive career trajectory, even though you have the necessary skills and experience.

I use this style of resume because it's easy to update and add to my LinkedIn profile, and I have enough job experience to fill out the page. But I remember what it was like first starting out and how desperate I was to fluff up my bullet points with any information that made me look better qualified. I cringe to remember it, but I even put my college grade point average on some of my early resumes. (Don't do this! I promise no one in the industry cares, and it screams inexperience.) Most people are familiar with this traditional form of resume, and it has a long history of successful use, so I won't dwell on it.

The Classic isn't exciting, and it's understandable that inexperienced writers want a more appealing layout. They try out colorful templates from Canva or FlowCV and follow the advice of career gurus to emphasize skills over experience. Many resume services hype a sort of "deconstructed" resume these days. The format gets this name because it pulls apart the information in the chronological format—the skills and experience—and lists them in separate sections. Here's an example.

The Deconstructed

It's easy to see why this format is popular with students looking for their first jobs in the industry, as it allows them to focus on what they can do rather than what they've *done*. It's great for hiding gaps in your career or plumping a slender job

A deconstructed resume.

KEY SKILLS

Leadership

* Planned and coordinated team events and deadlines
* Worked with product narratives
* Met deadlines in high-pressure situations
* Found key research locations
* World traveller and adventurer. I love kayaking!

Storytelling

* Creative writing for various formats, including stories, features, blogs, and various reviews
* Written effective dialogue for marketing use
* Worked within a broad range of genres and emotional tones for stories
* Written award-winning article in "house style"
* Written guides and reviews

Collaboration

* Team and independent work on mobile games projects
* Time management- juggling multiple freelance writing projects
* Effective communication and social skills
* Worked with team on events for shows
* Collaborated on cat-based content with local media

Technical and Tools

* Coded and wrote interactive Twine story adaptations of novels
* Self-taught Trello and other organisational tools
* Self-taught Gamesalad creation as part of a game design course

AWARDS

* Best Display Design - 2020
* Manfred Holt Award for Excellence in Fiction -2019

Nona Magley

BRAND STORYTELLER

VIEW MY PORTFOLIO

EMPLOYMENT

Narrative Designer/Writer Now
Created exciting interactive content for multiple game companies.

Cats Are Awesome! 2020
Created interactive cat content, and coordianted design

Global Adventures 2017
Travel, blogging, research

SKILLS

* Writing and Editing
* Collaboration
* Customer Service
* Copyediting and Collation
* Product Promotion

PROFICIENCIES

* Twine
* Microsoft Suite
* Trello
* Mailchimp
* TikTok/ YouTube

history into a nice meaty resume. So, what are the pros and cons of a format like this?

Pros

* Highlights your strengths. If you know how to do something, like use Perforce or manage a project, then you can list that here—regardless of whether or not it was professional work. If you learned leadership through managing a group project at university, then it's still a valid skill to list. Because work history and skills have been decoupled, you're not limited to a professional skillset.
* Surfaces soft skills. You can create categories for "soft" skills that often go overlooked, like collaboration and communication. It lets you lean into your strengths.
* It's more visually interesting than the standard resume. You can add a nice pop of color to draw readers eyes to the broad categories of skills.

Cons

Oh boy. When I bring up deconstructed resumes to recruiters and hiring managers, they all get the same look on their faces. It's an expression I can only describe as "sour." With hints of rage. They *clearly* have a problem with these resumes, so I asked them to break down their dislike for me.[1] Here's what they said:

- **No standardization.** They're hard to understand at a glance because recruiters aren't sure where to look for the information they need. It takes time to decipher the layout and answer a simple question like "what did this candidate do at their last job as a writer?" Remember that thirty-second rule? This resume violates it.
- **There's no context for the skills.** One manager called it a "mix-and-match" resume because she kept trying to match the job information in one column to the skills in another—without success. It's difficult to get an idea of how the candidate will perform on the job from these resumes. Compulsion Games Narrative Director Lisa Hunter noted that she "had to fish through the whole CV looking for games."
- **They're deceptive.** Lisa also said this resume is "one of the sneakiest I've ever seen. It's clearly designed to conceal a lack of game experience." One recruiter looked at it and rolled her eyes. "I'm not stupid," she said. Everyone I spoke to said the format made them suspicious. It makes them look for what you're hiding rather than focus on what you're highlighting.
- **It treats all skills equally.** Leadership skills are leadership skills, right? Well, not exactly. It's great that you led a team of five designers to victory for your school game jam. Definitely mention that somewhere! But that's not the same as leading a team of professional writers through an entire AAA game development cycle to release. Are you a good communicator because you persuaded a team of designers to go with your pitch or because you persuaded your dog to "fetch"? It matters! And you need to show that you understand the difference. It's okay that you haven't used your communication skills in a professional capacity yet. They're still valuable skills. Just be honest about the context.
- **It's fluffy and repetitive.** Look how much extraneous material is in here. There are skills, proficiencies, and jobs that have no relevance for a game-writing or narrative design role. Fantastic that you love kayaking, but why include that in a resume for a game-writing job? "It would need a heck of a cover letter to explain" why you're a good fit for the role, Lisa observed.

---

[1] I can't share the resume I showed to the recruiters and hiring managers because that poor applicant! Instead, I borrowed a template from a kind volunteer and imitated the particular deconstructed resume as best I could.

Sachka Duval agreed. There's "no experience, no visible knowledge or interest in games, and very little that says the person has their own 'universe' to bring to the table."

- **The information gaps are red flags.** The resume lists narrative design and scriptwriting work for "multiple companies," but doesn't say which ones. Uh … that's not irrelevant information. "I'm going to assume that they're concealing that information for a reason," one hiring manager said, describing the omission as "bizarre."

Overall, this format seems designed to highlight positives and conceal negatives, which is a reasonable goal, but it overcompensates and ends up feeling fluffy, unfocused, and dishonest. I asked all my recruiters and managers if they'd interview this candidate for the role based on this resume and every single one said no, even though they thought the applicant sounded interesting personally. "Vagueness almost never conceals experience and competence," Lisa said. "If someone has written a vague CV, I don't quite trust them to write documentation."

Also, please stop putting these weird little charts in your resume. They're useless. Nobody knows what they mean but you. What the heck is 90% of writing?

SKILLS
Writing
Proofreading
Research
Content Creation
Social Media
Rapport Building

An indecipherable graph.

So what should you do? How do you highlight the good stuff you're bringing to the table without undermining confidence in your ability to perform the job? Fortunately, they told me exactly what they're looking for. So, straight from recruiters and hiring managers themselves, here's what they want.

Content

Across the board, the golden rule was "make it easy." Make your resume easy to read and easy to understand. Make the reason they should hire you easy to see. Look through the job post and pull keywords for the role. Remember that job listing in Chapter 3? Here's where you speak to the requirements it listed. If you were applying for that job, some critical phrases to include in your resume would be: collaboration, communication, experience, transmedia, screenplay, writing and design, imaginative, interactive storytelling, marketing, and short fiction. These keywords will get you through any automated resume scanners and jump out for recruiters. In fact, all the recruiters said a variation of this. It doesn't have to be experience doing that exact job or even be work in the games industry, but you need to demonstrate how your skills apply specifically to the role you want.

KISS Them

One recruiter specifically invoked KISS (Keep it simple, scribes!). They said that their ideal resume would be

> clear and simple. I want the information to be easy to find, where I don't have to hunt for it, and I can easily understand where you've been, what kind of position it was, and what you've done. Also, it should be something that loads well, regardless of format.

So, that's what you want to do. Create a resume that borrows elements from the previous two formats. It doesn't need to be as plain and straightforward as The Classic, but it should be more focused and grounded than The Deconstructed. Let's look at what it needs to get right.

Petteri was emphatic that layout doesn't matter "as long as you include important information about your skills in a way that doesn't require much thought work and as long as they are not super jumbled up and difficult to understand." Natalie agreed, but gave some pointers for a recruiter-friendly layout:

- Your resume should be laid out simply, with the most important information at the top "above the fold."
- I would like a short paragraph summary at the top, then I want to see your most relevant experience/why we should hire you for this job/what makes you the right choice?
- Keep the layout simple and easy to read, you should be able to get all the most important points after a few seconds looking at a resume.
- Writing candidates sometimes include a lot of text. A resume should be short. Most of the time they aren't being read all the way through.
- It might make sense to not start with a timeline of your experience, if you are changing direction or a lot of your experience is not directly relevant to the role you are applying for.
- Be very careful of being different for no reason, if you are doing something unusual then there should be a reason.

Her advice gives us an excellent outline for the format. But what about that last bullet point? Don't you want a resume that stands out from the rest?

How to Stand Out

Obviously, the best way to stand out with your resume is to have an impressive work history on successful projects. But barring that, how do you get recruiters and hiring managers to notice you without getting creative with your format? Eevi Korhonen recommends focusing on what makes you special as a candidate. What can you bring to this role that nobody else can? "Always try to bring forth your unique experiences and interests. You never know if your interest in knitting or exotic animals happens to be a match for something we've been wanting to explore in our narrative." However, Eevi adds that "a candidate would have to be a true unicorn to stand out without any experience working on games."

Hiring managers think of teams holistically when we hire. What skills do you have that other team members don't have? Here's where your wider knowledge of game writing comes in handy, that Swiss-army-knife skillset we discussed before. Make sure your list of skills and proficiencies is comprehensive so a manager can understand what you're bringing to the table. Your experience playing romantic sims might be exactly what the team needs!

An Ideal Resume

So if we compile all this advice into one resume, it might look like the one on the next page.

Pros

- A quick and easy read. It sticks to the golden rule and delivers all the critical info in under thirty seconds. One glance tells recruiters that you have the skills and experience necessary for a game-writing role.
- Nothing is extraneous. Everything in this resume points toward a game-writing role. It includes skills from outside games, but also highlights how those skills would apply in game-writing-relevant work. No more fluff!
- It provides context for career gaps without trying to disguise them. This feels more honest and opens a door for discussing them in your cover letter. You'll get fewer suspicious looks and eyerolls from recruiters with this resume.
- You can add a pop of color in the text without cluttering up the layout with patterns. You'll stand out more than with a Classic resume, and it's more legible than a Deconstructed.

NONA MAGLEY

Tiny Town, Norway | Nona.Magley@NM.com| NonaMagley.com

GAME WRITER

An experienced game writer with a passion for storytelling. I can write in a range of styles and tones have a "communication and collaboration first" approach to my work. I'm familiar with a range of interactive media programs, including Twine and Trello. I'm a huge Bubble Time fan!

WORK EXPERIENCE

Writer | Indie Darling Games   Oct 2020 - present

- Write text and dialogue according to house style for award-winning independent titles.
- Collaborate with designers and other disciplines to realize the game narrative.

Writer | Cats Are Awesome! Website   Jan 2019 - Sept 2020

- Wrote interactive stories for popular cat-themed website
- Collaborated with Design and Marketing on weekly releases of cat-related content
- Coordinate the release of timed "events" with local media outlets

Blogger | Global Adventures   May 2017 - August 2018

- Created articles and "adventure stories" for travel-themed website
- Met deadlines in high-pressure situations around the world
- Wrote guides and reviews to high standard for marketing purposes

SKILLS

- Able to write in "house style"
- Interactive writing and narrative design
- Excellent communicator
- Team player
- Creative
- Thrives under pressure

EDUCATION   Sept 2014 - May 2017

Local College | College Town

- Studied Process planning, coordination, and efficiency
- Worked with various industries on launching efficient Process Systems

AWARDS

- Most Innovative Employee of the Year, IndieDarling (2020)
- Overall Best Employee of the Year, Cat Fancier (2019)
- Project Leader, Local College (2018)

An ideal resume.

Cons

- You'll need to tailor this resume for each role, carefully picking out keywords from the job listing. That can be time-consuming if you're applying to every open job, but it's ultimately more efficient because your chances of an interview are better.
- It's hard to hide a lack of experience. This part will take some thought, but it's genuinely okay to list work outside the industry for mid-level roles. Focus more on finding the parts of your past work that apply to the role you're going for.

Notice that the header says "an ideal resume" and not "the ideal resume." That's because it's not prescriptive. Interpret the advice from our recruiters and hiring managers in whatever way works best for your experience and feels comfortable. I am 100% sure that you can write a better resume than this example I tossed together for you!

You heard it from recruiters themselves that format doesn't matter, so experiment with various colors and styles as much as you'd like. If you "have a passion for graphic design," then feel free to show it. My only advice is to not let it overshadow or interfere with the information in the resume. That's the important stuff.

LYING TO WORK

As you've probably gathered by now, recruiters and managers can tell when you're bullshitting and will hold it against you. Nobody likes being lied to. It's fine to show your best side. We expect you to present your work in a flattering way. Writers are good at shading meaning and you should absolutely find ways of phrasing your resume to showcase your talents. Just make sure that putting a good spin on your experience doesn't cross the line into lying.

DON'T

- × List a skill you don't have
- × Say you wrote something you didn't
- × Say you worked somewhere you didn't

This is a small industry, and the world of game writing is even smaller. Everyone knows everyone. If you claim you were a writer at, say, Ubisoft Montreal, then I guarantee that someone will have a contact there they can ask about you. If you get caught lying on your resume, it's almost an insta-rejection. If you're lying about that, what else are you lying about? Who would trust you with their top-secret game story after that? I'll choose honest inexperience over fake credentials any day.

Tara J. Branigan said she's seen an increase in dishonest resumes:

> There is a trend I'm seeing right now in game development resumes and cover letters that I dislike, that is the idea of "whatever gets you an interview is best." Intentionally misleading or otherwise stretching the truth to get the interview may get you that first introduction, but under false pretenses. For some teams, this is not only not going to get you the job you applied

for, it is going to reduce your chances for future opportunities. The fields I work in are heavily communication and trust based. If the first impression is that you are being willfully deceptive, that is a huge red flag. With so many candidates applying for roles, is it worth the risk?

If you lie to get a job, you'll eventually get caught out. More companies are instituting trial or "probation" periods to make sure the job is a good fit, and that's usually when it becomes clear that someone fudged their resume. Even if you think you can "fake it till you make it," you'll be expected to do work you're not ready for. Wouldn't you rather start a job with realistic expectations for your performance? Also, you're not safe from consequences even if you manage to pass your probation. One hiring manager "had to let someone go who was doing a great job but hadn't quiiiite finished his diploma program listed on his CV." It's much safer to tell the truth.

Beware Resume Services!

Why warn you about something as commonplace as resume services? Kim Belair says:

> Whenever I see someone paying for that kind of mentorship or paying for that kind of service, I always say, 'Who are these folks? Why are they charging money for it?'

It's an unfortunate thing, but desperate writers are vulnerable—and people will swoop in to take advantage of their vulnerability. An entire industry has been built to craft the perfect resume that will "get you past the gatekeepers" and help you find work. Many of these career coaches have no familiarity with the games industry and don't understand its specific requirements. Do your research before paying one of the companies for their advice. Be wary on these points:

- **Qualifications:** What are their credentials? Are they qualified to advise you? Go look at that credentials checklist in chapter two and apply the same standards here.
- **Uniform Solutions:** One size does not fit all. If they don't work in the games industry—and specifically game narrative—they don't know the unique requirements of the discipline and can't give you accurate advice. What might be great advice for a corporate or general tech job doesn't work for games—especially for creative roles. An engineering lead isn't looking for the same things as a writing lead. If the service promotes one "job-winning"

template for every discipline, run away! I'll talk more about this in the next chapter.

- **"Career Coach":** I became extremely skeptical of this title while researching this book. Anyone can call themselves that. It's meaningless. There's no required training or regulatory agency to set standards for these services. *None.* Coaches are often very nice, upbeat people with good intentions, but that doesn't make them experts. If you want a cheerleader for your efforts or someone to make you "feel seen" as an applicant, then by all means get a career coach. But understand the limitations of that role.

- **Us vs. Them:** Some services promote a hostile or adversarial attitude toward recruiters and hiring managers. "*We* will get you past *Them.*" Beware this attitude! Your best ally for getting a job is the person hiring you. I've seen recruiters fight *hard* to secure an interview for candidates who made a good impression. Why start that relationship with resentment?

- **Magical Thinking:** Some of the advice I've seen is plain nonsense. It plays into the belief that if you want something badly enough, you can *will* it to happen. They offer instructions that read more like FBC incantations.[2] More on this in the cover letters section, but get your salt shaker ready.

- **Dubious Results:** It's infuriating when a resume service crows about getting candidates interviews and you, as a hiring manager, know a writer got that chance *despite* their bad application. Many leads said they've learned to look past the "deconstructed" resumes these services encourage and see what candidates are truly offering. Or if the resume is too mangled to decipher, they simply go to the applicant's LinkedIn profile. Candidates secure interviews because of the content of their resumes, not the format.

I had long discussions with devs across the industry about predatory services and schemes for hopefuls. I found a deep concern, dismay, and fury at the people who use newbie writers as stepping stones for their own careers. These "helpers" especially love to target marginalized writers, who are already vulnerable and who don't have access to the same networks and safeguards as their more privileged peers. Protect yourself. If someone offers to help you, ask what they're getting out of it. Don't take everything they say at face value. I could rant about this for a while because I hate seeing new writers exploited, but instead I'll end here with a final warning from Kim Belair.

---

[2] Yes, I referenced my own game. It won't be the last time!

People who make a business out of the dream of being in video games are so toxic. One of the most toxic things about our industry is that we always act like it's a dream job. Don't get me wrong, anyone who gets creative space has a dream job in that way. But it's a job. I see it as predatory when a solution feels like a quick fix or pretends it's a meritocracy.

Many resume services prey on the dreams of desperate game writers. Be careful. Be smart. Don't pay for advice you can get for free. And even when the advice is free, check their credentials and make sure they're not misleading you. They might be doing more harm than good.

I hate to end this chapter on such a stern note, so here's a picture of my cats, Nixy and Kijeu.

Kijeu and Miss Nixy.

Now that you know who's really writing this book, let's talk about using cover letters to make your resume sing.

CHALLENGE

Write a resume tailored to each of the 3 job roles you broke down in Chapter 4. Make sure each resume includes the following information:

- Your name in large letters
- Contact information
- Your experience that relates to the specific job you're applying to
- A list of skills related to the specific role you're applying to
- The keywords you've pulled from the job listings.

Save the three resumes as pdfs in this format: FirstnameLastname_Studio nameResume. I sometimes add the year for my own tracking purposes.

Examples: JohnSmith_DoubleFineResume, NonaMagley_TextboxStudios Resume2022.

And now you're ready to send those babies off!

Chapter 6

Cover Letters

> Is it bad that I just don't like cover letters? They rarely actually tell you much about people and far too often are used in ways that make my face scrunch.
>
> —Ann Lemay, Narrative Director, WB Games, Montreal

"Do I even need a letter?" The short answer is yes. All the recruiters I spoke to recommend writing them. Natalie thinks they're a polite and helpful gesture, while another recruiter says seniors rarely need to send them, but juniors should if the application doesn't have questions to fill out. "When you're just starting, if written well, it could help differentiate yourself or explain elements not in your CV." They're both right, but ... I'll be honest. I kinda hate cover letters. In my past few years as a hiring manager, I've moved decisively into the "no letter required" camp. Very few cover letters do what they need to: give information that your resume can't provide or persuade me to change my mind after seeing your work history. The vast majority of them are stiff, awkward, and—frankly—boring to read. I'm perfectly happy to assess you based on your resume and samples, so if you don't want to write one, feel free not to. I'm sure you have plenty of other things you'd rather do instead. Many modern application systems don't even have a place to add cover letters, so take advantage of that tech quirk.

However, not everyone feels the way I do. Strix relies on cover letters as a hiring manager.

> If someone doesn't try, that's a chuck-out-able offense. If they can't meaningfully reify their resume and tell me that they understand the position and how their skillset fits, then that's a big strike in my book. I also try to get a sense of personality from the letter.

DOI: 10.1201/9781003282235-7

Knowing that it depends on the hiring manager, it's probably safer to send one. It doesn't matter to managers like me, so focus on writing your letter to managers who want them.

Purpose

Your cover letter should convince a company they need to hire you, above all the other candidates. It puts a face to the cold, hard facts of your resume. Remember that your cover letter and resume are a one-two punch. They should inform and play off each other. Your letter needs to do one (or better yet, *all*) of these things:

- Explain or clarify your resume.
- Add information that doesn't fit or belong in your resume.
- Dazzle!

If it's not doing that work, then don't waste anyone's time. Take that time back! Go eat some chocolate or invent a new TikTok dance. But if you want to use this opportunity to make a case for yourself, here's how you do it.

What to Say

So if you decide to write a cover letter, what should it say? Career guides tell you to sum up your resume and explain its bullet points in more detail. That's bad advice. Whatever you do, don't do that. Make sure you're providing new information that hiring managers can't get from the resume.

Use the cover letter to tell recruiters who you are. Introduce yourself. Talk about why you want to work at that studio specifically or on that particular project. Tell them why they should hire you. What can you bring to the job that nobody else can? Why should they hire you over the other 2000 candidates who applied? Here's your chance to tell your story and make your case. Use your cover letter to give a glimpse of what you're into and how you write. Talk about your love for creative puns or what your lifelong obsession with horror movies brings to your writing. Tell them why their latest DLC[1] is the best part of the game. Information like that doesn't belong in—or fit into—a resume, but it's the kind of stuff hiring managers want to hear. It helps them understand what interests you.

---

[1] Downloadable content = additional material for a game that's added after the game is published. This can be anything from new weapons to entire levels and new stories.

Twice the Reading

A major rule of writing is to "know your audience." In this case, your audience is twofold. You need to impress the recruiter *and* the hiring manager, who have different tastes and requirements. The recruiter wants to understand your resume better and the hiring manager wants to understand you as a writer and potential colleague. So how do you walk that line? It seems impossible to balance these (often opposing) needs and sell yourself to both audiences. But that's the essence of game writing, isn't? To educate and entertain as wide an audience as possible. So, you got this! Let's break it down.

Audience 1: Recruiters

When you're writing to recruiters, you're explaining who you are as a potential employee. They've seen your resume, so they know you've held, say, three positions at three different studios and have the basic skillset for this job. What they want to know is what your job history doesn't say. Why is there a two-year gap between jobs? What part of your job do like best? Where do you want to be in five years? Why are you applying for this job? Petteri says that your motivation is especially important, so be sure to include that in your cover letter. "Let's say you're applying for something like *Fable*. You want to write for *Fable*. Okay, why? I'd say something like 'I've played through all the *Fable* games, and this is the genre I'm interested in. I've also heard good things about Playground Games.'" And then you should build on that and explain all the reasons why. Recruiters like to know that you're interested in their studio specifically and not just any studio or any job. "Instead of saying 'You know, I've been trying to land a writing gig for ages. I've applied for all different kinds of things,'" let them know why you took the time to apply for *this* job. This is especially important if you're switching industries. It's a subtle bit of flattery, but it also lets recruiters know that you plan to stick around and they won't have to fill your job in a few months when something better comes along. So, motivation is important. After that, you should bring up any additional skills or talents that might be useful for the role but don't fit on a resume. Petteri is interested in your "educational background or marketing skills, or what you liked about being a games journalist. The storyline there." The story of your career is a good place to jump off and discuss audience number two.

Audience 2: Hiring Managers

Picture this: You're a hiring manager having a hectic day. You've been running from meeting to meeting, putting out fires, and trying to catch up with emails in the few spare minutes you can find in-between. You finally grab fifteen minutes to look at some applications for a scriptwriter role. You perch at your desk to read them, trying to ignore the pop-ups alerting you to upcoming syncs and missed chats. You pull an application and look at the resume first. It's solid. There's some good experience in there, but nothing that really stands out as a "must hire." You see they included a cover letter, so you open it and read this:

> Dear Hiring Manager,
> My name is Nona Magley. I'm interested in your scriptwriter role on Bubble Time. I have two years' experience as a game writer and a year of writing articles for a nonprofit website. I can write all kinds of game text, from barks and conversations to menu text. I think I'd be a fantastic asset to your team because of my education, work history, and love of video games. As you can see from my resume ....

Now imagine you read this instead:

> Dear Textbox,
> Holy crap, you're making a Bubble Time game! When I saw your script-writer role, I knew I had to take a shot. I've loved the series ever since Bubble the Clown danced at my 5th birthday party. I even designed a match-three game around the "floaty boat" song when I was in design school. I've honed my skills as a game writer for three years, hoping that I could write for a funny platformer like Bubble Time someday, but now you're making the real thing.

Which letter grabs your attention more? For me, it's the second one. It's high-energy and hyperbolic, and an interesting read. It gives you a sense of the writer's style. You might smile; you might cringe; but I bet you're not bored. And that matters when you're writing for entertainment.

In both letters, you're getting roughly the same information—what they're applying for, their experience, basic knowledge of game terminology—but one hooks a manager's fractured attention better than the other. If it were me, I'd skim the first letter and then go back to the resume for a more concise version of the same information. But I'd actually read the second letter because it tells me what a resume doesn't: who the candidate is *as a writer*. The writer's voice isn't buried in formal corporate-speak.

I'm aware that this advice directly contradicts most of the advice about cover letters out there. But here's the thing: that advice is generally not aimed at writing roles. For that first letter, I used the recommended template from a popular career service. The format is fine but utterly forgettable. It might work okay for programming roles or in more corporate settings, but for game writing, it's a sad blob of vanilla pudding. Writing is our craft. You should view every bit of writing in your application as an opportunity to show off your skills. Think of it as a writing sample the manager is *guaranteed* to read. Have fun with it!

Many new writers, especially marginalized folks, don't realize you can play around with the format of your application. As Strix notes,

> Cover letters are basically a vibe check. Which makes them both good, and dangerous. From a diversity perspective, minorities are less likely to be able to execute on the vibe check unless they've had good mentoring, as we're generally left out of this kind of soft knowledge instruction otherwise.

If you treat your cover letter like a writing sample, you put the focus on "here's what I can do" rather than the limiting "here's what I've done" history of a resume. That's a distinct advantage for writers who haven't gone to expensive game schools or landed high-profile internships. Now that you know hiring managers will give you room to express yourself, seize the opportunity.

NOTE

If you are uncomfortable taking this kind of risk, and I recognize that many people are, nobody will hold a standard form cover letter against you. It won't *hurt* your chances. Just make sure it's relaying information above and beyond what's in your resume.

Letter Dos and Don'ts

So! Now that you know what both your audiences want, you can write that letter and make it interesting. But do so strategically. Here's what your letter should do:

Clarify

A recruiter's goal is to match the right person to the right job. That's great when you're the right person! But you often won't be. Only one candidate can get each job, so recruiters and hiring managers have to make tough calls sometimes.

Having insight into your circumstances could make all the difference. If there's something on your resume that seems odd or detrimental, but you can explain, do that. Is there a weird two-year gap between jobs in your resume? Instead of trying to conceal it (we've heard how well that goes over with hiring managers), explain it in your cover letter. Maybe you went back to school. Maybe you took time off to care for your elderly father. Maybe you were burned out and needed a break from the industry. Here's your opportunity to explain that gap. Obviously, you want to put the best face possible on it. I don't recommend going into detail or sharing personal information: "I took time off from games because I got burned out from working eighty hours a week at Studio Crunchtime."[2] It might be true, but it's more information than you need to give and it sounds like you're criticizing the studio. If you badmouth Studio Crunchtime, the recruiter might wonder what you're going to say about their studio. Don't go there. Keep it professional.

Also, keep the explanation short and basic. Here's a good way to address that resume gap: "In the years between Job A and Job B, I focused on family obligations and worked on several personal projects ...." That's enough to sketch in the situation without getting into your personal business. It paints you as responsible, compassionate, and yet so committed to games that you continued to make them in your own time. There's a lot going unsaid here, and that's fine. You're making the important points, and now that gap in your resume has some context.

Other resume elements that might need clarification are dual roles—when you were performing the responsibilities of two roles for whatever reason. I was lead writer at a studio where the narrative director went on medical leave. I was acting director for five months until she returned, so my job title for that studio could easily read "Lead Writer/Narrative Director," which might need some clarification. You don't have to explain the title, to be clear, but you can. Just keep the explanation to one brief sentence in your cover letter.

Be Understanding

On a poignant note, I asked all the recruiters the same question: "What can my book do for you?" And across the board, the main thing recruiters wanted was for readers to know they're human. They make mistakes; they forget. They're "human." Most recruiters spoke anonymously or entirely off the record for this book from fear of backlash. It's heartbreaking, but I understand why. I've seen candidates go on angry rants about how inscrutable or unhelpful recruiters are. Some of that comes from sour grapes or frustration at not getting a job they want—and partly from an adversarial mindset. Many applicants don't think of "them" as real people. I imagine that's why there are so many dishonest

---

[2] Studio Crunchtime is fictitious. Or is it ...?

application materials: deceitful resumes, hostile responses, guarded answers. But recruiters are just doing their jobs. They're compassionate. They know what it's like to have sick parents. Or to go back to school after taking a hiatus. They aren't monsters, and they don't have it in for you. They're professionals who have a genuine interest in people. You'd be surprised by how far a little honesty will get you. But—and always keep this in mind—they are not your buddies. They aren't there to support you personally or listen to your problems or help you find work. It's possible to build a relationship with recruiters over time. One recruiter said that she enjoys seeing candidates grow and fill out their resumes with stronger experience. But it's not the kind of friendship where you ask for favors, remember that.

Mention Additional Skills

If there's something the studio should know that doesn't belong in your resume, put it here. You've played every game they ever made? Tell them. You run a blog dedicated to the lead character of their IP? Tell them! Their latest game is set in Scandinavia and you majored in Norse mythology? Tell them. You were in the army for four years and they make a combat game? Definitely tell them. Any aspect of your personal life, interests, or hobbies that isn't directly related to games work experience but gives you an edge, make sure you tell them about it. Every tidbit of information helps them understand what you're bringing to the table.

Dazzle

As I noted at the top, the best cover letters act as an audition for the role. I've seen two cover letters recently that changed my mind about the candidates. One started out "Holy shit, you're making my favorite game!"[3] and told the story of the applicant's personal relationship with this beloved game series throughout their life *as a writer*. By the end, I believed they had unique insight into the series lore and was ready to see their samples. The other compelling letter was a standard "why you should hire me" note, but it was structured so well and told with such wit that I skipped the candidate ahead to the writing test without seeing their samples. In both cases, they used the cover letter to show me what they could bring as writers. Show don't tell, right? They used the opportunity provided by the cover letter to give me a sample of their work. And it was Highly Effective.

But Dazzle Sensibly

Don't go completely off the map with your cover letter. It's a risk that might pay off, but it's still a risk. If you're going to use the letter as a writing sample, it might

---

[3] Yep, it inspired my second example letter.

get rejected like a sample would. If it's clear that you're trying to dazzle the reader but your writing is stiff or florid or way! too! punchy! then you're doing more harm than good. Mikki warns against getting "too cute" with it too. "If you're turning it into some kind of exasperating puzzle that I have to go through to figure out who you are, I just kind of go 'no.'" He says that unconventional cover letters are hit or miss for him.

> If you're like 'I'll tell you two things about myself, but if you want to know more, you have to interview me!' then I will never find out more about you. Because the purpose of the letter is for me to find out enough about you to want to interview you. I am not enticed by this mystery, and I literally have 200 other people like you here, so I don't have time to spend on this.

So, to sum all of this up: Be creative, but don't play games. Provide all necessary information and explanation. Let your voice shine through, but keep the letter brief and engaging. Anything that doesn't work to sell your writing or make your case should not go in the letter. In fact, there, are a lot of things that shouldn't go in your letter.

What Not to Say

This could be an endless category because I've seen some wild things in cover letters, let me tell ya. But I'll break it down into sections and try to keep it brief.

- × **Resume Rehash:** I've covered this, but it bears repeating. Or not repeating. New information only.
- × **Lies:** Ann Lemay notes that "many people lean on 'sell yourself' in these letters, but then make it … Too Much™ or just flat-out get advised to lie." The advice I gave for your resume applies here too. Present your best self, but be honest. If you never played the game you're applying for, don't say it's your favorite game. If you made a game on your own, be honest about the fact that "Couch Games LLC" is a one-person show. There's nothing wrong with that. Publishing your own game shows initiative. Pretending you're a big company that hired you to write a game is … weird.
- × **Templates:** Josh Scherr fervently hopes that your cover letter doesn't just fill in a template. Cover letters are annoying but important to him. They're "a way of personalizing yourself. So I don't want something that looks like somebody just filled in a Mad Libs. You know, 'Dear [recruiter]. I am very [adjective]. Your game looks [adjectives]. I would like to [verb] on it.'" Those are the letters he discounts "regardless of how much experience they have. Because if they can't be bothered," why should he?

× **Sexism:** Tara says, "Here it is, the year 2022, and I still have people writing in on job applications with 'Dear Sir.'" Address your letter to the studio. Even ye olde "To Whom It May Concern" is better.

× **Creepiness:** Tara also begs you not to "write your cover letter as a creepy ransom note complete with cut-out fonts and vaguely threatening wording should you not be given the interview. I really wish that was not an actual example, and yet …."

× **TMI:** There's a line between personable and personal that you should be careful not to cross. Don't talk about your long history of depression or your battle with drugs. Don't confess your secret fetish for pineapple. This is a form of job interview, so keep a professional distance.

× **Intimacy:** Don't talk about the recruiter, especially their appearance or habits or relationship status. I wish I didn't have to mention this, but it happens sometimes. Don't ask your recruiter on a date or flirt with them, thinking it will help you get a job. If flirting gets you the job, you probably don't want to work there. As we discussed before, the recruiter isn't your friend so don't get too familiar, even if it's the 100th time you're applying for the role. Follow their lead, and take the same tone they take.

× **Namedropping:** You should never—no, wait!

✓ Namedropping is okay! *If* it's relevant and true. Are you best friends with Hideo Kojima? If he's willing to give you a recommendation, then that's worth mentioning. If your "friendship" with Kojima is actually that you made eye contact once at an industry event and he doesn't even know your name, then maaaaybe you shouldn't namedrop him. But if you're applying for a job and you worked with the narrative director before—say so! If one of the writers suggested you apply—definitely tell the recruiter. Mention anyone at the studio they can ask for more information.

× **Aggression:** Petteri says the big dealbreaker for him is when a candidate applies "direct pressure on me or someone else on our team. Saying 'I really need this' and showing entitlement. Like saying 'I'm like the biggest fan of your games. If you don't hire me, you're insane.' When you're extremely passionate, that can materialize in different ways, but always try to be friendly, always try to be kind and not entitled." If you really are a super fan, you'll probably keep trying for a job there. And even if you get turned down at first, you might build up experience and qualify someday. "But if you mess things up at the start by being aggressive or super demanding, then they might have a bad feeling about you from the get-go. That might not even be true about you anymore! So, yeah. Don't do that."

HALP!

Right now, you're probably confused and overwhelmed and paralyzed by choice. Do I use a template or not? Do I sell myself or not? Do I even need a cover letter? Where do I start? Don't worry, I got you! I won't give you a template, but I'll give you a guide. Here's what your letter should do:

- Address the studio. ("Dear Textbox Studios" or "Dear Textbox.")
- Explain why you want to work for them *in particular* and not just any studio.
- Explain why they should hire *you* for the job and not any other candidate.
- Explain any issues with your resume.
- Show your personality.
- Showcase your writing skills.
- Be interesting.

All of this information should fit into two to three short paragraphs. That's it. That's the entire letter. Not so hard, huh?

YMMV

Your takeaway from this chapter should be that you can't please everyone. What one person likes, another person won't. What recruiters have to consider is different from what the manager is looking for. There's no one "right" or "perfect" letter that's going to tick all the boxes and guarantee you an interview. My best advice is to tailor your cover letter to the hiring manager and write a message to the recruiter in the application form. If you're following enough game folks on social media, you should know people from that studio and have a sense of how they talk to each other. Maybe the hiring manager is on Twitter? Their tweets or posts might give you a sense of what would go over well in a letter to them. Be respectful, be clear, be creative, and have fun!

CHALLENGE

- Take your current cover letter and throw it out. Look at your resume and ask the following questions:
  - Do I need to explain any gaps or oddities?
  - Is there any important information that's not on here?
- List the information you need to explain.
- Add any information that will help sell you: personal references, interests, passions, etc.
- Decide on your audience: recruiter or hiring manager.

- If you don't want to risk making your letter a showpiece, write a friendly-but-professional letter that hits all the essential information in under three paragraphs.
- If you're confident your writing is strong enough to make this a show-piece, then write your essential information in a compelling, entertaining way. Tell your story!
- Paste your cover letter into the appropriate space of the application or email.
- OR if there's no place for that, include it as an attachment with your resume and samples.
- Save the letter as a pdf. Label it in the same style as your resume: FirstnameLastname_StudionameCoverLetter. Example: NonaMagley_TextboxCoverLetter.

Chapter 7

Samples and Portfolios

The player's imagination is the most powerful storytelling tool we have. It's our responsibility to figure out the best ways to encourage and engage the imagination.

–Toiya Kristen Finley, freelance writer and editor in general; game designer, narrative designer, game writer, editor, narrative and diversity consultant in games

Here it is, my most-asked question[1]: "What kind of writing samples do I send?" It's a tricky question to answer because each studio is looking for different things. The short answer is "give them 2–3 samples that best suit the project you're applying to." The long answer involves thinking about tone, format, audience, time limits, and project needs. I know that sounds complicated, but it all makes good sense, I promise. Let's walk through it step by step.

The Purpose of Samples

If you've read my book this far, the purpose of samples should be obvious. This is where being a writer gets real. You can talk about writing on social media all you want. You can talk about journals and Scrivener and how to make a Twine game. You can be an armchair critic and rant about why you hate the movie *Predator* or love the game *Prey*. You can debate which *Final Fantasy* is best or dissect *RDR2* down to the last horsehair. You can take McKee seminars, memorize *Save the Cat*,

---

[1] Well, aside from the general "how do I break in?"

DOI: 10.1201/9781003282235-8

and read every game-writing manual in print. That doesn't make you a writer. A writer has to *write*. And here, now, with samples, is when you prove you can.

Once you're an established game writer, you'll have a body of work that speaks for itself. Studios will recognize your name and associate you with certain games in your portfolio. After a certain point, they'll come to *you* and ask if you're interested in heading their project. But until your star ascends, you'll have to show samples like the rest of us peasants.

Know the Project

If your samples demonstrate your writing ability, then you should send in your strongest work, right? Nope! Not necessarily. Your best writing might be a bad match for what the game needs. Your first step when selecting samples is to know what kind of game you'll be working on. If you've done your research about the studio, then you're already prepared for this exercise. You know the studio's ideology and what projects they're working on. If you're applying for *Space Opera: The Game*, send science-fiction samples. If it's an epic fantasy, show them your best Tolkienesque work. If Textbox Studios is making an "open-world RPG" and they haven't released any project information yet, go look at their website. Mikki suggests looking for the thread that runs through their work. "Studios tend to have certain styles. If you're applying at Naughty Dog, it's going to be totally different than if you're applying at, say, Avalanche. They just make very different kinds of games." Look for commonalities in their projects, a similar tone or themes. That's the studio's signature style. Say they're known for a series of dark-and-gritty detective games with realistic cinematics. You can guess that their "unannounced RPG" will likely have a similar dark-and-gritty style and realistic cinematics on top of standard RPG features like branching dialogue. It might even be a sequel to their hit game, *Shoot Me*. What does that mean for you? It means you should dig through your samples and find work that suits a project with those characteristics. Tone and style are critical, so look for pieces with a serious tone and contemporary language. If you don't have work that matches, then send the closest thing. Don't send fantasy writing or your favorite comedic one-liners for a project like this, even if you think it's your strength. You want to show the studio that you can write what the project needs. Make it easy for them to picture your writing in their game. That's the goal.

What to Include

Most studios will tell you exactly what they want from you. If we look back at the job ad in Chapter 4, we can see that the studio requests "2–3 short writing samples, including at least one screenplay sample." But if they don't tell you, or say something like "a few samples of your best work," then use your knowledge of their project to select pieces from your portfolio. You've already matched the tone of your work to their signature style, now you want to match the project's genre. Choose work that suits the needs of an open-world RPG: branching dialogue or ambient scenes.[2] If they're making a story-driven AAA game like *The Last of Us*, then sending a screenplay sample is critical.

"But, Anna," you say in dismay, "I've only written barks and item descriptions. I don't have any dark, gritty screenplays." That's absolutely fine! Matching your work to the project is ideal, but it's not required. Send whatever you have. Hiring managers are usually writers too. We remember what it's like to be a junior. We know you don't have a wide range of samples yet. We just want to see what you can do. Ann Lemay has interviewed junior writers on "the strength of a really good poem, just as much as a TV script (dialog), or a section of fanfic (long form narrative, can respect an IP)." She looks for potential in her juniors and "an understanding of what makes a good conversation, a good moment, a good story." Nobody expects a junior to write independently or at the level of an established senior. We're applying different criteria to samples from seniors. So if all you have are barks, then great. Send them. You can also include some unvoiced samples if you want. Maybe "a short email, weapons descriptions, or a short bio." That's enough to get a sense of your abilities, and you'll have a wider range of work to share in the future. For more experienced writers, Ann recommends including

> ambient conversations (4–6 lines, make them pop with interesting topics), barks (yes, boring to write but every writer has to do these) and one or two cinematic scenes (3–4 pages tops each). Show you can write ANY kind of game writing.

Range is important, but don't dump the entire contents of your portfolio into an email and call it a day. You definitely want to curate your selections. If you can't figure out what the studio wants, it's absolutely fine to ping the recruiter and ask for guidance.

Who's Reading?

Writing for your audience can also give you an edge in the process. This is another place your studio research will come in handy. If you learned that a

---

[2] Ambient scenes fill out the open world to make it feel alive. If you walk by some NPCS, and they're gossiping to each other about an upcoming archery competition, that's an ambient scene.

popular writer recently announced their role as lead writer on the game or you saw an interview with the project's narrative director, use that information to your advantage. Find out what other games they worked on. Look for a signature style in their work. Do they say in their interview that they enjoy reading bark sets? Have they tweeted about their love for puns? Take those insights to heart! Those people will likely be the ones evaluating your samples. Learn what they're looking for. For example, Josh Scherr wants to hear "an interesting sounding voice, and that's not something that's easy to define." He had one applicant who wrote their samples with a unique diction "that made it stand out. It didn't read like something I'd read before. Or they take typical ideas and put their own interesting twist on them. Or they're funny, or they're concise. It can be a lot of different things." If you can find a fresh take on a classic trope, that will definitely get you noticed by me and Josh. Other hiring managers might focus more on the game beyond your samples. Kim Belair looks for an awareness of other disciplines.

> It's the difference between someone who does a mission design and understands the constraints of a mission versus someone who does a mission design and just goes all creative and has a lot of great ideas. It's clear that the person with great ideas doesn't get what's going to happen to those ideas as they go through the development process.

She looks for writers who use only core mechanics or limit dialogue to one scene because "it's showing that on-the-job utility and teamwork." And she looks for a writer who approaches their work holistically, because they'll have to work with other disciplines. Detailed insight like Kim's is exactly what you're researching. Leads share explicit advice like this to help, but also to make our lives as hiring managers easier. So, take those tips and run with them! Of course, it's not always possible to find out who's leading a project or what they want to see in writing samples, but do your best to find out. It's valuable guidance.

Time Limits

You might be scratching your head over this parameter, unless you know the rule of "one screenplay page equals one minute of recording time." But that's not actually what I'm referring to here. I'm talking about time limits for you and your reader. As we discussed in previous chapters, most hiring managers unfortunately don't have a lot of time to spend vetting samples. You have to make a good impression *fast*. It's not as brutal as the recruiters' thirty-second rule, but you'll want to hook a manager immediately and keep them reading. That means submitting samples that get to your best writing right away. "If you send us a 120-page screenplay, we are probably not going to read the whole thing," Mikki admits. He recommends that you limit your submission to three samples and edit them down to

> what you feel is your best work. Sometimes we get 20 things, and they're all like 60 pages long, and ... well, you're prolific! But I don't know what to look at, and I have to look at 300 other things.

Editing is crucial. If you spend two pages throat-clearing or setting up characters and scenarios that don't pay off in the sample itself, nobody is going to see the brilliance of your plotting or character development. Cut to the chase—literally. Trim the sample so that readers will get to the exciting or well-written bits right away. Think of the sample as a complete work. It's not just a snippet from a bigger story. I mean, it could be exactly that, but ideally it also stands on its own. Remember that readers won't see the other 85 pages of your screenplay to understand how the seeds you're planting bloom into glory by the end of the story. Your reader is seeing a few scenes at most, so make sure you contextualize them. Help readers understand how brilliant you are by framing the work in these few sample pages. If you have the time, craft the sample so that it feels complete. A short quest or cinematic scene with a beginning, middle, and end is great. If you can, do all your narrative set up within the writing itself. Maybe a line or two that explains why the characters are where they are at the start of the scene. That's the most elegant way to do it, but it's not the easiest thing to pull off without awkward exposition. Especially if you need to get that application in fast or produce samples by the next day. If you're pressed for time, it's completely fine to write a brief introductory paragraph explaining the scene and characters. And I mean *brief.* A few sentences, tops. Framing like this is absolutely vital for barks. I can't tell you how many times someone has sent me an excel sheet of barks with no explanatory notes at all. Look at this:

Combat barks with no context

Soldier	Watch out!
Soldier	Got a live one!
Soldier	I've been hit!
Soldier	Man down!

It's nice that you can write standard combat barks, and there's even a hint of progression, but that doesn't tell readers anything about how they're being used in-game or what this moment means to the larger narrative. And to be blunt, this sort of generic, low-tier writing isn't going to impress anyone. An impressive set of barks would showcase the character's voice, react to an in-game occurrence, and reflect an aspect of the world. But short of that, at least set the scene and give prompts. Here are the same barks with some added context:

> Scene: A soldier stands inside the door of a bustling 1940s canteen. It's his first time out on the town since he returned from the front line, so his social skills are rusty. He keeps falling back into military habits.

Combat barks with context

Role	Line	Note
Soldier	Watch out!	*Someone spills a drink on him*
Soldier	Got a live one!	*Sees an attractive NPC*
Soldier	I've been hit!	*(suggestive) The NPC is* very *attractive*
Soldier	Man down.	*(glum) Gets rejected*

Now, aren't those more interesting to read? They won't win any awards, but at least your reader understands the work they're doing in the game. The same thing goes for conversation lines. If I can't tell who the characters are and what the context of their conversation is, it loses all of its depth. Just keep the introduction short and sweet. There's no need for lengthy character bios or a half-page of plot summary. Give readers enough information to appreciate the scene and no more. You saw how I sketched in the scene for our lovestruck soldier above, but here's another example:

> Two visitors surprise Marjorie in the dining room of her manor house. It's the anniversary of her daughter Lily's death. She wants to be alone with her grief, but her guests are clueless. They unthinkingly brought a bouquet of lilies as gift.

That's all you need! Now I have the critical information and might understand the subtext of a line like "Get those flowers out of here!"

Project Needs

Trimming and rewriting samples lets you tailor your work to the project. Is it a game with branching conversations? Then match your samples to that requirement. Is it a text-based game with lots of expository writing? Then revise an existing sample to meet that need. I'll tell you a little secret. As a freelancer, I applied for so many game jobs and needed such a wide variety of samples, that I wrote my own game. I created some characters, mapped a plot, and wrote out the entire game story. I didn't write every last conversation and cinematic, but I wrote enough of them that I had raw material for every sample need that might arise. My game and characters were admittedly bland—I won't be pitching that game to studios as a possible project anytime soon—but it was a good foundation for all my samples. I knew the characters, understood their motivations, knew exactly how to enter and exit each scene, and had a big picture in mind that helped me with subtext and foreshadowing. I knew what the characters were supposed to know in every scene. Then, whenever I applied for a job, I'd grab a relevant part of my game and tweak it to match the style and tone of the studio and project. If you don't already have work that's a match, it's the best way to create samples fast. However, I only recommend this method for confident, experienced writers who have the time to invest in tailoring samples. It means that you're submitting raw work and that's risky when you're less experienced. You want to submit your strongest work that aligns with the project, remember? That means work that's been feedbacked by critical eyes and polished to a high gloss. New writers should choose polish over a custom fit. Stick to samples you're confident in and adjust them slightly or frame them with a short intro to align them with the preferred tone as much as possible.

HOW TO MAKE A SAMPLE FROM EXISTING WORK

1. Let's say your brief is "2–3 pages of a dramatic screenplay" and you already have a longer screenplay ready to go.
2. Pick one moment to showcase. To meet the brief, this should either be a high-action moment or an intense character-focused moment. (Ex: A team breaks into a high-security lab and discovers a big secret.)
3. Cut the scene down to its key beat. (The moment they discover the secret, right?)
4. Frame this beat with the information you need to understand it: backstory, setup, payoff, and climax/aftermath.
   a. Backstory (Why they're going to the lab)
   b. Searching the lab (setup)
   c. Finding a monster (payoff)
   d. The monster breaks free and comes after them (climax)
   e. They escape the lab. (aftermath)

5. Make the sample just the good stuff: the search/reveal and the climactic chase scene.
6. Write a 2–3 line summary of the backstory and setup, just like the ones I did for the barks before. Put that at the top of the screenplay as a note. Instead of bios, reveal character through dialogue.
7. Rewrite the scene to focus on the reveal and chase. Match the tone and style to the project. (This lab scene is versatile and works for scifi, horror, thrillers, romances like *The Shape of Water,* or even a comedy like *Ghostbusters.)*
8. Include a single line at the end to indicate what happens in the next scene. *Voila*!

The more you practice reworking your samples, the better you'll get at it. In fact, it's good practice to make up briefs for yourself and try to fill them. I like to give myself writing prompts like a funny picture or gif and then write, say, three ambient scenes about it. Or a short cine. Whatever method you use, keep writing! The more you practice, the more work you'll have to polish into portfolio pieces.

Interactive Samples

Many studios request interactive samples these days. Some studios specifically ask for short Twine games as samples. Why do they want them? To see if you understand the specific needs of interactive writing. In the past few years, there's been increasing overlap between the entertainment industries. Game writers are working on Netflix shows and comic book IPs, and there's been a flood of writers from other media entering games. Some types of writing transfer easily to game writing. If you've worked in theater or written screenplays, you've probably got a good understanding of what writing for games requires. But some other forms of media make for tougher transitions. You can be a talented novelist, for example, but you might struggle with voiced dialogue. What reads well on the page doesn't necessarily translate to the spoken word. Some prose writers make excellent game writers, to be fair! Cassandra Khaw, Antony Johnston, and Rhianna Pratchett, to name just a few. But to write games, you'll need to show that you understand the specific demands of interactive writing and how it differs from traditional media. The best way to do that is by making your own game, of course. But if you don't have time to learn Unity, you can whip up a short interactive sample with Twine.

Twine Samples

I've played many Twine games as a hiring manager, but, I'm sad to say, few good ones. I get it. It's difficult to write a compelling interactive story that plays in under five minutes. But that's usually how much time managers have to spend on it. Some games ask interesting questions of the player or make good use of conditionals. Bravo for those! But most of them don't. Basic choices and conversation options aren't going to dazzle a hiring manager. ("Open the door: Y/N?" is common in these samples.) The worst is when a writer submits their exploratory work, and you can tell they're being silly and messing around to figure out how interactions function. I'm glad one of us having fun! Okay, that was mean. But I want you to feel my frustration. There are incredible Twine games out there: *The Uncle Who Works for Nintendo*, *Depression Quest*, *Howling Dogs*, and *With Those We Love Alive*, to name just a few. (Not to mention multimedia games like *17776* that transcend their simple formats in mind-blowing ways.) They're works of art. I don't expect your Twine game to be anywhere near that level, but I do expect more than a few jokey options and a "thanks for playing!" If you don't want to put effort into it, then please don't include a Twine game just to tick a box. Make playing it worthwhile. Otherwise, include a flowchart or script instead. *Please.*

What about Fanfiction?

The old-timey days when fanfiction was scorned by the mainstream are long gone. Archive of Our Own contributors have won Hugo Awards, and Marvel movie stars ship their own superhero couples. Hazel Monforton credits fanfiction for landing her first industry job.

> My best piece of advice is "write fanfiction." I wouldn't be where I am without having written a lot of fanfiction about the franchises that I was eventually hired to write for professionally. It is great practice for writing in-house styles and for thinking deeply about characters and where you might take them. Fanfiction asks questions and tries to answer them. "What would a character do in X situation?" "What would happen if a character was Y?" "What if characters A and B kissed?" It's usually that last one, but there's a lot of interesting things happening in fanfiction around big franchises.

That's solid advice from an expert, folks. Hazel also reminds you "to remove your fanfiction from the internet once you've been hired." But to be serious, absolutely submit fanfiction as a sample if you think it's good work. I've read some extraordinary fanfiction—better than published work in many cases. As both Ann and

Hazel noted, it's important to show that you can write in an existing game universe. That's what game writers do. Our individual voices disappear into the house style and character's voices, so it's important to show you have that adaptability. You might get lucky and work on the franchise that inspired you.

The Dos of Samples

We've already covered most of the dos for samples. Tailor your samples to the project and house style. Know your audience. Get to the good stuff as fast as possible. Provide context for the scene. Submit polished work over risky reworks if you're inexperienced. Keep your total samples at ten to twelve pages maximum unless told otherwise. Put a fresh spin on old tropes if you can. And if you have to submit samples as an attachment, put them all together in one PDF. That about covers it!

The Don'ts

I wish I didn't have to include this section, but I do. Over the years, I've read some truly astonishing samples—in every sense of the word. We writers put ourselves into our work in ways we don't realize. Our speech patterns, our observations about life, all our rich and varied experiences infuse our work. But we also betray our worldviews in our writing, so think carefully about what you send. It's fine to have your friends read your samples, but try to get some objective feedback from readers who don't know you. An online writing group is great for that. Ask them how you're coming across *as a person* through your writing. Do all your samples sound angry? Are there no female characters *at all* in your three samples? Are your characters racial caricatures? Is there pointless profanity sprinkled through the work? Those are the kinds of things you should watch for. I see these problems mostly with younger, inexperienced writers who are trying to mimic the voice of an established writer they admire. They might see a character who swears a lot and think he's funny, so they write their own character that swears a lot. Only they miss a critical trait of the original character that gives the swear words meaning. So, their character swears pointlessly, where the original swears a lot only when he's nervous—as a tell. One of those is empty profanity, the other reveals character. Be careful with that stuff!

Plagiarism

Also, and this pains me to say, don't plagiarize. I'll say it again: don't steal other people's work. I'll say it one more time: don't take other people's work and try to pass it off as your own. Not only is it unethical, but you're going to get caught. The games industry is small, and the AAA game-writing space is *tiny*. Everybody knows everybody. And everybody knows everybody's work. Your hiring manager will likely recognize stolen work. Heck, I once had someone submit *my own work* to me as a sample. They took one of my *Guild Wars 2* quests the IGDA had posted as an example, tweaked the wording and changed the format slightly, then submitted it as a sample of their work. To me, the person who wrote it. I wasn't expecting such brazen theft, so it actually took me a moment to recognize that it was my work. But after squinting at it for a bit, there was no mistake. It was mine. I sent them a blistering email telling them to stop. Then I pulled my samples from the IGDA site so nobody else could rip them off. Lesson learned!

Oh, and they didn't get the job.

Pornography

Yes, people submit it. No, it's not forbidden. But think deeply before submitting straight-up pornography. Is it relevant to the project? Is it your best work? Will it read well in the bright light of day? If you decide to submit pure smut, definitely submit additional samples to prove you're not just a, uh, one-trick pony.

Okay, that's enough. I don't want to discourage you! All of this sounds very complicated, I realize, but it's not. Stick to strong work that aligns with the studio's needs and you'll do just fine.

Showcasing Your Work

So you've got a handful of samples you like, and you've matched them to the studio style. What's next? How do you showcase them in a way that gets you noticed? If the job post asks you to email the samples or attach them to the application, then collate all three samples into a single pdf. If they asked for two to three short samples like our example job post did, your final pdf should come in around ten to twelve pages maximum. That's enough material to showcase your skill and demonstrate that you're capable of writing at the level they need. I know some studios ask for more work than that, and that's fine. Give them what they're asking for. But most hiring managers I spoke to don't have a lot of time to spend on samples and will scan the material just to get a sense of what you're bringing. In all of my years of reviewing work, there have only been a handful of times when I got so caught up in the story that I wanted more. That's how you *should* leave a hiring manager—wanting more—so shorter samples are still good. Keep that in mind when preparing samples.

You might be reading through this chapter with a sinking heart. It's so much work! Adjusting samples to suit the studio's style. Trimming and reworking your existing samples. And then cramming all of that into a pdf. Who has time? And how do you share your Twine game or other interactive samples? Is there a better way to show your work? Fortunately, the answer is yes. You can create an online portfolio.

Set Up Your Portfolio Site

Now that you can create perfect, fully contextualized samples, you should set up a portfolio to show them off. Don't wait until you're applying for jobs to create your portfolio! Have samples and a way to host them ready to go. Opportunity could knock at any time. Keep your work in a safe place, update it with recent work over time, and have the space ready to show hiring managers before you apply for a position.

It doesn't matter where you put your portfolio. Wordpress, Wix, and Squarespace offer templates that are easy to fill in and post. But you can also use Dropbox or Google docs if you just want a place to stash your work. When you're posting the samples, break up the text or links with images or videos. Make it easy and enjoyable to read. I want to see what your work looks like on the page because that's the format we're working in at a studio, but I also love seeing links to videos of how it actually plays. Some game writing looks dull on the page because it's *doing its job*. But see it working in-game with all the other storytelling elements available to interactive writers, and it can suddenly come alive. A smart portfolio shows me that transformation. An even smarter portfolio walks me through the process of creating the final product.

Portfolios are an opportunity to tell your story. Your resume tells me what you've done. Your cover letter tells me why I should hire you and not somebody else. Your writing samples show me what you can do. And your portfolio shows me your journey. It's the story of you as a writer, so tell it with care.

Your Story

It makes me sad when I open a portfolio and there's a bunch of folders jumbled together in there all willy-nilly. If you don't want to arrange your portfolio, then at least suggest a few samples in your cover letter. That way I go into the portfolio knowing what to look at. If I look at something else then that's on me, right? Or you can arrange your samples chronologically and cross your fingers the hiring manager goes for the more recent work and not your student samples. In those chaotic portfolios, I usually read a few samples at random, but I have no way to know what's your best and strongest work. It's a lost opportunity. "People get afraid to put themselves in the portfolio," Kim says.

> Every piece you include in a portfolio, it's great to go 'Here's why I'm including it. Here's what it's saying,' because sometimes you'll get someone who goes 'here's a cut scene that I wrote' and you're like, 'okay, buy why did you choose to include it?'

She wants to understand the decisions you've made about your work. Her favorite parts of the portfolio are when writers speak in their own voices through their notes and comments. "That's where you're not writing in the character voice, you're writing in the voice that I'll hear on Slack every day." A well-crafted portfolio can humanize your work and show your personality as a potential colleague. My favorite portfolios walk me through the writer's growth. I like seeing how far a writer has come. Look at the projects page on my website, for example:

My public portfolio.

My most recent (and notable) projects are at the top, with my current project in the spotlight. As you travel back in time, you're basically reading my resume, right? Humble beginnings on small browser-based projects all the way through to the big AAA games I work on now. The thumbnails link out to the game websites. That's my public portfolio. I also have a site for a private portfolio and that's where I keep my samples under lock and key. (See my plagiarism story.) This is the space that I curate and use to tell the story of my work. Here's a small slice of what it looks like. This is the index that lists all of my samples.

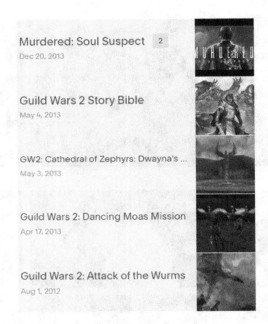

My private portfolio index.

Here's some of my older work. As you can see, it's grouped by date and project. I have scripts available for download in pdf format and video versions of key scenes.[3] My strongest work is at the top of the page, so it's the first

---

[3] I reverse-engineered many of these scripts from videos of published gameplay or blogs, and the story bible entry is a single page with key information altered. It's more for tone and layout. No NDA violations here!

thing people see if they start randomly scrolling. It's not entirely in chronological order, although it could be. My work has definitely improved over time and my strongest work is my most recent work. But do whatever feels right to you. It's okay to express yourself! Sometimes Kim sees a portfolio "that is a completely different form, but the person's put something really great down and I'm willing to go and figure out the shape of this." Sweet Baby Inc. offers portfolio reviews as one of their services, so she's seen a lot of them go by. And she's noticed that some writers follow a strict, dictated format, even when it doesn't work for them.

> They're afraid to freestyle. And if I'm going to keep it 100, my portfolio for years was not super gamey. I was starting out in video games, so it had prose and different forms of writing. And I was showing that I can adapt to different voices, and I can adapt to different responsibilities, and I can write small, and I can write big.

She was telling the story of her versatility as a writer. Another approach is the one taken by Amy Shaw, who did a piece on portfolios for Sweet Baby's website. "She'd done a portfolio that was originally for a spy, open-world game. And her portfolio focused on that one fictional game." Every sample in her website illustrated different aspects of that one game. And at the end, if you look at her portfolio, she's shown that she can write everything you need for a video game. "I know the mechanics. I know bios. I know that it takes a bunch of building blocks. And I'm going to show you how those building blocks come together in a mission design." Just like resumes, there's no one-size-fits-all solution. Be wary of anyone who wants to force you into a template. You're a storyteller. Tell your story!

Unreleased Game Samples

If you have work from unreleased projects and you've scrubbed it 100% clean of any identifying markers, go ahead and include it in your portfolio. Here's an example.

I found a picture that captures the style and mood of the game,[4] and I titled the piece by genre rather than naming it. Now the sample looks like any other professional sample in my portfolio. Presto! It's that easy.

---

[4] I replaced the unreleased project artwork with a copyright-free image for sharing in this book.

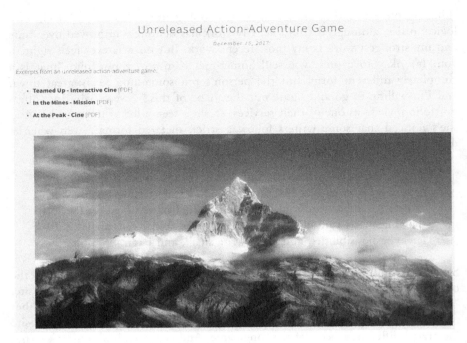

Example of an unreleased project entry.

Here's Your Mnemonic!

If you put all my advice together, you get a nice, writer-friendly acronym: PROSE. It stands for polish, range, order, style, and ease. Follow these steps to create a solid portfolio.

POLISH

Your portfolio should showcase your skills, so only include your best, most polished work. Never include unedited work. You can't see your mistakes, but employers sure can. I know this seems obvious, but I've seen some sloppy samples over the years. It looks unprofessional.

RANGE

Show the hiring manager that you understand all the writing needs of a game: dialogue and cinematics, of course, but also barks, objectives, item descriptions, letters, codex entries, and various other bits of text. I've written song lyrics and poetry for games, so I include links to that material too. You never know what the needs of the project might be, so cover your bases. Have samples of each type of writing, from screenplays to UI strings. Here's where you include links to your interactive writing, too, like Twine games.

ORDER

Decide on your presentation. It's tempting to list your work chronologically, like a resume, but that might not be the best presentation of *your* history. Maybe your last project wasn't successful, but the one before that won Game of the Year. You want to lead with the stronger work, right? If the studio likes it, they'll read more. But if it's not great, they'll never skip down to see the dazzling cinematics you wrote for a project three years ago. The important thing here is to guide readers through the story of your work.

STYLE

You will end up writing for some wildly different IPs in your career. Each project has its own style and tone: comedic, cyberpunky—even New Weird. Your samples should show that you can write to order in any of these styles. If all I see in your portfolio are high fantasy cutscenes, then I might not hire you to write for a thriller.

EASE

Above all, make your portfolio easy to access. Many studios will ask you to submit a few short samples as pdfs. Give them what they ask for, but also include a link to your full portfolio so they can read more. Make it easy for them to find and read all your work.

As the person who wrote these guidelines, I promise that it's okay to break them. Just like resumes, or cover letters, or samples, or game-writing itself, there is no one true way to share your work. Arrange your work alphabetically if that's what works for you. Only list your One Perfect Sample if that's all you think you need. It's your story, tell it the way you want. Tell studios who you are as a creator and what journey you took to reach their door. Show them what you can offer, the depth and breadth of your skill, and how well you'll fit into their project. Tell them that story, and you'll land the gig. Good luck!

CHALLENGE

- Create three samples that display your best work. For this challenge, create a five-page screenplay sample, a contextualized conversation, and a sheet of contextualized barks.

- Combine all three samples into one pdf and save it in the following format: FirstnameLastname_StudionameSamples. Ex: NonaMagley_TextboxStudiosSamples.

OR

- Create a space online to hold your samples. It can be a webpage, a dropbox, or a space on google drive. Whatever you prefer.
- Arrange the samples in a way that tells your story as a writer. Link to videos from the project. If there's no video of your work specifically, link to a trailer that gives the game's flavor. MAKE IT CLEAR that the trailer is for tone and isn't your work
- Ask a friend to look through the portfolio and samples and give you feedback. What does it say about it you? Have them tell you in their own words.
- Check your portfolio for PROSE and you're ready to go!
- Add a link to your portfolio on your resume and mention it in your cover letter. If you use one portfolio for multiple applications, tell each studio which samples to look at.
- IMPORTANT: If your portfolio is private, *include the password* in your cover letter.

Chapter 8

Interviews

Don't try to "game the system." Always be your authentic self.

—Petteri Tuomimaa, Senior Recruiter, Noice Inc.

You've filled out your application, sent in your tailored resume, and linked the studio to your dazzling portfolio. You check your email and there it is: the interview! They want to schedule a chat with you. Pat yourself on the back: You've done well to get to this point. You've made it out of the slush pile of applicants and now have the opportunity to make your case and sell yourself in person. But interviews are nerve-racking, even when you're confident in your social skills, and they're agony for introverts. Don't worry! I'm going to walk you through the whole process and give you some tips to make it all easier. By the time you're done with this chapter, you'll be ready for anything.

Types of Interviews

If you think about it, an interview is a strange interaction. It's an artificial process, that's nothing like the work you'll do on the job. (Unless you're a recruiter.) Both sides of the interview process have a tough task: trying to decide from a few hours of contact what years of work together might look like. On the hiring side, we're trying to see how you approach ideas and briefs, how you respond to critique, how you think about the writing and game development processes, how you navigate disagreements and setbacks, how creative you are,

DOI: 10.1201/9781003282235-9

how combative you are, and how enjoyable it would be to work with you. It's like a vertical slice[1] of your character.

The first thing to know is that there's rarely a single interview. The process is different at every single studio—actually, that's so important I'll say it again: *The interview process is different at every studio.* But after talking to various studios and recruiters and having seen both sides of the process during my career, I've noticed a standard pattern of progression. It looks like this:

- **Phone Screen:** This is a short, get-to-know-you chat based on the materials in your application. It's usually a half-hour call with a recruiter to discuss your skills and find out if your expectations for the role match the company's.
- **Manager Interview:** If your application looks good and the recruiter believes you're aligned with the company on salary, benefits, etc., then they'll schedule a chat for you and a hiring manager.
- **Follow-Up Interview:** If the hiring manager was on the fence about you, there might be a short follow-up interview for you and another person on the team. Maybe a principal or a senior writer.
- **Team Interview:** If you make it to the team interview, you're a serious contender for the role. You'll meet the team you'll be working with and learn more about the project.
- **Onsite:** At this stage, you'll meet members of other disciplines, such as producers, designers, and artists. You might have a chat with the studio head or creative director.

I'll say it one last time: Every studio has their own, individual hiring process. I've applied to places where I interviewed first, took a writing test, and then got the job without another step. I've interviewed at places where I went all the way to the onsite and then took a writing test. It all depends on the studio. But if you prepare for the interview process outlined earlier, you'll be ready for any version of the process they throw your way. So, let's walk through all of the interview types step by step.

The Screen

This step used to be a short phone call, but nowadays it's a quick Zoom or Teams meeting. Whatever the format, it's a routine part of the recruitment process. If you're invited to a screen, that means that you've successfully ticked the

---

[1] Vertical slice = the section of the game shown to publishers/investors as a project milestone. It's like taking a core sample of the game. The VS might get polished into the shiny demos you see at E3 and other industry events.

requirement boxes and the recruiter believes you're a viable candidate. Sometimes they'll ask for more information about your experience or clarification about some of your skills, but they're generally trying to get a sense of who you are as a developer. What do you want out of this job? What are your salary expectations? Are you able to relocate? The recruiter wants to make sure that you and the studio are aligned on all these important issues before they take the conversation further. After all, what's the point of going all the way through a rigorous hiring process only to discover at the onsite that you need double the salary they can offer? Better to find out now at an early stage before any more time is wasted on either side. Go into your phone screen prepared to clarify your expectations and availability.

You've done your homework on the studio and the role long before this, so you should have a solid idea of what the studio is about and whether you'd be a good fit. I have a whole chapter on contract negotiations later, so definitely read it before your phone screen and be prepared to start the salary discussion.

The most important point is to be upfront about what you want. This is the time to put your cards on the table and learn if the studio can match your expectations. Recruiters have access to information about salary bands and benefits for the role that your hiring manager may not know. Ask them! Seize this opportunity to ask hard questions. Is salary important to you? Ask about the salary range for the role. Are you interested in growth? Ask what career development options are available for the role. Does diversity matter? Ask about the company's D&I initiatives. Willow recommends asking about employee resource groups (ERGs). If that feels too risky, then ask about outreach programs. You learn valuable information and it also shows you are interested in the company as a whole rather than just the job itself. The recruiter expects you to be curious and have a lot of questions, so go ahead! You can learn a lot about the studio culture during these phone screens, so don't miss your opportunity.

Another thing to keep in mind during this interview is that you'll be talking about a subject you're an expert on: you! Nobody knows your experience and strengths better than you do, so share what you know. Here's your chance to explain gaps in your work history or fill in more detail about past roles. In Petteri's phone screens, he likes to "discuss a bit about the company culture and the project and hygienic things like moving or maybe compensation expectations." He describes it as "laying the foundation" for your relationship with the studio and making sure no "big question marks pop up later in the process." After that, the recruiter will likely open the floor for questions. They won't ask tricky questions about game narrative because that's not their field. They're only learning if you fit the role well enough to pass on to the hiring manager. Just relax, have a nice chat with them, and find out more about the job. The first interview at any company can be a little intimidating, but there's no reason it should be. Remember that the recruiter *wants* to hire someone, and they're rooting for you to be that person. If you're not an axe-murderer, then you'll do fine. (If you are, uh … maybe you've got bigger problems.)

In or Out

The phone screen is when you should ask about remote work and relocation. Don't assume you know what the company wants. Many ads say "remote work possible," so now's your chance to find out what that means. You have two goals here:

- Be clear about what you want.
- Find out what the studio wants.

If you *only* want to work remotely and they *only* want someone who can be onsite, this is where you bow out. I'll repeat what I said before: You are unlikely to get the job if they want you onsite and you can't do it. Maybe they can't compromise for legal reasons. Maybe you can't compromise because your family is settled and your kids are in a good school. Now's the time to have this discussion and find out. There might be room for compromise or for a hybrid solution, so know what your options are. But if they're clear remote work isn't possible, you'll have to make a decision. If you decide to continue the interview process, be aware that you're at a disadvantage and that it might end up being a dealbreaker. If they want you to work onsite, then now is also the time to ask about their relocation package. Ask them to send you the details in writing. You'll be able to negotiate changes later, but make sure the basic reloc stipend covers moving and visa costs *at a minimum.*

Manager Interview

Once the recruiter decides you're a good candidate, they'll pass your information along to the hiring manager for approval. We usually get an email from the recruiter saying, "Hey what do you think of this person?" Hiring managers will look through your materials (especially your resume and writing samples) and decide if they're interested in learning more about you. If they are, then recruiters will arrange an interview. You'll probably get an email saying they want to set up a chat for you and the manager. The person you speak to at this stage is usually someone from your discipline: a lead writer or narrative lead. Most AAA companies are good about listing the name of your interviewer. This is valuable information! Do a little research and find out what they've worked on and what they're interested in, narratively. (If you don't already know.) You absolutely want to prepare for this interview. This is the interview where you'll be asked to discuss your craft. Every hiring manager is different, and they'll ask different questions and be interested in different aspects of game writing, but they're all trying to find out the same thing: Who are you as a writer and is there a place for you on their team? Your challenge in this interview is to convince them that you're who they're looking for. Easy, right? I'm being sarcastic here, because of course it's not easy. They can't hire everyone who applies. Heck, they can't hire every candidate they *like*. Hiring managers hate writing rejection notes. We know how hurtful it is to receive one, having received plenty in our time. But with so many candidates and so few roles, it's inevitable that you reject 99% of the writers who apply. So when we go into these interviews, we have to be discerning and ask some tough questions about the craft and process. Be prepared.

- **Know Your Craft.** Here's your chance to show off what you know about game writing. Are you an expert on narrative structure? Talk about it! Do you see similarities between comics and game writing? Share your insights! It's exciting to chat with other writers about innovations in our field or explorations they're doing on their own. These are my favorite conversations as a manager because I learn new things all the time.
- **Know Your Application.** I shouldn't have to say this, but know what you put in your resume, samples, and portfolio. If you submitted interesting work, the manager will want to talk about it. They'll ask about the work you did at past jobs or unclear information from your resume. This part of the interview should be easy, but unfortunately, it's where many candidates get exposed. Ed Stern, Lead Writer at Splash Damage, cautions you to "never lie or exaggerate about your involvement on a project. We'll find out, sooner rather than later. The difference between 'I made this decision' and 'I was in the same room when it got made' is not small." If you have to admit that the professional "project lead" credit on your resume actually means "I wrote a Twine game in school," then it looks bad. Really, really bad. I had one candidate who'd clearly been coached not to give a straight answer about her work history. Someone had taught her to deflect the conversation from that topic and talk about her strengths instead. If I ask you three times, point blank, to explain what you did at your last job and you can't answer that question? I'm going to assume you're hiding something. It's a huge red flag, and you probably won't get the job.
- **Know the Development Process.** Craft is critical, but in AAA you're a small part of big team. If you have real, hands-on knowledge of game-making, be clear about it. Shipping a game from start to finish is a long, hard process that teaches a lot of valuable lessons. What did you learn? What knowledge can you share? I can't stress enough what a leg-up this kind of experience gives you. Collaboration is such an important part of game dev that it covers missing skills in other areas. When Kim interviews a candidate, she thinks "Well, they're 75% of the portfolio. But talking to them, they're so collaborative that I don't even worry about that 25%. We're going to make it work."
- **Know the Project.** You won't know much about the project at this stage—especially if it's unannounced—but that's okay. Discuss the project in

general terms, or come prepared to discuss any previous games in that series or other games in the same genre. Try to get more information. If you haven't signed an NDA yet, managers won't tell you much. But they can drop some tantalizing hints! Tara says the worst candidates "didn't put in any effort to understand what sort of company they would be joining. I don't expect (or want) candidates to come in with a scripted list of answers, but I do expect that you can show that you've done at least a little research into the games you'd be working on, and the larger company." She described an applicant who looked good on paper, but "who had clearly not played or even researched any of our games. This was at a free to play mobile publisher, so I told her that before the in-person interview, it was critical that she take a look at a few of our games ahead of time." But when she showed up to the interview a few weeks later, she still couldn't "answer any questions about them or speak towards how she would approach working on them." Don't be her. Find out what you can on your own and come prepared to ask questions!

- **Know Your Interviewer.** As we discussed, see what games they worked for and look for interviews and articles about them. Look for patterns in their talk about craft. That's probably what they care about most. Remember that this research isn't about digging into their private lives or stalking them on Insta, it's about understanding their interests and taste as professional writers—who might be your leads someday.
- **Know What You Want.** You should be asking a lot of questions and interviewing the hiring manager right back. Find out what kind of lead they are. How do they feel about crunch? How do they help their writers achieve their goals? How does the role you're applying for fit into a career path? Don't be afraid to ask tough questions! Nobody will be upset if you try to gather information about the job. You're expected to. Quite frankly, it's disappointing if you don't. A good interviewer will make it clear that you can jump in with questions at any point, so take them up on it. If you forget what you wanted to ask and remember later after the interview, don't be afraid to email and ask. Studios want you to get the answers you need.
- **Share Your Interests.** Try to steer the discussion to (relevant) subjects that you care about. We can usually tell when a candidate is passionate about a topic, and it's always cool to see what lights someone up inside.

Above all this, though, just be yourself. Your interviewer *wants* to like you. The hiring process is incredibly time-consuming, and everyone wants to find the perfect person as soon as possible. They're hoping it's you!

If you impress the hiring manager, they'll move you on to the next step. This usually means they ask you to take a writing test or send you straight on to the next interview.

Follow-Up Interview

Of all the interview steps, this is the least common. If you're asked to do a follow-up interview after meeting with the hiring manager, it probably means they weren't fully convinced of your skills or weren't sure about your experience. They're calling in their colleague so they can get a second opinion. Don't be upset! Remember that they didn't reject you outright. That means they see something in you worth considering. Treat this as an opportunity to really sell yourself. Don't be afraid to be blunt and ask about their concerns. "Is there anything about me as a candidate that I can explain in more detail? Is there anything that makes you hesitate to hire me? I can answer your questions right now." This will allow you to focus on the area of doubt and persuade them that you're the right candidate.

Alternatively, you might get a follow-up interview with the hiring manager after taking the writing test. In this situation, they'll want to discuss the decisions you made in the test. This is a fantastic moment to walk them through your test and highlight all the clever little details they might have missed. Don't be afraid to show off! There's a time to be humble, but a job interview isn't it. Don't be arrogant or conceited about it, but be clear that you made smart, informed choices that you're willing to stand by. It's persuasive, trust me.

If you get this follow-up opportunity and have signed an NDA, ask about the project in detail. Now's when you can get some really juicy information about what you might be working on for the next few years of your life. Carpe that diem!

Team Interview

This is the interview I always enjoy most as a candidate. You get to sit down with a bunch of other writers and geek out about your craft. What everyone's looking for at this stage of the interview is chemistry. Do you get along with the other writers? Do you click? Do you challenge each other in interesting ways? I won't speak for other leads, but I'm always looking for writers who can fill out any gaps in my team. I don't want a team that's all military experts, or who all went to the same game-writing program, or who *only* play card games. I'm looking for people with unique perspectives and knowledge to round out the skillset of my team. This is the place to talk about unusual hobbies or experiences. Talk music, or sailing, or calligraphy. If you have an interest that's near to your heart, bring it up! The people you're talking to could be your closest colleagues for years to come. Some of them might end up being your best friends. Try to make a genuine connection with them. Even if you don't get the job, you'll l have made some new contacts. And you might meet someone who shares your interests. Honestly, I don't have much advice for this interview beyond "have fun!"

The Onsite

The final boss! If you make it to the onsite, you're almost there! Onsite interviews are time-consuming and hard to plan because so many senior devs are involved. The goal of this interview is to have you meet the extended team. As a writer, you'll meet people from disciplines like design, production, and art. They'll all have to work with you, so they're interested in seeing what you're all about. They're mostly interested in how you view their discipline and how familiar you are with the process. You should already have a decent understanding of how things work at the studio by this stage, so be comfortable and confident with your answers. Your main goal here is to let them know you respect their crafts and are open to compromise. Nobody expects you to know about their disciplines in detail, so there's no need to pretend. Acknowledging another team's expertise is a smart way to go.

The hardest part about the onsite is that it's physically grueling. You have to be "on" and razor sharp for eight to ten hours straight, and that's exhausting! It's especially draining if you had to travel or fly to another time zone to visit the studio. You might be fighting jet lag on top of the usual stress. For one job interview, I flew internationally across four time zones, arrived late in the evening, got up early for a day-long interview, then went out to dinner with the lead and a producer until 9:00 PM. A twelve-hour day of being on my top performance! I was so tired I was sleepwalking by the time we left the restaurant. (Fortunately, I got the job.)

On top of being exhausting, the interviews can be repetitive. You'll give the same answers over and over again—and that's okay! Petteri explains that the repetition is there as a check, to see if "you're talking the truth and are who you say you are. I've seen cases where people answer a question one way in one interview and then in a very different way the second one." Be consistent and you'll be fine. Petteri advises that you don't try to guess what the team wants you say. Answer questions with "whatever you feel is right. And sometimes the right answer to the question is 'I don't know' or 'I've actually never heard about that. Could you explain more?'" It's easy to panic and start babbling the first thing that comes to mind, but just take a breath and get back on track. Again, treat this as an opportunity to learn about the devs and the studio. Even if you don't get this job, you might get a job there in the future. Make the most of this moment.

If you're at the onsite meeting the bigshots, then the role is yours to lose. But don't get cocky! You *can* still lose the job at this point. As someone who participates in interviews with candidates for other teams, I've vetoed one or two people in my time. And I've sometimes had other teams come to me and make a case for not hiring someone I was excited about. It's rare, but it happens. In the end, the hiring manager will make the call, but they will take feedback from other teams very seriously. This is not the time to slack off or get overconfident. Be on your best behavior and sell yourself. If you do an interview that's actually onsite, then you'll get a studio tour and probably some swag, so you won't come out of it empty-handed no matter what.

Perspective Shift

I'll be honest, I used to tie myself into stress knots over job interviews. I'd have anxiety attacks and sometimes throw up before the interview. During the interview, I'd blank out on my answers and freeze up when it was my turn to ask questions. I was not a good interviewee, to say the least. But then something happened. I don't remember what caused the shift in my thinking. Maybe I just grew more confident about my own abilities. But I started going into interviews with a different attitude. I started thinking of them as networking opportunities. It became less about the job and more about getting to know people. I became genuinely, humanly curious about the people I was talking to and started connecting with them personally. I liked them! They were interesting folks who had a lot to teach me. I started seeing interviews as a chance to educate myself and expand my horizons. They became ... actually fun? And exciting? Once it stopped being about A Job and became about the people in the industry that I admire and want to meet, interviews became easy for me. I'm at a place in my career where I occasionally accept job interviews just for a chance to chat with folks and hear them talk about their craft, even if I'm happy where I am. You never know where it might lead. Samantha Wallschlaeger seconds that perspective.

> I had interviewed with Crystal Dynamics a few years ago and really liked the narrative team, but the studio just wasn't the right fit at the time geographically. But when my most recent studio went through layoffs and I was affected, the narrative director reached out to me with an opportunity to work from one of their new locations, which happened to be the city I live in. This time around, I was thrilled to accept. It just goes to show you—the connections you make during your career don't go away.

Even knowing that, you still might be nervous in interviews. Sometimes, you'll meet people you've admired for years or the writer of your favorite game. It's easy to get a bit starstruck. That's okay! The best thing to do acknowledge it. If you don't want to admit you're nervous (or anxious), say you're excited. "I've really been looking forward to this interview." That way the interviewer will interpret any awkward silences or stumbles as adrenalin. Again, we've all been there! It's totally understandable and nobody is going to judge you harshly for it. Well, nobody worth working for. Whitney has a strategy to prepare for these moments. She recommends interviewing yourself in the shower. Ask yourself interview questions and practice answering out loud. She admits it sounds weird, "but it helps you get used to the feel of those words and ideas coming naturally out of your mouth."

A Note on Fashion

This might seem like a strange section to have in a book about game writing jobs, but I remember what it's like to look in from the outside and not know what's appropriate for an interview in gamedev. There's less pressure if your interview is online, but if you're going to an onsite, you'll need to choose an appropriate outfit. Many articles about interviewing have a corporate focus and suggest business casual attire. This is perfectly acceptable in most industries, but I promise you'll feel overdressed if you show up in their recommended jacket, nice shirt, and trousers or skirt.

> I wore a black wool suit to my first job interview in games. People thought I was a cop. I pretty much undressed during the interview.
>
> —Geoff Ellenor, Game Director, WB Games Montréal

The games industry prides itself on being the opposite of corporate culture and the dress code is best defined as "chill" The gamedev uniform is a hoodie, t-shirt, jeans, and sneakers. For both women and men. Women have specifically called out Mattel's Game Developer Barbie for nailing their office look. You'll fit right in if you dress like her. Of course, you can dress up more than that if you choose, but you'll definitely stand out if you go full suit and tie—or full-on costume. If you want to go to your onsite wearing detailed Garrus cosplay, do it! I'm not here to tell you no. Some studios might appreciate your tribute to a character they designed, after all. I wore a blazer over a hoodie to my onsite at Remedy Entertainment, and they appreciated my nod to Alan Wake. But that was hardly a daring fashion statement. In general, the more extreme your outfit, the riskier it is. The safest bet is to wear what makes you comfortable, while understanding what the studio norm is: a simple shirt, jeans, and sneakers. Just make sure your clothes are clean and not too worn. And don't worry about tattoos, brightly colored hair, piercings, and other standard body modifications. Nobody's going to blink unless it's something truly extreme.

Dressing feminine used to raise some eyebrows, and I would definitely have felt out of place wearing a flowery summer dress to my first gamedev job. But I wore one to work just the other day and felt perfectly at home, so things are definitely getting better. Considering it's an interview and you'll be stressed, focus on comfort over fashion. And speak up to let the recruiter know if you need something! I once got whisked into an interview so quickly that I was still wearing my windbreaker. Every time I moved—or breathed—the windbreaker made that nylon swishing sound. I was mortified. Especially when I had to whiteboard a game level to that constant *sshh-sssh-shsh* sound. I went through all that stress and embarrassment instead of simply asking to hang up my jacket. Nobody would have cared.

My advice is to wear something comfortable that is slightly dressier than your day-to-day clothing. You should look like you put in some effort. But dress for comfort. You might be asked to stand at a whiteboard and map a story or draw a level, like I was, or you might just sit in a conference room for seven hours. Whichever it is, it's a long stressful day, so you might as well get comfy.

NDA

You've heard a lot about those notorious nondisclosure agreements and how they're like a vow of silence. If you get far enough in the interview process, you'll have to sign one. My advice is to take them very seriously. These are binding legal documents and you shouldn't sign one frivolously. You can find versions of standard NDAs online. They all sound pretty much like this:

Dear Nona Magley

You have been invited to Textbox Studios for the purpose of participating in an interview, and possibly a series of interviews, for a position with our company. Textbox develops and publishes interactive entertainment software products. In the course of these interviews it is possible that we might share certain information with you in order to learn more about you, your skills and your technical expertise. This information may be confidential and proprietary information of Textbox; it is essential that these discussions be kept confidential. Therefore, before the interview(s) begin, we ask that you review this letter and sign in the appropriate space, indicating your agreement to the terms and conditions contained herein.

1. Confidential Information means all information disclosed by Textbox, or learned by you in the course of your interview(s) that relates to Textbox Studios' or its licensors' technology, intellectual property assets, financial c and affairs, financial statements, internal management tools and systems, equipment and assets, products and product development plans, marketing plans, customers, clients and contracts, and is designated by Textbox as confidential, or the reasonable person would deem to be confidential. However, Confidential Information will not include any information

An excerpt from a sample NDA.

Some are more detailed than others, but the message is the same: zip it. Don't talk about what you learn during the interview. Read the documentation carefully, especially any sections about privacy statements and penalties. Know what you're agreeing to. And stick to it! Your five minutes of fame on Reddit are not worth the legal headache you'll get if you leak confidential information.

Do Your Homework

It's a good idea to have some questions prepared ahead of the interview. Your interviewers want to see you interested in the experience and curious about the project and studio. Sometimes coming up with them on the spot is tricky, Petteri says. "You're blanking out because it's a stressful situation. You have a lot of adrenaline pumping. But it can be a bad look if you don't have any questions, because the team might take that as you not being that interested in the job." Maybe you already have the answers from your research or because you asked them early on and learned everything you need to know. Ask them again! It's better to ask something and appear active and engaged, then to seem like you don't care. This is your dream job, right? Several recruiters advised writing the questions down in advance and having them right in front of your during the interview. Or downloading a list of interview questions from career advice sites. But hoo boy! There are some awful "recommended" interview questions out there, so be careful. The best questions come from a place of genuine interest, so it's best to write out what you really want to know about the job and stick with that.

Red Flags for Interviewers

There are a lot of things that can go wrong during interviews. Most of the people I talk to are lovely, talented professionals, but they're simply not right for *this* job. Occasionally, however, you'll meet a candidate whose behaviour gets them an emphatic no from the team. One recruiter noted ruefully, "If people aren't aligning with our core values, we know it will be an issue. If you are rude, or don't seem to listen" or you're not prepared, those are bad signs. But "usually dealbreakers, especially at the beginning, come to the skillset and who we feel may be a right fit." Other red flags are more concrete than someone not sharing the company's values. Eevi spells it out with typical Finnish bluntness:

> The thing that immediately tanks my interest is just absolute lack of humility; treating the company as if they should be falling all over themselves to hire you. Healthy confidence and selling your skills is good; condescension and entitlement are not. Some people have this strange idea that to get the spot you somehow have to disparage others and prove your superiority over the existing team members. That's never gonna be the ticket. Almost always the existing team gets a say in who they want to hire and if you come across as an asshole, they're gonna say no.

It might seem incredible that someone would come into an interview and destroy their big chance like that, but, my friends, these eyes have seen things you would not believe. Most candidates are a joy to meet and a pleasure to chat with, but when things go wrong, they go seriously wrong. One dev told me about a guy who showed up drunk to his onsite and vomited into the waste basket between interviews. Nobody could figure out where the hideous smell was coming from until after he left. Tara's had candidates who are overtly sexist. "I once had a candidate tell me point blank that 'women don't play first person shooters' shortly after bashing his boss because 'she's a woman, so she mostly plays Nintendo.'" Years ago, I had a candidate who asked if I'd be his lead—because he didn't think he could handle a woman as his lead. I thanked him for letting me know and ended the interview. What else was I supposed to do with information like that? Step down from my job because he's uncomfortable? There are moments in an interview when you know it's simply a bad match. I could go on and on. I heard horror stories while researching this book. But there's no point dwelling on it, because that won't be you. In fact, you should be keeping your eyes open for red flags too.

Red Flags for Candidates

Just like you, the studio is putting on its best face, but there are some warning signs that you should watch out for.

- **Crunch Culture:** Samantha suggests that you keep an eye on how much the studio respects your time.

  Do they give you an impossibly long writing test with a short turn-around time? Does the recruiter call you without warning or schedule calls for later than 5pm? Do you get ghosted for weeks at a time only for the studio to suddenly resume the process without explanation? Do interviewers show up late? She calls out these behaviors as warning signs of crunch culture. If you see these signs, you should ask recruiters and leads about the studio's overtime policies. Many studios are surprisingly upfront about expecting you to crunch. I've seen mandatory crunch written into contracts before. It's best to find out now if they require it.

- **Who's on Top?:** Mary Kenney is "always very keen to see who interviews me in the final rounds. That, to me, indicates who gets promoted, who gets to be a lead, and who is listened to at the studio. Is it all white men? That's not a great sign." She recommends that you "ask if there are any people from marginalized groups in leadership positions at the studio. You need to know whether you'll have the opportunity to climb the ladder." Samantha agrees and adds "This is not only bad from a studio culture standpoint, but also probably says a lot about the variety of voices going into the game you'd be making, and the authenticity of those voices."
- **Diversity:** Many of the writers I spoke to mentioned that studio diversity is a concern for them. We've all seen those company "Who We Are" photos that show a bunch of guys who look pretty much alike. Unless you're one of those guys, studios like that can be alienating. Evan recommends "bringing up diversity in some fashion, just to figure out what the reaction is in the room." If you care about representation in your work and having diverse perspectives in the writing room, then it's good to mention it and see if "people will engage with that, or if they'll be sort of weird about it." But don't just ask if

they care about diversity, because of course they'll say yes. Approach the topic from a craft perspective. Evan usually tells a story about one of his characters who didn't fit in and always felt like they weren't getting respect. And if the interviewer doesn't respond or just sits there stone-faced, then it might indicate he's not interested in issues like that.

References

At some point in the process, they're going to call the references you listed and ask about you. You should line those up before applying, if possible, but make sure you have them locked in now without fail. Your best references are leads or coworkers from previous projects who know what it's like to work with you day to day. They can be your most passionate advocates. If you don't have any industry references, that's okay. Anyone who can speak to your professional behavior is fine.

Next Steps

Whew! You made it! The interview is over. The studio should tell you what the next steps are at the end of each interview. If they don't, ask them what's next. You can get an idea from the interview process I outlined, but companies will all have their own quirks. However, if you've gone through the screen, the lead interview, the writing test, the team interview, and the onsite, and the studio still sounds enthusiastic, you're probably close to getting an offer. Exciting! Wait, what's that? You didn't take the writing test yet? Oh. We'd better talk about that next then.

CHALLENGE

Record a mock-interview with you and a friend, then play it back.

- How do you come across?
- What are some tics or tells of nervousness?
- How confident do you seem?
- How clear and informative were your answers?
- Based on your answers, would you hire you?

Practice and rerecord the interview until you're satisfied you sound professional and knowledgeable.

Chapter 9

Writing Tests

> My screenwriting teacher once told me that our job is to find ways to hide art into our work. I think it's our duty.
>
> —Sam Lake, Creative Director, Remedy Entertainment

Good news! You've been talking to a studio, and they're interested in your work. Bad news! They want you to take a writing test. Maybe you've shown them samples and they liked what they saw, but they want to know if you can write in their house style. Maybe you've already chatted with the recruiter or the team and they want to see what you're like on the page. Maybe it's just a standard part of the hiring process at that studio. Whatever the reason, most large studios will ask you for a test.

There's no set point in the hiring process when you'll be asked to take a test. Some studios send them out right away to weed out candidates. If you're an established writer with a proven track record and solid samples, you might never have to take a test. But for most writing jobs, there is a writing test and it usually comes after an initial phone screen and samples.

I said that being asked to take a writing test is "bad news," but it doesn't have to be. Sure, the negatives of being asked to take a test are well known: They're time consuming and demanding, and it's tough creating work that you know will be scrutinized. Most writing tests are unpaid and nobody likes working for free—especially when the test is long and involved. And even when they're a reasonable length, a few hours of work per test can add up when you're applying to several studios. This is a barrier to candidates who can't spare the time for them. That's a lot of negatives! So what are the positive aspects?

- **They Level the Experience Playing Field.** If you're an inexperienced candidate with few polished or published samples, writing tests are your

DOI: 10.1201/9781003282235-10

friend. This is your chance to show the studio what you can actually *do*. It doesn't matter if you have ten years' experience or two on a test. Hiring managers are looking at what's on the page. This is your chance to show off your skill and outshine your competition.

- **Talent Beats Polish.** You might not know every rule of game-writing or grammar, but can you write interesting characters and witty dialogue? Here's your chance to prove it. Because writing tests are time-limited exercises, the bar is lowered for polished work. This means your raw talent can shine through.
- **You Can Learn a Lot from Them.** Writing tests are a window into the work that company expects from writers—and how they treat them. If the test asks for a specific format, tone, or style of writing, then you might be able to guess what working on the project will be like. When I applied for jobs in the past and struggled to match the required tone for a test, I realized the project wasn't for me. I couldn't write what the company needed—and usually they agreed. This is a good way to find that out. Also, if the test is long and involved—essentially an entire mission—and you've been given only a few working days to deliver it, note that. It might indicate that the studio sets unreasonable deadlines for the project and you'll be expected to crunch.
- **You Can Make Samples.** If you get the job, fantastic! If you don't get the job, you can still put the work into your portfolio as a sample.

Those are all the reasons you might agree to take a test. If you decide you don't want to or shouldn't have to, then fair enough! Some studios will assess you based on your samples alone and that could potentially be enough to secure you a job.

Getting Paid for Tests

You might be saying, "Hey, Anna, it's not that I don't want to take the test. I just want to be paid for my time and labor." Honestly? I get it. I (in)famously said on Twitter once that I was okay with unpaid writing tests. I thought of them as auditions and didn't mind giving up an evening for a test of reasonable length. The backlash was immediate, overwhelming, and humbling. I learned a lot that day. I heard from freelancers and students who are struggling financially and can't afford to miss even one night of work. People shared writing tests that were entire full-length missions for AAA games or that required extensive research of the IP to complete. And I heard from marginalized folks who feel that tests are too subjective and should be eliminated altogether. They opened my eyes and made me realize that I was speaking from a place of enormous privilege. For me, giving up one evening to take a test for a job I'm very likely to get is a calculated gamble. The odds are in my favor. But not everyone has my time, resources, and experience. Especially not for longer tests. In purely logistical terms, if you applied to four studios and they all had a week-long writing test, that's a month of free labor! A month's worth of unpaid work with no guarantee it'll end in a job. Looking at it that way, of course you should get paid. I agree with that wholeheartedly. Boo to unpaid tests! However, most AAA studios don't pay for testing. That's our current reality. And, whatever your personal views, you have to work with the existing system. My advice is to set a reasonable rate for your time and ask to be paid. The worst that will happen is that the studio will say no and then you'll have to decide if you still want to take the test or not. But it's worth making the case. Some people do get paid for tests. Some companies pay for them as a matter of course. The only way to normalize it is to keep pushing. And to keep educating people like me about the hardships of unpaid testing.

Should I Take an Unpaid Test?

If you ask for pay and the studio says no, then it's your call to walk away or not. Only you can decide if it's worth the trouble. Maybe it's not. Maybe you look at the role and say, "Eh, good luck. I'll look elsewhere." Or maybe you hang in there and hope your samples are strong enough to secure the job. In some cases, they might be. But Mikki warns that when a candidate doesn't take the test, it puts them at a disadvantage. "Would you rather have me say 'I don't see what I need in your writing samples. You're out'?" He explains that if a candidate refuses the test, he has to compare their samples to the work of all the other candidates.

> If the others are willing to do the test and you're not, and one of their tests is like, 'Holy crap, that is exactly what I want!', most likely I'm going to go with that person because I know for a fact that they can take direction.

Knowing it's a gamble, you'll have to make a tough call. And the choice is harder when you really want the job.

So, with all this controversy, why do companies insist on writing tests? Well, I already touched on one reason why: They give less experienced candidates a chance to shine. A test allows hiring managers to look beyond a resume's dead history and see a writer's living skill in action. Your samples might not be strong or showcase your talents as well as they could. Tests are an opportunity to show your unique voice and perspective. If your samples didn't show it, now you can prove you have an ear for dialogue, a sense of humor, or a creative approach to structure—you can show off your skill and versatility. Tests let good candidates shine, but they also catch out applicants who plagiarized their work, who can't write outside their comfort zone, or who can't follow a brief. This is important information for studios and hiring managers to know, so I don't see tests going away anytime soon.

Rhianna views tests as a chance to assess the studio.

> I actually don't mind doing them because I always appreciate a challenge and the way the tests are set out can tell you a lot about the people you'll be working with and their narrative sensibilities. Companies looking for long and unpaid meandering tests can be a warning.

Beware of Scams!

Unfortunately, game studios that ask for entire missions or weeks' worth of work have opened the door to scammers. There are unscrupulous companies out there that ask for "writing tests," but they're not offering jobs. They're making entire games from stolen work, one writing test at a time. Some of them even pose as recruiters from reputable companies, which is why you see legal disclaimers on those companies' job posts. If you look at a job listing for Bungie, for example, you'll see a note at the bottom warning about fictitious job openings. Their warning is more about a common scam where a "recruiter" asks for personal information or tries to trick money out of you, but a similar approach is used to scam free work from writers. The scam usually comes in the form of an incredibly detailed and specific writing test. Here's an example:

Story Outline & Writing Requirement			
Overall Guideline	1.Our stories are generally 15-20 chapters. The outline test requires only the first 6 chapters. 2.Chapter 1 should contain the hook/Inciting Incident/Meet Cute beat! 3.The end of every chapter should be a cliffhanger. 4. A relatively fast stroy pace should be kept.		
Genre	Subject: Genre: Theme: (select one or more,mark them with red.if you can't find a genre for you book above.then add your book genre)		
Book Idea: (within 300words)	EXAMPLE STORY HERE		
Prologue (within 300words)	EXAMPLE PROLOGUE		
Outline (every chapter within 200 words)	Chapter 1	Chapter 2	Chapter 3
Beginning			
Middle			
End			
Beginning			
Middle			
End			

A scam writing test.

They'll ask you to complete the test, which is very involved and time-consuming. When you submit that work, they'll typically ask for more "to help them decide." They will keep asking you for free work until you refuse. Some people say no after the first round. Some people go for a second round. Some people, desperate for work and thinking "well, I've come this far," keep going. The goal is always just out of reach, and so is payment. I heard from one writer who did get paid—but it was a nominal amount of about 100 USD for weeks of work.

These scams are clever and cruel. They take advantage of the existing system and of writers' willingness to audition for a good job. It's often difficult to tell the difference between a legitimate test and a scam. So how can you protect yourself? If you've been following my advice about research and credentials, you're well placed to spot red flags. Here are a few to look out for:

- **Identity:** Who is this company? What have they published? The reason scammers often pose as prestige companies is so they can trade on the studio's reputations. They're taking advantage of the trust writers have that their work could lead to a job offer. Do your research on the company—especially if they pop into your inbox unsolicited. Do you know anyone who's worked for them? If they're from a major studio, does their email reflect that? Ask a lot of questions and *do your research.*
- **Never Pay:** No legitimate game company is going to make you pay to submit an application or take a game test. Never. If they're asking you for money at any stage, run screaming away. Even if they somehow turn out to be legit, which is doubtful, they're not a company you want to work for.
- **Draw a Line:** If you decide the company is legitimate and they're genuinely testing your skill, you might agree to the test. Again, it never hurts to ask for payment. If they agree, set reasonable rates for your work and ask for payment up front. That way you get paid even if you're rejected, and it's almost like a mini freelance contract. If they refuse and you decide to take the test anyway, set a limit on how much work you'll do and stick to it. Don't do more work or constant revisions.
- **Retain Your Rights:** Don't sign away your rights to ideas. Some of these scam companies will ask for detailed game pitches. Do not give them the rights to whatever you're pitching. If they ask for them, say no. Unless they're interested in purchasing the pitch from you for a fair price, which is an entirely different conversation.
- **Trust Your Gut:** This is a big one. If something feels off or strange, it probably is. Don't be afraid to ask questions or push back. Ask your friends for advice. The scam artists usually cast a wide net, so they might have approached other writers you know. Post in writers' groups to see if anyone's worked with them. Get the advice you need to protect yourself and don't be afraid to walk away.

A SCAM STORY

A writer who got tricked into doing free work very kindly offered to share his story. Pay close attention so you can avoid the same traps.

> I initially responded to a recruiter's post on LinkedIn, which went nowhere—but then I was surprised with an email by a "colleague" of the recruiter about doing work on a different title. They had a game on Steam, and they wanted help to "optimize the story before launch." Next email, I got a game key and got asked about my thoughts—what needs fixing, how long will it take/what will it cost, etc. They basically asked for a small consult and some numbers. There were some red flags at this point, but it wasn't a huge ask so I spent about two hours of time on it and gave them what they asked for. The follow-up to THAT was where they went full mask off. They sent over more work materials for me to look at, and said they looked at my notes but couldn't come to a definite decision on who to hire due to "a lack of information about your writing styles." They asked for more in-depth analysis of storylines, characters, a new plot structure etc. Then they suggested that if I made some good flowcharts/diagrams/etc. of it all it would "help them make their final decision." All in all a ton of work that felt like they were going to directly use it for the final product. At this point I'd become very suspicious, and asked around about the company in some game writing communities I was a part of. I soon heard from another applicant who was fed the same lines, and we both decided to quote a rate for the work requested by the company. Never heard back from them.

Another writer took a writing test for a casual romance game. She checked their website and they seemed legitimate, so she took their test—which turned out to be pretty involved. When she completed it and turned in her work, they asked her to do more. "It was real crap," she said. "They post they'll pay 3000 USD for the work and then lure people in to give them 'free tests' with that held over them." She did six complete "chapters" of work for them, before giving up. She never saw the money.

In retrospect, both writers saw some warning signs that they'd ignored. "The initial bait-and-switch of applying to work on one title, and being offered work on another title by a different person was a red flag right out of the gate," admitted one writer. "And the emails (and in-game writing!) were all pretty bad, broken English." It might have been "a legitimate difficulty on their end, but it did make me suspicious—comms looked just like a spam email."

How is that these experienced writers, a senior in one case, fell for a scam like this? They should've known the moment they saw how involved the writing tests were, right? Wellll ...

What Does a Writing Test Look Like?

I have a nice collection of writing tests from my job-hunting adventures over the years. And for this book, I spoke with writers who shared their experiences testing for various companies. There are some wild tests out there! Some companies ask for "an entire self-contained Story Mission. The goal is for it to take somewhere between thirty and forty minutes to complete and offer a true storytelling experience." Some companies ask for multiple tests rolled into one, with a character biography and three examples of character arcs, a screenplay that incorporates the character arcs, and a playable Twine game. (In ten days!) Some companies give intense timed tests to get metrics on how fast your turnaround time is. Some companies ask you to write a full-length screenplay. Some companies want all the bits and pieces: barks, branching conversations, cinematics, item text, objectives—the whole enchilada. Looking at these lengthy, unpaid tests from some of the top AAA companies in the world, it became obvious how a writer would fall for a scam test. Especially if the scammer was posing as a reputable company, there's no way they'd know the difference. I have to be honest, I was shocked by some of the demands these legitimate writing tests made. I understand now why not getting paid for this work is so harmful. Writing this chapter was an education for me. By comparison, the writing tests I give are simple. They're usually something like this:

> Write a scene that involves two characters searching a building and finding something that leads them to a new location. The scene should contain the following:
>
> ■ A conversation
> ■ A choice
> ■ A short cinematic
>
> Please use a contemporary setting and language, but don't set it in the universe of any existing IP. The scene should be no more than three to five pages long. You have a week to complete the test, but please don't spend more than one evening on it.

That's it. In my eyes, if you're not going to pay for tests, they should be a reasonable length. And I prefer to see what writers come up with when they have room to stretch their imaginations, so that's what I test for. Clearly, there's wide variation in tests from studio to studio and project to project, but they do have some things in common. Across the board, the question tests are asking is "Can you write for *our* game?"

How to Ace the Test

By the time you're asked to complete a writing test, the studio already believes you can write. What they don't know is if you can write the kind of games they make. That's what the test reveals. I'm sad to say that samples are not a great way to judge whether someone is right for the project. I know writers with twenty years of experience who write mind-blowing work in certain genres—but who fall to pieces if they step outside their comfort zone. Not every writer can write everything. A good writing test might say, "Yes, yes, I see that you write excellent fantasy stories, but can you write gritty noir dialogue?" And often the answer is no. Better to find that out with a short test than to hire someone, onboard them, and have to let them go after a few frustrating months because they can't write to the standard you need. It's no fun for the writer, either. Imagine starting at a new studio, full of ambition, only to come in and feel like a failure day after day. I've been on both sides of that equation, and it's demoralizing for everyone. A writing test isn't a guarantee of good performance, but it's a reassuring indicator that the writer will be able to meet the project needs. I'd rather know right off so I don't waste my time or the studio's. So how do you ace it?

Do Your Research

We included a writing test. We didn't think we needed to explicitly state "this will be a test of your ability to conduct and display basic due diligence, research our company and IPs and competitor titles, reverse engineer the technical restrictions and game tone, and then write tonally appropriate, feasible, actable, implementable dialogue." So few of the writing tests were anywhere near tonally right or actable or implementable in that game. I felt like I'd pulled a sneaky trick on them. Is it misleading to call it a writing test and not an initiative test? Would you apply for any job without researching the company or project first? Is this a generational thing? Help!

—Ed Stern, Lead Writer, Splash Damage

■ I hear this same cry from hiring managers around the industry. It's getting better now as more devs talk about it, but we still see the problem. Do some research. You know the drill by now: find out what kind of games you'll be writing for. If it's a huge company such as Ubisoft, check the news to see what projects are currently in development at the studio where you're applying. Your *Assassin's Creed* test will be different from your *Just Dance* test. If it's a just-announced title and there's no information about the kind of game it will be, look at their other titles. Do the same research you did for your writing samples. Naughty Dog isn't looking for high-fantasy writing. Failbetter doesn't want your Marvel-inspired contemporary superheroes. Take a good hard look at their games, then write your test in the studio style.

Follow the Instructions

■ This seems obvious, right? Why would you ignore the instructions? But so many people disregard explicit requirements. If the test asks for "no more than five pages," don't write ten. Brevity might be part of the test. If the test asks for a fetch quest, don't write a long cinematic. Write what the test asks you to. Studios want to see if you can write within constraints. Josh Scherr notes that Naughty Dog's test "had very, very, very specific guidelines. One of them stated 'this character you introduce cannot be a character from one of the existing games. It has to be your own creation.' And then we got a test that had Joel in it, and we're like, nope, sorry."

So yeah, folks, follow the instructions.

Don't Cheat

■ Look, I get it. Writing tests are time consuming. It's tough to write a good, sharp script in the short amount of time allotted. You might end up tossing something together at the last minute because your careful planning went wrong. Game studios know this. Professional writers understand. But they want to see how well you write to specifications. If you tweak an existing sample into kinda-sorta matching the test—or worse, outright send pages from a pre-written script—you're not helping yourself. Studios can usually tell when you fudge the test. Setting aside the fact that your kinda-sorta-fits test will be outdone by a test that ticks all the boxes, it makes you look careless. Do you think the job isn't worth the effort? Do you not care about your work? Will you cut corners on tasks if you get the job? Cheating raises questions, none of them good. Just like I think bragging is fine during a job interview, I think earnestness and hard work are good for assessments. If you decide to take the test, give it a fair shot.

Minimize Risks

■ Writing tests are your chance to dazzle the studio. This is where you show off your command of language, your genius for witty one-liners, or your tight narrative design. Tests are not the place to innovate or try to hit the "inverted hero's journey" beats you saw on a fanfic site last month. Write what you know you're good at.

Have Fun!

■ No, I'm not joking. Most professional writers I know enjoy writing tests. Treat it as a fun exercise, and write something that entertains you. That way, even if you don't get the job, you'll have another sample for your portfolio.

What Are Leads Looking for in a Test?

As a hiring manager, I've learned the unfortunate truth that work experience does not necessarily mean talent. I've met writers with twenty-year histories of steady games work who are, uh, not the best at their craft. And I've already mentioned writers who fall apart when you ask them to step outside their comfort zone. My writing tests check for proficiency in a house style. Mikki Rautalahti often looks for more specific traits. He was the narrative lead at Remedy Entertainment, which "is known for a very specific kind of character approach. They are very story driven, very character driven, very atmospheric." Their writing test focused on paying a lot of attention to storytelling and the quality of that storytelling, because "how many people have writing samples that address those things?" He designed their writing test to see if a writer could "produce work that is compatible with Remedy approach and the Remedy formula."[1] In a similar vein, Ann Lemay thinks a "good writing test will specifically focus on what was lacking from a candidate's portfolio, or will seek to be specific to your project as a last check." She likes to include "a round of feedback and second submission part of the interview process to get a sense of a candidate's personality and reactivity to feedback." All of us agreed that it's important to limit the test to one scene and to respect the candidate's time. Naughty Dog tries to make their writing test as "short and unobtrusive as possible," Josh says. But it makes a big difference in who they interview during the hiring process. Josh was more impressed by candidates who found an angle on the test's particular scenario that he hadn't seen before.

---

[1] I took that test, by the way, and enjoyed it. But it was one of the harder tests I've taken.

In a given genre, there are so many tropes that are easy to fall back on. We've done it ourselves. So it's a question of what is the interesting spin on your best friend, that you did this whole journey with, suddenly turning on you? And how well can you convey that in your dialogue, place, structure, scene? That was very informative.

If a company gives a test "with no parameters and then criticizes the applicant for not writing what you expected them to," Ann advises you to simply "walk away."

Turning the Test into a Sample

Once you've finished the test and received your answer (hopefully an offer!), what should you do with your writing test? You can tuck it away in a folder and never look at it again, if you want. But I strongly recommend turning it into a writing sample. Here's how you do that:

- **Ask for Feedback.** I always write a few notes about what I liked and didn't, but I know my thoughts don't always reach the candidates. Ask for it! Worst case scenario, you don't get any notes or you get vague high-level feedback. Or you get a hurtful letter like the one in Chapter 4 that you can safely ignore. But you also might get genuinely insightful feedback that helps you improve. Use that feedback to improve your test as you turn it into a sample for your portfolio.
- **File Off the Serial Numbers.** You must have signed an NDA to take the test. Don't break it! Ask the company for permission to put it in your portfolio. Make it clear that you're willing to change any identifying information, and then make sure you understand what those identifiers are. It can be as simple as removing any proprietary information from the test. Swap out any IP-specific names for unconnected names:
  - **Bad:** Lara Croft becomes Tara Kraft. Spartans become Schmartans. Hyrule becomes Lowrule. It's too easy to tell what you've swapped them for.
  - **Good:** Lara Croft becomes Lisa Parker. Spartans become soldiers. Hyrule becomes Wondruh. Unless there are other identifying markers in the test, nobody will connect the new names to the originals.

In an extreme case, they might ask you to remove any signature narrative features that might connect your game to unpublished features of the test, such as an unusual tone or narrative branching. But generally, studios are okay if you turn the test into a sample that's "in the style of" their published IPs. A good rule of thumb is "Could I have written this test as fanfic without knowing anything about the current project?" If the answer is yes, then you're probably safe.

Never publish test materials (like the scene prompt) without explicit permission. That's a direct violation of your NDA! I've known some writers who posted the entire test and their work for it on their websites and got found out by the company. There was one writer who had to be asked three times to remove a writing test from his public website. He grudgingly adjusted it each time he was asked and then reposted it. He finally pulled it down after being told point blank he was violating his NDA and the company was prepared to enforce it. (There is no doubt in my mind that he simply included it in his private portfolio.) Think he'll ever get a job at that company after that? Who's going to hire someone who brazenly breaks their NDA? And I'm here to tell you all, when I'm looking through a writer's portfolio and I see an unaltered writing test, it's a *huge* red flag. Why take that risk? It's so easy to make a few simple changes and post it publicly.

Also, don't—for the love of all games—*don't* include an unpaid writing test in your resume as a sample of "contract" work the company hired you to do. If you were paid for the test and it's technically true, check with the company to make sure they approve you characterizing the test as contract work. Otherwise, it's dishonest.

Grow That Portfolio

Over the course of your career, you'll take a lot of writing tests. If you're smart about anonymizing them and polishing them afterward, your portfolio will eventually overflow with samples in all styles and genres. Some of the best work I ever did was for a writing test I took years ago. It has a place of honor in my portfolio even though I didn't get the job. Good work is good work. Be proud of yours, no matter how the test goes.

CHALLENGE

■ Take any writing prompt you want and make your own writing test. The prompt can be an image, a song, an existing game mission—whatever catches your interest and inspires you to write. Here are some example prompts and assignments, based on real-world writing tests:
- Write a highly cinematic five-page scene in screenplay format about a confrontation between characters. Have them fight. I mean, really go at each other! Then, write a second version of the scene that has an entirely different mood and ending.

- Write a bio for an original character and then write a cutscene with that character and your all-time favorite game character teaming up to rescue a hostage. Focus on their motivations and the interaction of their personalities.
- Start with a blank canvas and write a conversation between three and five enemy NPCs, in a scenario of your own design. Do anything you want, but the scene has to end with an explosion. The only other constraint is to make it interesting!
- Write two pre-mission monologues with [videogame character of your choice] as the protagonist. It should recap what happened in the previous mission and set up the next mission's objectives. Invent whatever you want for all missions!

■ Set a deadline for the work. Keep it under a week, especially for shorter "tests."

■ When your test is complete, ask your friends or a writing group for feedback.

■ Address the feedback in revisions to make the work better.

Bam! You've practiced taking a writing test *and* created a new sample for your portfolio. Post that baby online!

Chapter 10

Contracts and Negotiations

> Be pragmatic, be commercial, be reasonable, and focus on the important things.
>
> —Peter Lewin, Senior Associate, Wiggin LLP

It's been a nail-biting few days after your onsite interview with the game studio. They loved your writing test and the recruiter says she's "hearing good things" about you. Everything seems to be going well, and you're confident they plan to make you an offer. Is there anything to do now except sit back, relax, and wait? There sure is! Now's the time to start thinking about your pay.

A Fair Wage

The Dutch government recently announced that all companies must post a pay range with job listings to promote better salary fairness. Candidates applying for jobs will be able to see exactly what each role pays and avoid many of the traps of "blind" negotiations.[1] Great news for folks working in The Netherlands! (And now some US states and EU members.) For the rest of us, however, negotiating contracts and salaries remains a troublesome process of information gathering and

---

[1] Performa HR. "Salary Indication in Vacancy from August 2022 Past." 2 November 2021. https://performa–hr-nl.translate.goog/nieuws/salarisindicatie-in-vacature-vanaf-augustus-2022-verleden-tijd/?

DOI: 10.1201/9781003282235-11

guessing. Women, BIPOC, and other marginalized groups are especially vulnerable in the current pay negotiation systems. So, what can you do when the company has the advantage? How do you secure a fair wage and contract?

Authority

First, I'll admit that I'm not the best person to advise you on this topic. You'll notice an abundance of resources and interviews from experts in this chapter. That's because I know this isn't my area of expertise, and I rely on other people to help me with my contracts. I strongly recommend reading all the books and articles on negotiation that you can find. Tarah Wheeler offers invaluable negotiating advice for female candidates in her book *Women in Tech: Take your Career to the Next Level with Practical Advice and Inspiring Stories*, (Sasquatch Books, 2016). She even provides a script to take with you into negotiations. Believe me, you'll want one. Even if you've done your research, salary discussions can be thorny.

The painful truth is that we writers undervalue our work. That's partly because creative work is undervalued by society in general, but also because writing games for money seems like a dream. What, you mean you're going to *pay* me for doing this thing I love? Incredible! Negotiations are especially scary when you've struggled to break into the games industry or fought hard to win a coveted role. You're afraid to lose it by pushing back on a low offer. On top of that, there are very real and well-documented penalties for women and marginalized devs who negotiate. It seems safer to just take the first offer and not rock the boat.

Even if you do negotiate, you're at a disadvantage compared to your more privileged peers. They often have access to insider information and connections that you don't. Despite my best efforts to research and haggle, I've been severely underpaid many times in my career. I've also been one of the highest-paid people at a studio. Where I landed in the pay band depended on my research and who I knew at the studio more than any other factors. You have to have someone on the inside. Companies are looking out for their bottom line. They won't start with their highest bid when you might accept a lower amount. It's on you to talk them up to a number that works for both of you.

I'll share my tactics for going into negotiations armed with solid figures, but I've also asked some very smart people for their advice. We'll give you tips for securing the best agreements with a studio, but our advice should only be your starting place. There are fantastic resources out there for all aspects of the negotiating process, so read up and know your stuff before you enter wage discussions. Remember, you're setting a salary baseline that will ripple out across time to affect all your future raises, promotions, bonuses, and even game credits. Those are the stakes, so you need to get this initial agreement right. Knowing that, where should you begin?

Step 1: More Research!

You knew I was going to start with research. Knowledge is a useful tool in every aspect of the hiring process, but it's especially critical now. You should already have much of the information you need. You've learned about the company benefits through their website and interviews, and you've looked on sites like Glassdoor for employee reviews. Glassdoor makes you register to see salary information, but it's worth it to get an idea of wage bands at the studio. However, time to pull out your salt-shaker again: the information is self-reported and therefore not guaranteed to be accurate. Companies curate their profiles to put on a good face, and disgruntled employees go there to extract revenge with bad reviews. The figures on a company profile give you a ballpark range, though, and that's an excellent place to start. For our purposes, let's say that Glassdoor shows the salary for a mid-range writer in Seattle to be $75,000–85,000.[2] Now what?

Your next stop should be finding more accurate information from industry sources. Annual reports like the IGDA Game Dev Survey and Skillsearch's Salary and Satisfaction Survey can give a snapshot of general salary information across the games industry by studio size and experience. That's interesting to know, but not the hard numbers you need. So, let's check out the independent and developer-run salary surveys to see if Seattle writing salaries are listed there. These wages are also self-reported and anonymous, but the sheets are for "devs helping devs," so the numbers are generally honest. Let's snoop through Evva Karr's Global GameDev Salaries[3] and the GameDev Salary Check[4] spreadsheets. There's nothing for Seattle writers, but you can get an idea of what writers in other tech centers are making. This is important to know! Salaries for major cities are substantially higher than smaller towns because the cost of living is higher. Salaries in West Coast urban centers like Seattle, Los Angeles, and San Francisco are generally higher too, so let's see if we can locate any of those. Okay, I see some LA and Bay Area salaries in the $70,000–100,000 range. Let's note those. What do we have now?

- Glassdoor 75–85k
- Dev Surveys 70–100k

We're starting to get a sense of the salary band with these figures. But there's still a lot of open air between 70k and 100k, so you'll need more data. At this point, your

---

[2] All the numbers in this chapter are made-up and meant solely to walk you through the research process. Seattle writers, please don't use these figures!

[3] Karr, Evva. "Global GameDev Salary Database 2021." http://bit.ly/GameDevSalaries2021.

[4] Goodbrand, Cairo. "Game Dev Salary Check." (There are several sheets like these, so ask around.) https://docs.google.com/spreadsheets/d/1RCujW4PYQO0abNW3GjFNnknaQVx3 kJQPMGtNcJQx4fc/edit#gid=1759958873

best bet is to see if you can talk to someone in Seattle to narrow it down. Consult your network, find a good match, and talk to them about working as a writer in that city. If your network comes up dry, look through Twitter's #GameDevPaidMe hashtag to see if someone there can advise you. If you're lucky, you'll find someone at the exact studio you're talking to and they can give you the inside scoop on salaries.

Caution: Be gentle when approaching someone to discuss their salary. I've noticed that younger generations have no qualms about swapping wage figures, but older generations have to fight years of indoctrination to open up. There's a lot of shame and fear swirling around compensation, and it's often tied to people's sense of self-worth. They might be devastated to learn that a company lowballed them or that they're earning far less than the industry average. Don't let this stop you from asking, but be aware that money can be a surprisingly emotional subject for some people.

You find a helpful writer to chat with and learn that they have roughly the same experience and professional background as you. They reveal that they're making $80,000, but that's after a few years and a couple of raises. Okay, good to know! That aligns with your researched range and confirms you're on the right track. You can guess the company's first offer will align with the lower end of the pay scale, $75k, but you can make a case for at least $80k because someone with your exact skills and experience makes that amount. Now you have a solid idea of what to expect as a baseline offer and a figure of $80k to shoot for.

Step 2: Time to Math!

Your next step is to visit Numbeo and check out the cost of living in Seattle. Wow! It's an expensive place to live, huh? Look at the prices for rent, groceries, transportation, etc., and try to work up a monthly budget based on the lifestyle you'd lead there. How much would you spend each month on rent? Would you take public transportation or would you need a car? How much would groceries cost? Try to think of everything. Your budget might look something like my estimated figures on the next page.

These are my estimated expenses for a one-bedroom apartment outside the city center, for a single person with no children who takes public transportation. I didn't include health insurance costs, which are considerable in the United States, because most studios offer a company plan as a benefit. If you're going for a contractor role, make sure you know what basic expenses aren't covered by the

An estimated budget with figures from Numbeo

Item	Cost[5]
Rent	1,800
Transportation	150
Food	700
Bills (electricity, phone, cable, etc.)	250
Debt (student loans, credit cards, etc.)	300
Other (entertainment, streaming subscriptions, etc.)	250
TOTAL	3,450

company, so you can account for them. But insurance aside, your budget likely looks quite different than mine and that's fine! Everybody has different needs and priorities. Whatever your budget, total your estimated expenses to get a number for your monthly living expenses.

Your next step is to go to a US tax calculator and find out how much of that $80,000 salary you'd have left after taxes. I used us.icalculator.info.[6] According to them, you'll have roughly $63,500 to spend on rent and bills after federal taxes, which leaves you with 5,300 a month. If you're working remotely from another country, use a currency converter like xe.com to interpret the amounts. You'll also need to research the tax laws regarding foreign income.

Once you know your monthly salary, deduct your estimated budget from that amount. In my hypothetical example, you'd have $1850 left once your bills were paid. Is that enough for you to live on? Does it cover clothes, vet bills, travel, books, and any other expenses that might crop up? No? Then how much more money do you need to survive? You need to come up with two figures here. One is the minimum amount you can live on *comfortably*. And by comfortably, I mean you can afford everything you need and have a little left over for savings. This figure is your "ground floor." Then calculate how much you'd need to live *well*. Staying within reasonable bounds (you're not going to get 150k for a job that pays a comparable writer 80k), what's your shoot-for-the-moon figure? This should be

---

[5] These numbers are averages from Numbeo and solely for the purpose of illustration, so no angry letters, please

[6] Federal Tax: $80k Salary Example | US Tax Calculator 2022 (icalculator.info).

an amount that's considerably higher than the studio's likely to offer, but not so high that you'll price yourself out of the job. That number is your "ceiling." For our example, let's say your floor is 80k and your ceiling is 90k. Now you have a range to maneuver within and you're ready to negotiate.

Step 3: Know Your Worth

Lead Writer Samantha Wallschlaeger has advice that sums up everything I have to say about negotiations:

> This is something I learned early in my career and it's served me very, very well: go into a negotiation knowing exactly what your labor is worth. If you're a marginalized person, try to ask someone who is from a more privileged group than you. Then take that number into your negotiations and ask for exactly that, even if it seems outlandishly, ridiculously high. It's the number they'd give to the person you asked, so why not you? If the studio comes back with a lower counter-offer, ask if they can make up the difference in the form of a signing bonus. If they refuse, that's okay—you gave it a shot. Then you decide whether you want to give your labor to this studio at a discount, or hold out for a studio that will pay you your exact worth.

I encourage you to read about successful negotiation strategies from wiser people than I. In addition to Tarah Wheeler's book, I've heard recommendations for *Never Split the Difference* (Random House Business, 2017) by Chris Voss. "It is written from the perspective of a former FBI hostage negotiator, and some of the tools in it are extremely effective when applied to salary negotiations," Tara Brannigan says. "He outlines certain tactics from direct experience, and how they can be applied to more everyday negotiations. I have found it to be extremely useful." Tara also recommends going into negotiations with other job offers. It's good to know what other companies in that area are paying in case your studio pays below-average wages. "In one negotiation, the offer on hand was $20k lower than what I knew were the going rate for similar roles in the immediate area. Being able to go back with concrete numbers raised the offer by $15k with a statement in writing to review in one year's time. At the one-year mark, this was raised an additional $10k." There's really no downside to having another offer, aside from having to apply to multiple studios. But that's a small price to pay for the luxury of choice—and the freedom of walking away from a bad offer.

If you've been smashing your face against the glass wall of the industry for a while, you're probably grateful to have any offer at all. You're afraid if you ask for too much, you'll lose your shot. I understand feeling that way, I really do. But hiring candidates is a long and arduous process for studios. The more senior you are, the harder it is to find someone with your unique set of skills. After investing all that time and energy in finding a great candidate like you, the company wants to make things work. Trust me on this. As a hiring manager, there's an immense feeling of relief when we locate a writer we want to work with. I'm happy to reclaim my time from vetting resumes and writing tests and spending hours a week interviewing people. The whole team gets excited to bring the new writer into our creative circle. We're committed to getting you on board. I won't say you *can't* mess things up at this point, because it's still possible. I know a senior writer who asked for a wage higher than our CEO's salary and ... no. That's just not going to happen. But we still tried to work with him until it became clear he wouldn't budge. But in all my years of gamedeving, that's the only time I've seen someone price themselves out of a job. You've done your homework and have a reasonable range in mind, so that won't happen to you.

To feel more secure, prepare a list of your skills, awards, experience, and unique abilities. Write them down on a reference sheet with your salary research and keep it handy. You might need it during the negotiations to remind both parties what you're bringing to the table. Tara likes having the facts with her when she's negotiating asynchronously or via video conferencing. She recommends including information like "your goal in taking the new position, your target salary, how you fit this specific role based on their requirements" and any other information you might need to make your case. Once you've assembled your list, you're ready.

Step 4: Negotiate!

The recruiter contacts you a few days after the onsite with some good news. Everybody loved you and they want to offer you a job! Congratulations! You did it! All your hard work has paid off. It's tempting to shoot back an acceptance email right away but stop. Take a deep breath. Now is when the negotiations start.

At this point, things usually go one of two ways: You'll either receive an offer letter or the recruiter will ask for your preferred salary.

- **Offer Letter:** Ideally, you'll receive an offer letter. That means you have a concrete number and a list of benefits to look over and negotiate. Read it carefully to make sure your title is correct and that the salary isn't completely off what you discussed. Don't just say yes!
- **Preferred Salary:** The correct response to "What salary would you like?" is "What's the pay band for this role?" Never, never, never, *never* say a number first. Your number is almost always lower than it should be. You already had some initial salary discussions back during the phone screen, so the recruiter has a ballpark salary figure. It's fine to remind them of those talks and request a number from them.

Once you get a firm offer from the studio, counteroffer with your "ceiling" number. Don't worry if they say no! Remember Samantha's advice: shoot for the moon and you just might hit it. At least you tried. You'll probably go back and forth a few times before you agree on a salary. It's up to you what number you settle on, just remember not to accept an amount below your "floor." You can't survive on less than that amount. If the studio doesn't make you an offer that's at your "floor" or higher, then, I'm sorry, but you need to walk away. Or if you're in a desperate situation, take the offer and immediately start looking for work elsewhere. But do your best to negotiate for a better wage.

I won't walk you through every detail of the negotiations because, again, other people have already done an excellent job of charting your path. However, marginalized folks should stop right here and read Tarah Wheeler's "Minute Zero in the Gender Pay Gap"[7] before taking another step. Her strategy works.

Remember that it's the recruiter's job to sign you on for the lowest cost possible—but to still sign you on. The process is called a negotiation for a reason. There has to be some give and take on both sides. Whatever salary you settle on, make sure it aligns with your needs and your budget. Don't be afraid to lay out your reasoning to the recruiter. Recruiters have their own calculations to make, and it's important to make sure you understand each other. Petteri describes what this process looks like from the recruiting side:

> Let's say we're comparing you with other people on the team. I'd think that you are between this person and this person in terms of experience. We're willing to give you the benefit of doubt because you have a lot of potential, so we're going to maybe give an extra amount for that. That puts your level around here, and we'll give you that number as a salary offer. If there are things that we should know as a company, like you need to make a certain amount of salary to be able to make ends meet or you need a housing allowance, make those things known as early as possible because it might be a blocker for us. Maybe we can't hire you because of that. Or maybe it can help us take a position of "Okay, we need to pay at least this amount of money for this person." Be forthcoming, open, and honest about your needs, but also showcase that, "Hey, I bring this much value to the team."

In other words, if you ask for a high salary, be prepared to explain why you need it and what skills or experience you have that make you worth the money. That's where your reference sheet comes in handy! You can make a case for your salary based on your research, and you can remind them of your invaluable skillset.

---

[7] Wheeler, Tarah. "Minute Zero in the Gender Pay Gap." Medium. Last updated 25 June 2015. Minute-Zero in the Gender Pay Gap | by Tarah Wheeler | Tarah Wheeler | Medium

Mind the Pay Gap! It Starts Here

There's a persistent myth that women don't negotiate, and that's why they earn less. There's a modicum of truth to this, but there's a reason: studies reveal that women are penalized when they negotiate.[8] There's also some evidence that companies lowball women and negotiate harder with them, as Petteri can confirm with his experiences as a recruiter. He said that he's had some great female candidates who stepped up to negotiate their salaries. When that happened, supervisors would sometimes contact him to say "'Oh, they seemed really bossy' or 'They're just after the money.' And I don't understand. I ask, 'What's this really about?' So many women get swindled out of proper salaries because they don't know any better. And it's like a balancing act because you can't get too aggressive." There are plenty of depressing studies out there that show how the cards are stacked against women and marginalized communities during the delicate negotiation process. Harvard Business Center has some great research—and some great tactics for countering biased behavior. It's worth an afternoon of reading to arm yourself against discriminatory behavior.

Exposure

What if a studio comes back with a low offer, or worse: they ask you to work "for exposure"? This expression is now widely recognized as a joke thanks to the @ forexposure_txt Twitter account—and it should be treated as a joke if a studio offers it to you in lieu of a salary. Should you ever work for exposure? My answer is no. Never work for free. I repeat, *never work for free.* There should always be some material benefit to you. I could rant on and on about this, but the Writer's Guild of Great Britain infographic says it better than I could.[9]

Step 5: Sign on the Dotted Line

Once you agree on a salary, the studio will draw up a contract. In AAA, these are enormously complicated documents that are written in legalese. The contract outlines your relationship with the game company. How many hours a week is "fulltime"? How are your bonuses structured? How much of your writing do you own and how much is the company's property? Can you take on projects outside of work? All of those terms are laid out in your contract.

---

[8] Bowles, Hannah Riley. "Why Women Don't Negotiate Their Job Offers." *Harvard Business Review.* 19 June 2014. https://hbr.org/2014/06/why-women-dont-negotiate-their-job-offers

[9] Writer's Guild of Great Britain. "Videogames: Should I Work for Free?" https://writersguild. org.uk/resources

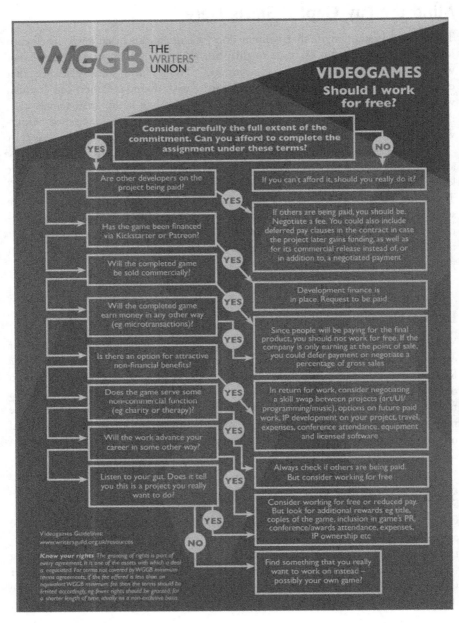

The WGGB's guide to working for free.

Once you get it, read it carefully. Many people think that once the contract is written up, it's set in stone. And some companies will push back if you ask for changes. But keep trying. Agreement on the terms of the contract is part of the negotiation process. You should absolutely ask for adjustments. Remember: once you sign it, it's a legally binding document. Breaking the terms could lead to serious consequences for your career and even land you in court or forced arbitration. Make sure you're absolutely comfortable with what you're agreeing to.

Do I Need an Agent?

If you're one of the rare game writers who has an agent, then lucky you! Your agent will negotiate for you and secure you the best possible deal. Rhianna's agent deals with her contracts and fee negotiations, which she hates doing. Her agent understands how much writers are paid in other fields and brings his TV and film experience to the table. This gives negotiations an extra sense of professionalism and protection. "He's also helped me receive contractual elements such as occasional signing bonuses and a better class of air travel for long-distance flights. Stuff that's not uncommon in other fields, but I'd probably find harder to negotiate on my own. He keeps me one step removed from the sordid topic of coin and allows me to fully focus on the creativity." As we discussed earlier, agents are fairly unusual in AAA games. Even though Mary Kenney has a literary and a TV agent, she doesn't have one for her job at Insomniac. "That said," she adds, "if I decided to go back to freelance games writing … I'd probably want an agent who could help me negotiate games contracts as well as books and TV." I've personally never had an agent and never felt the need for one, but I've often hired lawyers for contract negotiations and been very glad that I did.

Do I Need a Lawyer?

Short answer? No. If you can't afford the fees and can't get donated services, do your best on your own. I managed without a lawyer for many years and did just fine. But I often had to agree to clauses that made me uneasy. Some organizations like the WGGB offer legal services as a membership benefit, so you can submit your contract for review and get excellent high-level legal advice that way. But they don't have the time to go over every section and clause with you, or negotiate on your behalf. For that, you'll need to hire a lawyer. It can feel like an overwhelming and very adult thing to do, but if you are juggling multiple projects—like writing a book, teaching seminars, and working on games—I strongly recommend it. It's worth the investment to protect your creative output.

To find out more about hiring a lawyer for game contracts, I spoke with Peter Lewin, a senior associate at Wiggin LLP in the United Kingdom. I expected him to sell me on the idea of hiring a lawyer, but he actually thinks game devs can handle some contracts on their own. It's no different from any other negotiation. He suggests that "you take the pen yourself, and mark up contracts with the changes that you want. Or you can go back with a bunch of discussion points and say 'this clause is giving me concern. Can you explain it?'" After that, you talk it through with your employer and see if they'll make changes for you. Or have their lawyers make the changes. Pete says there's some trust involved there, that they'll do it well, "but it saves you a bit of time and fees." He cautions that when you're looking at a fresh contract, the quality of that starting paperwork can "vary quite a lot across the industry. The starting position, what's the impact, how much you're going to have to push back on and the bargaining power of the two parties."

My ears perked up when he mentioned the power differential because that's the position most AAA devs will find themselves in. One small person looking at a contract that was drafted by lawyers for powerful corporations. I explained that I've pushed back on clauses a few times, but my change was rejected. Pete acknowledged that "sometimes the bigger companies can push through a bit more because they're doing 100 or 200 of these agreements. They don't have time to negotiate them all the time, understandably so. You might have to accept a bit more there." But he also said that devs "shouldn't be afraid to ask questions to understand things. You should always understand it. At the very least, don't be afraid to request changes. You can make those changes yourself or just talk about them." So, if you're not in a place where you can afford a lawyer, read your contract carefully and make sure you understand what you're signing. I've successfully changed some contracts, especially as a freelancer. It can be done. But let's say you look at the contract, it all goes over your head, and you decide to hire a lawyer. How do you do that?

How Do You Find a Good Lawyer?

Most people don't know where to start looking for a lawyer. It seems like a scary process and you might not be sure how to find one who handles game contracts. Wiggin is one of the few firms in the United Kingdom that offers services for the games industry. But do you need a games-industry-focused lawyer to review a contractor agreement? Pete says it depends on the deal. If it's a really serious games-publishing deal (you're selling your screenplay for a million-dollar project) or a high-value consultancy contract, you might want to get someone with publishing experience or a games industry lawyer. "But having a game specialist is probably slightly less essential for a writer. So just a good commercial lawyer would probably be a good starting point." Okay, but how do you find one? Do you just google "video game lawyer"? As it turns, out, yes! You can definitely find legal services that way, but Pete says the best route is to get a recommendation from friends, if you can. Just like any other professional service. Contact the lawyer and set up a consultation. Pete walks us through what that first meeting should look like:

> Most lawyers will have a chat with you, like a free initial consultation to give you some additional pointers and see if you're the right fit. That goes both ways, to see if you're happy working together. And then on that call, if you can share a copy of the agreement, then that could be helpful because then the lawyer might be able to give you a fixed fee for, usually, a review and maybe some edits. They probably wouldn't be able to give you a fixed fee for beginning to end because you don't know how much negotiation it's going to take. But ask for a fixed fee. Failing that, get their hourly rates.

Ahh, the rates. When I was working in Washington, DC, I ended up paying about $900 USD for two hours of an entertainment lawyer's review time. That was back in 2016 though, so I figured rates would be higher now. But Pete says that's still about right for straightforward writer contracts. Rates vary significantly from place to place, and "if you're in Scotland, lawyers are going to be cheaper than probably if you're in London." If you take regional differences into account, then a lawyer will run you "probably a few thousand currency wherever you are" for more complicated writer agreements.

What Should I Ask?

When you're looking at the contract, what sort of things should you be aware of? Is there anything in particular that writers should double-check? Pete has looked at a lot of game contracts in his time, so he's familiar with some of the more arcane clauses they contain. He says one of the biggest things to clear up is whether you're classified as a contractor or an employee. We've already discussed that contractors don't have the same benefits or protections as FTE writers do, so you can understand why you'd want to know that. Pete says, "There's certainly some mis-categorizing of people within the industry. People that maybe should be employees being classified as contractors. There's not a really bright line as to when you tip from being a contractor to an employee." He suggests asking yourself some questions to nail down the definition. "Are you only working for one studio? Are you dedicating all of your time to working on this one project? Do they provide you with all of your laptops and equipment? Do they dictate when you come to work and what you do? It's not a super simple test. But yeah, figuring that out is an important one."

In the United States, most contracts are for "at-will" employment, which means either party can end the contract at any time for any—or no—reason. Make sure you understand the specific details of your at-will clause because you might still have a notice period to serve. If you have an FTE contract, you'll have a bunch of additional benefits. "There's going to be protections around working time and minimum wage and holidays and sick pay and things like that." Pete points out that most FTEs don't get a writer-specific contract; they likely get the same general employment contract as everyone else, possibly with a few minor modifications. But contractors have agreements that "can really differ quite a lot in terms of how well they're written and how long they are, how complicated they are." He had a long list of clauses and concerns that contractors should watch out for. Too many for me to include in this one little chapter of one little book. Contractors, my advice is to get legal counsel before signing anything. There are too many ways for you to get in trouble.

The Usual Suspects

Over the years, I've learned to look out for some tricky clauses before signing any contract. Here are the key points I always make sure I understand:

- **Salary:** How much do you make? When do you get paid? How do you get paid? Do you get overtime or wage-based perks?
- **Bonuses:** What are the requirements to receive a bonus? If it's profit-based, what is the formula for determining it? When are bonuses handed out?
- **Notice Period:** If you decide to leave, how far in advance do you need to notify the company? If they lay you off or (horrors) fire you, how much advance notice do they need to give you?
- **Raises and Promotions:** Are you guaranteed an annual salary review or raise? When do you qualify for a promotion?
- **Title:** Make sure your official title is what you agreed upon. It's never happened to me, but I've heard stories of some last-minute title changes. Titles matter! It can affect your pay, your future roles, and your credits.
- **Credits:** Speaking of credits, this is a hot new issue in contracts. Under the current credits system, game devs are vulnerable. You've heard the stories. Some devs have worked on a project for years, left a few months before the game shipped, and got left out of the credits. Some studios have a blanket policy that if you leave before ship, then you get "Special Thanks" and that's it. Devs have been demoted in the credits, put into subcategories, or had credit for their work given to someone else. There are no industry-wide rules for credits, and devs have almost no recourse when there's a problem or a dispute, beyond the goodwill of the studio. Pete recommends negotiating it right from the start. Get a guarantee in writing.

- **Noncompete Clauses:** They can also be called "restrictions after termination." Basically, they're rules for what you can do and who you can work for after you leave a company. Here's what Pete says: "Sometimes it could be three months long, sometimes it could be twelve months long, sometimes it might be you just can't work with someone you might have been working with when you were at your past employer. Sometimes, it might say you can't work in the same industry." He says they range in length and strictness, so definitely know what's in your contract. These clauses can be quite restrictive, but I've had good luck pushing back on them.
- **Intellectual Property:** This is another sticky wicket that you see in a lot of AAA contracts. The gist of it is that anything you create while working for the company belongs to them. *Anything*. As a writer, that means anything you write or create. If you write a personal journal at home, technically your company owns it. I've never seen this clause enforced, but it's a frightening thing to have in your contract. There is a way to claim some IP as your own, however, and you do that with deeds of variation.
- **Deeds of Variation:** Let's say you want to work on a side project like, oh, I don't know, a book of game-writing advice while you're working for a studio. Does your book automatically become their property? Nope! You can secure a deed of variation from the studio to work on side projects. And you can do this at any point, not just when you're signing the contract. Let your lead know that you have a side project you want to work on and then submit a proposal. They'll probably run it up the chain and get approval from the legal department, but I've never been turned down. I know plenty of game devs who've worked on their own games on the side. Most studios are fine with it, but make sure you clear it with them.
- **Relocation Pay:** If you're moving for this job, you should negotiate a relocation package that covers all your needs. You should never pay for the cost of visa paperwork or moving fees on your own. If a company wants you to relocate, they should pay for it.
- **Signing Bonus:** This is a one-time payment usually offered to entice you away from another studio or job offer. Some bonuses can be a hefty sum of money. If your salary isn't what you hoped, here's where you can make up that deficit.

There are plenty more things to look out for, but that covers the big stuff. If this all seems scary and overwhelming, don't worry! Pete says unreasonable clauses that are "restraints of trade on your business" may not be enforceable. You have to be able to earn a living. But some employees may "follow it out of fear of rocking the boat, whether it's legally enforceable or not." Don't let that be you. Read your contract carefully, make notes, ask questions, and push back on anything that seems unreasonable. If you meet any resistance, keep pushing! Here's some final advice from our lawyer Pete:

If you've got the time, the persistence and the negotiating power to push to actually get it removed, then I think you're in a pretty defensible position to keep pushing on it. I've been in circumstances where it just took pushing on it three or four times on the same issue, being persistent, to get something out of a contract. It's a bit like a war of attrition, and it feels like sometimes when you get the first no, you kind of go, "Oh, that's it then." But that's not always the case.

So ... DO I need a lawyer?

Your long, long, long answer is no. You can read your contract carefully and make adjustments yourself. However, in an ideal world, hire a lawyer if you can afford it. Look over your contract and note any problem areas, then see if you can retain legal counsel to review some of your concerns. It might cost a thousand pounds or more, but it's an investment in your future and security and could prevent all sorts of headaches down the road.

Now What?

Once you've bounced the contract back and forth a few times, you'll reach a point where everyone agrees it's a deal. The studio will send the final contract over—most places have a digital signature form now—check to make sure all the adjustments have been made, and then sign! WAIT what are you—ah, just kidding. You're good. Save a copy of the contract for your own records and go get yourself a treat. You've earned it.

CHALLENGE

Find a job you want and do the research as if you were taking the job:

- What does the company usually pay for that role? (Glassdoor, Numbeo)
- What do similar roles in that region pay? (spreadsheet) The industry? (GSA survey)
- What is the cost of living in that region?
- What would your specific cost of living be there? (Transportation, rent, bills, etc.)
- Set your lowest range based on that figure. This is the figure you won't go below.

- Do your research to determine how much savings you need to put away and what your labor, experience, etc., is worth. Set your high range.
- Try to talk to someone who works at the studio to confirm your range is realistic.

Go into negotiations with confidence!

Chapter 11

First Day

Know your worth. This includes monetary worth, yes, but also your worth on a team. Many studios mistakenly see writers as just "handling the dialogue" when the scope of our job is so much wider than that. Ask to be included and respected as a collaborator who brings something important to the table.

—Samantha Wallschlaeger, Lead Writer, Crystal Dynamics

Holy moly! It's finally happening. The contract is signed, and you start tomorrow. Exciting news! Of course, you want your first day to go smoothly and set you up for success at the studio. And of course it will. But if you're anything like I was on my first day in gamedev, you're panicking. There's no need. Treat it like the first day at any office job.

The Night Before

You shouldn't need to prep much for your first day, but read through your correspondence with the company carefully to see if they gave you any special instructions. The important things to look for are the classic Who/What/Where/When. Note who you're supposed to report to and any paperwork you need to bring. I've had studios refuse to let me start working until all paperwork was completed, so get that out of the way as soon as you can.

Once you know what your schedule looks like the next morning, decide on your outfit. Dress the same way for your first day that you would for an onsite interview: casual, but slightly dressier than your normal day-to-day. Make sure the clothes you want to wear are clean and ready to go, and that's it! You're free to

DOI: 10.1201/9781003282235-12

spend the rest of the evening however you want. Relaxing and resting the night before are the best things you can do to set yourself up for success the next day. I can't stress this enough. Remember that you already have the job, so there's no need to study or prep. Do whatever you usually do to have fun: read, hang out with friends, play games. Try to get a good night's sleep. You'll want to be rested and sharp the next day.

Getting There

If you're working from home, lucky you! All you have to do is connect at the right time and then follow your company's instructions. But if you work onsite, make sure you anticipate the commute so you can plan accordingly and be on time. Some companies are built on campuses or have security checkpoints, so factor those in to your schedule. If you're driving around to find the right building or waiting for clearance at a security checkpoint, that can slow you down. Don't stress if you're late! People understand that it can be tricky to find a building the first time and that problems can arise while you're sorting out your commute. They're not going to fire you for being ten minutes late on your first day, I promise.

At the Job

Unless they've already given you an assignment or you're jumping in for a high-intensity workshop, your first day will be an easy one. It's more about getting you set up and introducing you to people than it is about starting work.

Your schedule this first day will likely be tightly structured. You'll need to get your workstation set up properly and make sure you have access to all the programs and resources you need to do good work. That means meetings with your lead, team, and IT. Human Resources will probably meet with you to review studio policies and procedures, and to go over health care plans, pensions, and similar concerns. You'll go to a variety of meetings where you have to introduce yourself. You'll have your first stand-up![1] And you'll meet an overwhelming amount of people. You might get handed some swag. It'll be a blur of activity, but hopefully a happy one.

I wrote a long chapter full of advice for your first day, but in the end, I decided to cut it. Your studio will hold your hand in the beginning and your colleagues will help you find the answers you need. You'll be fine. So instead of a lengthy spiel on standard office advice, I offer you a short checklist. Here. Take this.

---

[1] A short, daily meeting where devs talk about what they're working on that day. You often literally stand up at your desk for it, ergo the name.

First Week Checklist

- **Take a Studio Tour:** Learn where the important things are, like the biggest whiteboards and best coffee machines. Find out everything you can about the routines of daily life at the studio.

- **Take a Virtual Studio Tour:** Learn the ropes of studio life online. How do you book a conference room online? How do you submit an expense report? How do you set up a meeting on your calendar? That sort of stuff. Read the employee handbook cover to cover. I can't stress that enough. Know what's expected of your behavior. If you sign a new NDA or social media policy, make sure you understand every last word of it. You can get in serious trouble for a "harmless" Reddit comment or a throwaway tweet. Know the rules.

- **Read ALL the Documentation:** In very early pre-production, that might be as simple as reading a few design documents. If you're joining late in the project there will likely be a wiki full of designs, plans, schedules, and lore. If you're lucky, someone will have put together a starter pack of critical information. Read all of it now, while you have time. I can't tell you how often a barely remembered fact from my first week on the job has proven to be useful. Focus on the key project information: What are the game pillars? What are the key project features? How does narrative fit into the game? What are the story and main characters? What is the project schedule (ship date, key milestones, etc.)? Get a sense of the shape of the project and how your writing fits into it.

- **Feedback:** Write up feedback on your reading. After this first week, you'll never see the project with fresh eyes again. Your impressions at this stage are invaluable, so write them up. Keep your feedback neutral and constructive, but don't be afraid to point out issues with the story or production plan. Your team may be so deep inside the project at this point that they can't see the problems. Who knows? You might be able to dazzle them with solutions to longstanding plot issues. As long as you're not a jerk about it, this can be a great way to get your team talking about the hows and whys of the narrative and to understand how they landed on this version of the story. Diplomacy is very important because the team is more attached to the story than they are to you at this stage. Phrase your concerns as questions, and explore the story together. For example, let's say you've read the story and think the antagonist is passive and uninteresting. How should you bring that point up to your team?
  - **Bad:** "Your villain is boring and not scary."
  - **Good:** "I'm not sure I understand the villain's motivations. Can you explain them to me?" or "This is an interesting approach to a Big Bad! Would you walk me through the villain's arc and how you plan to get players emotionally invested in stopping him?"

If your team is missing critical information, make sure to point that out too. Sometimes everyone knows the story so well that they don't write it down because "everyone knows that." Well, new people don't! Make sure you alert your team to any knowledge gaps in their documentation.

- **Learn the Hierarchy:** Ask for an organization chart. It's good to know who's in charge of what and who your colleagues are. You'll need this information to chart your career path.
- **Meet Key People:** Talk to your lead and compile a list of the people you'll work with the most. I like to set up short, individual "get to know ya" meetings with everyone on the list in my first few weeks at a new job. Establish relationships and lines of communication early on.
- **Ask Questions:** You're going to have a gajillion questions at this stage and that's great! Ask them! The first week or so of a project when everyone knows you're new is when you should ask questions. After a while, people will expect you to have a certain level of project familiarity or to know where you can find answers on your own. But now? You're an innocent baby who knows nothing. There sincerely are no stupid questions about the project at this stage, and that's a glorious bit of freedom. Dig in, dig deep, and learn everything you can while expectations of you are low.
- **Be Kind to Yourself:** Nobody expects you to pick everything up instantly. Some people hit the ground running and some people take longer to ramp up. You might get frustrated with yourself in the beginning because you don't know everything you think you should or you worry that you're not performing as well as you should. My advice is to stop and breathe. I mean it: BREATHE. You're not expected to know everything at this point. You have time to learn. Be curious, thoughtful, and willing to learn, and you'll be fine.

Start Collaboration Early

Learn to speak the language of teams around you, especially folks in narrative-adjacent disciplines. Every aspect of the game should tell your story. Most devs recognize this and are storytellers in their own disciplines. They're usually excited to collaborate with Narrative. It's important that you convey your ideas in terms they understand and can apply. Understand what they need from you and your work and try to meet them on their territory. Willow's "main question for Narrative is often 'What key features about the narrative of this space am I trying to convey?', or more often the case 'So, what is this place?'" Willow is a story-driven designer and likes to use a space's larger purpose in the story of the world to inform her design. When you're talking to level designers like her, you'll collaborate better if you understand how her work can tell your overarching story. "Is this building a factory, building weapons for the war or a hospital for injured civilians? Is this a lost temple to a forgotten deity, or a secret research facility, or both?" Collaboration unites the physical space of the game level with the emotional space of the narrative. Make it your mission to find out how every discipline approaches storytelling and how you can support their work. In the first few weeks, that means asking questions about their features and processes, looking over their plans, and talking through ways to help each other out. Find out what excites them about their work and what parts of narrative pique their interest. Many people you meet at this point will become your staunchest allies later in the project.

Probationary Periods

First-day performance anxiety can be exacerbated by probationary periods. Knowing that a company can let you go at any point for no reason is terrifying. (Sorry, my US friends on at-will contracts. For you, the terror never ends.) But keep in mind that's what probationary periods are *for*. To give you and the company a chance to see if you're a good match. I used to think it was silly. I was like, "Well, of course it's a good match. Don't you know that by this point?" But honestly? No. I've seen enough people start at a studio, get a better sense of the project and processes, and decide, "Nope, this isn't for me after all." Sometimes people leave for personal reasons. Something changes in their life (a parent dies, a partner gets an unexpected opportunity), and a job that seemed like a good fit turns out to be the wrong move at the wrong time. It happens far more often than people realize. It's especially tragic when you've moved internationally for a job and it turns out to be a bad fit or there's a sudden turn of events that takes you back home again. If you give it a shot and it's not for you, then better to know now. Make sure you know what the consequences are for leaving early, and talk to HR about how to extricate yourself. Some contracts have clauses that require you to repay relocation costs and hiring bonuses if you leave during the first year. If you negotiated your contract well, you already know what those penalties are.

Probationary periods are generally for the benefit of the company, to protect them against hiring someone who can't do the job, but they can protect you too. Spend those first few months asking yourself if this place is right for you. Do you see a future here? If not long term, at least for a year or two or until you get the project done? If not, then better to get out now. Go talk to your lead and HR about what your options are. In general, if you feel it's a bad fit, they'll understand and will work with you to end an unhappy relationship. But remember that the hiring process costs a lot of money and they *want* you to work out. They're rooting for you to succeed. If you're struggling, tell them what you need. They'll almost always help you get it.

Imposter Syndrome Part 1

This might be your first job at a game studio. Or your first time working on a AAA game at all. Or maybe your first time working with people you've admired for years. It's easy to get intimidated and think that everyone knows more than you or that you don't know what you're doing and you'll get exposed and fired. Imposter syndrome is a hell of a thing. And that's just the voice coming from *within*. On my first day at a job early in my career, my lead told me that I wasn't her first choice. She'd wanted to hire a different candidate, but their schedule didn't align with the studio's. So they hired me instead. I spent the rest of my (brief) time at that studio knowing I was second choice and feeling judged for it. But even with a supportive lead, it's tough to fight off imposter syndrome. I'm sorry. I have no advice for how to fix this, only how to live with it. Keep a folder of accomplishments on your desktop to look through when you doubt yourself. Look at the list of your skills and awards you wrote up for salary negotiations. Talk to your friends and colleagues. Some places are tougher than others, and you might be afraid to show any weakness. I get that. Keep reminding yourself that you're here because the studio thinks you can do good work. They don't expect perfection, only progress. As long as you're steadily learning and getting better, you'll be fine. *You belong here.*

Take a Moment

At the end of your first day, stop for a moment to appreciate how far you've come. You've learned and grown an incredible amount to be where you are right now. You set a goal, made a plan, and followed it step by careful step to reach your dream. You broke through that glass wall around the AAA industry, and now you're a professional game writer. You have so many incredible firsts ahead of you: The first time players react to your game trailer. Your first zing of anticipation and fear after the game ships and it's too late to change anything. The first time you see your game in a store and think, "I made that!" Your first launch party. Your first awards show. Your first AAA game credits. Your first fan letter. Your first story being played and loved by people all over the world. So many wonderful things lie ahead for you.

The first half of this book ends with your moment of triumph, as it should. In the second half, we'll focus on turning your first job into a successful career. When you're done savoring the moment, let's get to work.

CHALLENGE

At the end of your first day of work, make sure you can answer all these questions:

- Who is on your immediate team and what is the hierarchy (who is your lead, reports, etc.)?
- What software programs do you need for your day-to-day job? Do you have them all?
- What does your schedule look like for the next week?
- Who do you contact about workplace concerns (the room is cold, you need dry erase markers, you need a key to the garage)?
- Who do you contact about administrative concerns (what's my health insurance, how do I enroll in a pension plan, who do I talk to if I'm having personal problems)?
- How do you submit a ticket to IT?
- If you're on a probation period, when does it end and what does it take to succeed? (A list of concrete goals.)

You'll need to know more than these essentials of course, but this list will get you started. It's a lot to take in on the first day. If you learn nothing else, know about your team and where to go for more information on various subjects. The rest you can learn as you go.

Chapter 12

Moving Up

If I could have a superpower as a writer, it would be to know what my players are thinking at all times. I do my best to try and figure this out! Listening to feedback and observing playtests and live streams all can help. But if I could just know with utter certainty, then I could always write in a way that aligns as closely as possible with my players' experience, or effectively subverts that experience, which can make for moments where players feel extraordinarily connected with what they're playing. It's like the game is reading their mind. I think good writing in games is a factor of the innate quality of the writing, multiplied by the presentation quality of that writing, multiplied by how the writing is used. So, I think whenever game writers can be involved with or at least highly aware of how their work will be surfaced to the player, they improve their work's chances of having the highest positive impact. This is another way of saying that having deep knowledge of the constraints of the work can be extraordinarily important to unlocking the writer's creativity and the work's potential.

— Greg Kasavin, Creative Director, Supergiant Games

Now that you've got a job and you're off to a good start, most advice books pat you on the bum and let you toddle off on your own. But this is when you need a mentor the most. You'll have friends in the industry (I hope!) and can talk through a lot of problems with them and ask for advice. I encourage you to do so. Your colleagues will get you through the roughest part of every project. The jokes you share, your tales from the trenches, the little acts of kindness and support, and the friendships you build will stay with you long after the game has shipped and you've all moved on to other projects. My wish for every one of you is that you find fellow

DOI: 10.1201/9781003282235-13

travelers to share your game-dev journey. The friendships and shared adventures make it all worthwhile. But your friends won't have all the answers you need. They might not know their rights and responsibilities or understand how to solve your unique problems. They might lack the experience to help you grow in your craft or advance in your career. That's why you need a mentor. And these next few chapters are why I wrote this book.

Now What?

Your first day of work is exciting. You play pinball in the game room and learn about the free food, beer fridge, tutorials, and other employee perks. A dev wanders by in a Totoro onesie. But once the novelty and glamour wear off, you realize that it's just an office job like any other. And honestly? Parts of it are dull. When the daily routine of game writing becomes tedious, you need the three Ps to survive: *Patience, Persistence, Passion*. I know passion is a dirty word these days because some folks have taken advantage of it to encourage overwork. What I mean by passion is finding something in your job to inspire you. You'll spend most of your time doing un-fun tasks. Updating documents and spreadsheets. Writing UI text and objectives.[1] Sitting in long meetings. Revising and revising and revising. You'll need to keep your goal in mind and find things to love about the project if you want to stay invested. Are there days when you'll come in and get all heart-eyed over your amazing job? Absolutely! I have days when I can't believe my luck. I write video games for a living! How cool is that? But I also have days when I don't want to get out of bed because there's a big pitch or a tedious day of spreadsheets ahead of me. That's when you have to dig deep and find reasons to go in. Find the parts of game-making that light you up, and focus on them to get through.

The Writing Routine

So, what does a day in a game writer's life look like? Is there such a thing as a typical day? Yes! There are some broad strokes that color everyone's daily tasks, and those come from the project phase. By phase, I mean where you are in the development process. There are many stages to making games, from Pitch to Patch.[2] We'll focus on Preproduction (or Prepro) and Production because that's when writers do most of their work. Prepro is where you brainstorm and pitch all

---

[1] Objectives are the bits of UI text that direct you around the game and tell you what to do. "Talk to Eddy" or "Return to Headquarters." They're often found in the upper right corner of the game screen.

[2] Pitch = the proposal for a new game. Patch = an update to an existing game that adds new content or fixes bugs.

the ideas for stories, prototype your narrative systems, plot and plan, and generally map the game out on paper. Production is when you actually sit down and make the thing.. If you're working on a narrative-driven game, writers will often enter Production before other teams so they can lay the track for other departments to follow.

Preproduction

In Prepro, your team will pitch story ideas and characters to leadership on a project. There's commonly an existing IP: a publisher wants you to make *Big Superhero Movie: The Game* or your studio is making the sequel to a successful first project. In both cases, you'll inherit a game universe that's already well-defined, and your task is to tell a story within those parameters. The project will come with lots of documentation: world guides,[3] art, characters, and perhaps plot proposals. A franchise with multiple existing titles might have a guide hundreds of pages long. It's your responsibility to know the rules of that universe and create work that fits comfortably within its confines. Personally, I enjoy the challenge of constraints. And when it's a franchise I adore, like the *Dishonored* games, it's gratifying to write work that becomes part of the canon for that universe. (Fans will help you get the details right. Trust me.)

Sometimes, rarely, you'll start with a blank canvas. No existing IP, no defined universe, no fan-favorite characters, no canon. Pure possibility as wide as the sky. *CONTROL* was like that, for me. We spent a lot of time during Prepro defining the rules of the universe, specifically the Oldest House. What was it? How did it work? What's happening during a House shift? What *exactly* is a threshold? If you can define these rules clearly, players will experience the world as cohesive and real, even if you never tell them what the rules are. Most of this work happens during Prepro. It's when you define the game universe and how different systems will express it. To be clear, I'm speaking primarily of story-driven games here. Plenty of games start as a series of systems and game physics, and then the writing team figures out what story they can tell with those tools. Either approach involves intense collaboration with other disciplines to make sure you're creating the universe holistically. If you dream up an epic, cinematic, high-fantasy story but Game Design wants streamlined match-3 mechanics, you'll have a challenge making those disparate elements work together without the story feeling like a "wrapper" for the gameplay.

---

[3] World guide aka story bible, lore bible, tone bible, IP guide. They're all terms for a compendium of information about the game universe. Their contents and purpose vary slightly, but I hear the terms used interchangeably.

The Prepro process varies from project to project. My experience has been different at every studio. There's no right or wrong way to approach this phase. Only what's right or wrong for your game, your team, and your resources. Daily work may involve pitching "big picture" story ideas and outlining major plot moments. This is when you write the game's foundational documents: biographies for the key characters and lore for creatures and regions (the story bible), and descriptive briefs for Concept Art. You work with other teams to create narrative tools—not just the systems that deliver story in-game, but the actual tools and programs you'll use to get the text *into* the game. You consult with producers to establish workflows and timelines for your work on the project, and staff the writing team. Here are some narrative deliverables[4] for the Prepro phase of a game:

- **Story Pitches:** These are sweeping, high-level pitches for the entire game story. You'll also pitch regional storylines, key characters and themes, and stylistic elements like genre, tone, and narrative devices (e.g., *CONTROL* has recurring imagery, symbolic vignettes, live-action overlays, and stylized signage). The narrative director and lead writer usually pitch these ideas to leadership, the creative director, and possibly publishing stakeholders. But the entire team contributes to the ideation process.

- **Story "Bible":** This document is sadly misunderstood and misused. The purpose of a bible is to gather all the plans and ideas floating around in Prepro, from every discipline, and bind them to a page. This gives the universe its shape. It's also a one-stop reference for teams to see what other disciplines have planned. As such, it's an incredibly valuable document. The task of assembling them usually falls to writers, and frankly, I love them. Worldbuilding tickles my creative mind. To give you an idea of what's in a bible, look at the table of contents on the next page. As you can see, it encompasses the whole game. Ideas and plans will evolve over time, and a bible should be a living document that evolves and grows with them. The best bibles are searchable wikis that link out to the work other teams are doing and whose pages get updated and archived as the project progresses. Keeping the wiki updated is a Sisyphean task, though, and there's either a dedicated loremaster for the job or the pages lose accuracy and relevance.

- **Story Synopsis and Treatment:** These are exactly what you think. The synopsis is a short summary of the story, usually only a few pages long. And the story treatment is a more detailed version of the synopsis. Eventually, these documents will become a scene breakdown or macro.[5]

---

[4] Deliverables are the work you hand over at the end of certain time period, like a sprint or milestone. For Narrative, these are usually concrete documents like screenplays and spreadsheets of barks.

[5] A "macro" is a detailed blockout of all questlines and missions. It contains plot, character arcs, gameplay, cinematic types, and other narrative needs. It's often a massive spreadsheet that updates regularly.

Story Bible   **MY SUPERCOOL GAME**   by Anna Megill

CONTENTS

Table of contents from a AAA story bible.

- **Character Biographies and Maps:** You know these already. Character bios explain who the character is, define their backstory and personality, and offer a guide for how they behave and sound. These insights are important when you're casting actors. Maps show where the character is at each point of the story. They "map" the character arc against the storyline.
- **Prototypes:** You'll collaborate with other teams on this work. It involves creating the narrative tools and delivery systems for the game, determining what "verbs"[6] your story will have, and generally supporting other teams with their Prepro work.

Every project is unique, and every game has different deliverables. As a junior or mid-level writer, you'll help brainstorm and write up story ideas and bios,

---

[6] Verbs = gameplay actions. What players can do to express story. Common verbs: walk, talk, investigate, fight.

and support other teams. This is my favorite part of game-making when it's all blue skies and limitless imagination. Preproduction involves *far* more work than I can list here, but it all adds up to one end: laying the foundation of the game and ensuring everything's ready for the go-go-go work of Production.

Production

Once you leave Preproduction, your focus shifts and your routine changes with it. Mary Kenney describes a typical day for a senior writer at Insomniac.

Writing

- Brainstorm, pitch, and write quest lines, characters, scenes, sequences, and so on.
- Write cinematic, gameplay, and emergent dialog (aka barks) scripts.
- Write or edit on-screen text alongside UX and design teams (hints, skill names, menus, fake social media feeds, all that good stuff).

Communication and Collaboration

- Meet with other departments to figure out the best way to tell parts of the story.
- Help with hiring for the story dept. and for other departments that work closely with us (design, audio).
- Mentor new writers or other devs who want to better understand storytelling.
- Help direct actors in the VO booth and on the PCAP stage.

Feedback

- Give feedback in animation and level design reviews and live playthroughs to improve storytelling in cutscenes and gameplay.
- Give feedback on other writers' cinematic, gameplay, and emergent scripts.
- Play the game! Write up narrative bugs and advise on scripting/timing updates.

I simplified Mary's tasks and broke them down into a few broad categories: writing, collaboration and communication, and feedback. Most of the work you do will fall into those categories, in one way or another. (Now you can see why "communication" is the top keyword in job listings!) The details of your day-to-day will change, but this is very much a typical day in Production.

Most mid-level writers, especially contract writers, join a project during Production. This is when the bulk of the writing gets done. When you exit Prepro, you (should) know the design of conversation systems, combat barks, UI text, the different types of cinematics, and how much of each thing you need for the game. Now you just have to write it all! Your team fills the dialog "buckets" for each feature and writes the letters, journals, signs, item descriptions, and general UI text that make the game come alive. There's a tremendous amount of work to do and never enough time to do it. There are too many Production deliverables (including the *entire game*) to mention them all here, but here's a very rough list of what you'll work on.

- **Cinematic Screenplays:** everything from shiny "gold" level cinematics to less costly "bronze" cutscenes.
- **Ambient Scenes:** Scenes that trigger as you move through the world to bring it to life. They often intersect with the main storyline to set a mood or provide non-critical information.
- **Systemic Writing:** The barks, greetings, "foffs,"[7] and various one-off lines that play through the game systems. NPCs usually have a "bark set" or collection of lines that they respond with depending on various game conditions. For example, depending on the time of day, an NPC might say "Whew! It's a hot one today!" or "The night is young."
- **Vendor Lines:** These are lines for shopkeepers or other item sellers in the game. They occasionally work on a separate system from general barks because of transactions.
- **UI Text:** This can be anything from loading screen text, to objectives, to journal entries.
- **Letters and Notes:** There might be an in-game and UI version of these, so they require collaboration with other disciplines.
- **Signs and Posters:** These depend on context for their effectiveness, so the Narrative has to work closely with environment art, quest design, and level design to get the most out of them. (A "stop" sign means different things at a traffic intersection versus a lover's leap.)

Concurrent with these deliverables, you'll pitch ideas for characters and sidequests to your leads, sit in on recording sessions as talented actors bring your work to life, collaborate with Audio to nail the pacing of recorded lines in the games, answer questions from QA and Localization, and write marketing materials like trailers and demo scripts. And, aside from the act of actually typing words on the page, you'll share responsibility for these tasks with your fellow writers.

---

[7] Foff = "eff off" or get lost. The lines an NPC says when they have nothing left to say. "Oh, are you still here?"

Friends and Allies

It's the people who make game dev worthwhile. I heard this refrain over and over when interviewing people: their colleagues were like family. Your fellow devs make life at the studio exciting and fun, while your immediate team affects your day-to-day happiness more than any other factor. They'll understand you and the work you do better than anyone else. Sometimes, they become your confidantes and dearest friends. A writers' room atmosphere brings you closer together too. People throw out their raw thoughts and emotions and reveal who they are on a profound level. You might be talking about a characters' development in the story and someone brings up abuse they experienced as a child and how it affects their behavior now, as an adult. Their experience serves the narrative, but their vulnerability deepens your understanding and your bond.

Choose your friends because you care about them, but choose your allies strategically. What's the difference, you ask? Friends can be allies and vice versa, but sometimes you make alliances with folks you don't care for at all. An ally is someone you work with toward the same goal. Maybe you don't like that guy in Audio[8] but the two of you are the only ones who understand the serious ramifications of a change to the dialog system. Team up with them to get your point across. The more voices speak out about a problem, the more likely it will get attention. I realize this advice sounds mercenary and terrible, and for some people, it is. But Eevi Korhonen has a pragmatic attitude toward it all. "Wherever there's power structures, there's gonna be politics. And if the people in power don't look like you, it's usually gonna mean that you have to fight harder to get some of your thoughts and initiatives across." She admits it can be exhausting and require constant vigilance—and that can affect your creative output. She's had to "derail a whole week's work to suddenly come up with a pitch or rally coworkers to save a feature or a story beat" because higher-ups don't see its value and want to cut it. That's when allies come in handy.

> I've found it really helps to cultivate personal connections in a team, so you can have a group of allies— preferably from across the whole team— who feel similarly on the topic and leverage that group power to show you're not the only one who feels strongly on the topic in question. And it's even better if you can find an ally who's more senior or ideally even on the leadership level in the project or company.

Sometimes, politics and power games are so bad they get in the way of project deadlines. In these extreme cases, Eevi says "it helps to document the lost work and lost hours and make a case to higher-ups in the language they understand. And that's the language of business." She suggests that you outline the problem in a

---

[8] Before I get bewildered messages from the Audio folks I know, this is just an example.

clear cause-and-effect format: "By having to rewrite locked scripts, we've lost X hours. This will likely result in us not meeting the milestone goals. Now these critical features are in danger of not meeting our internal quality standards. Has this been accommodated into our roadmap? How can we prevent this from happening in the future?" That's how you focus attention on your needs! And when management investigates, make sure your allies are ready to fight for your common goal. It doesn't even have to be a work-related goal. Maybe you and your colleague want a different brand of tea stocked in the break room. Team up! Demand your Yorkshire Gold.

Collaborators

Game writing *is* collaboration. You can't make a AAA game without a team of talented people. Josh says the fun of working with other departments is "figuring out how to really sell a moment in the game, whether it's a little one-off joke or whether it's some really dramatic moment. Making either of those moments work requires a lot of cross-disciplinary collaboration." Remember when I talked about the interweaving of story, action, and mechanics to produce the "holy grail" of game narrative? That's collaboration.

In AAA, some teams break into small collaborative groups or workstreams (called "pods," "feature teams," or "strike teams") to make sure every discipline has a voice in the creative process. Pods focus on a specific feature or region. So, if your game is made up of four sectors or maps, there might be a dedicated pod for each one. When you're in a pod, your responsibility—regardless of seniority—is to represent Narrative's interests and keep your team informed of updates, changes, and ongoing work. Your pod might plan the web of sidequests in a town or slip secrets behind waterfalls. Through your collaboration, you'll start to see the world holistically and understand how the work of other departments melds with Narrative to create a playable game. It's eye-opening how every discipline views the same problem through a different lens and how their solutions never crossed your narrative mind. Pod-level collaborations can be the most creative and fruitful interactions on a project. Some of the happiest times in my career have been turning words into worlds with my pod colleagues. I wish you the same joy.

The Game Writers' Room

A writers' room runs on collaboration too. Many game writers work alone or do piecemeal work as contractors, so working in a collaborative environment might be new to you. I've got some wonderful news for you: this is the fun stuff! I've never worked in any type of writing room except game-writing rooms, and I hear they're different from the film and TV versions—but not by much. Game-writing teams have specific roles and responsibilities for members in day-to-day work, but, occasionally, the entire team gets together for what I like to call "story summits." At Remedy, these were days-long offsite meetings, where we answered questions about the game universe. At other studios, it might be an afternoon brainstorming in a conference room. The purpose is the same: You "break story" as Hollywood types love to say—which simply means figuring out the parts of your narrative. What are its beginning middle and end? What are the major story beats? You've probably done this sort of work on your own plenty of times. What makes a writers' room special is the raw creative energy. There's a strange and wonderful alchemy that occurs when a group of talented people combine forces. They one-up each other in a glorious back-and-forth of ideas and inspiration, until the story becomes much greater than the sum of its parts. It's magical. A writer's room is a great way to brainstorm, workshop scripts, and solve story problems. And, as I mentioned earlier, it's a great way to deeply know the people on your team.

KEY ELEMENTS OF A GAME WRITERS' ROOM

■ **A goal.** Perhaps a question to answer, story to break down, or specific topic to discuss.
■ **A leader.** They run the meeting and keep the discussion on track.
■ **A notetaker.** Someone has to write it all down.
■ **A flat hierarchy.** This is vital! A good idea can come from anywhere and junior writers must be empowered to challenge leads and directors.

What comes out of a writing room is work in the form of individual tasks. These should be familiar assignments like bios and screenplays, but don't hesitate to ask for clarity on what's expected. You might worry that asking questions makes you look stupid or inexperienced, but it's actually a sign of diligence. It's much worse to fumble your way through an assignment and produce work that doesn't fit the brief. Ask! It's your lead's responsibility to give you clear instructions and assignments. If you don't understand and your lead leaves you to figure it out on your own, you'll inevitably run into problems. Head that off before it becomes a crisis.

Managing Your Manager

Your lead can make or break your career. They will nurture your talent, help you better your craft, and get you the tools you need to shine. A good lead will prepare you for the next step in your career and guide you along that path. They'll give you focused critique and actionable feedback. They'll be as invested in improving your work as you are. They can also shield you from the drama and stress of the development cycle and look after your well-being. Nobody will help or hinder your career path as much as your lead, so invest in that relationship.

To get the support you need, you might have to "manage your managers." This means setting up short daily check-ins to get clarity on your tasks. It means starting emails with a summary of work that you've done and why your lead should care. In some cases, I've taken over the management of my own schedule and created a bullet-pointed list of tasks to review and check off with my lead as they're accomplished. The goal is to get their guidance so you can do good work.

It's easy to become resentful of your lead. It's their job to, well, *lead* and they're not doing it, right? I'm not here to defend leads who leave their teams to flounder, ignore cries for help, or worse. There are some awful leads out there. Believe me, I know and have the scars to prove it. But, in most cases, your lead is just buried in work and can't find enough time to help. Evan has always approached managers as "human beings who are busy and need to be reminded that your guidance is a part of their work. That's what they should ultimately be trying to deliver on." Like me, Evan has come up with strategies for getting the support he needs from overwhelmed management. "One small thing is meeting them on their terms, like how do they like to give feedback and when do they like to give feedback. Stuff like that." He points out that every manager has a preferred style and a smart writer learns to accommodate it. "Some people prefer to be grabbed, so say, 'Do you have five seconds to talk?' and have a chat. Some people prefer a scheduled meeting. Some people prefer to give feedback asynchronously. Work with whatever your manager prefers."

When you're asking for a manager's help, it's important to understand your own process. Every writer has their own system and individual needs. Maybe you can't write in an open office and need a quiet space to think. Maybe you need written feedback after every draft. Some writers thrive with detailed direction and extensive oversight. Personally, I like my lead to set clear parameters and then free me to do whatever I want within those boundaries. Whatever you need, articulate it to your manager. For Evan, constraints are critical. "I think deadlines are helpful for me personally and writers generally, but I think they're helpful for managers too." He points out that it can help you both set a quality bar. A sort of "you have one week to get me a first draft" understanding. He also notes that "a lot of younger managers think they're being kind by not giving you deadlines. But that's not good for my creative process, and it doesn't teach you how to write professionally—which is really different than just writing."

It's unusual for managers to push back when you're asking for guidance (they want you to get the work done too), but it does happen. Sometimes, you'll ask your lead to explain feedback and they think you're being precious about your writing. Stick with it! Be clear that you're happy to change the problem; you just don't understand what has to change. Also, absolutely push back on your workload. If you have too much work and you can't get it done within the expected timeframe or to the expected quality level, let your lead know right away. Don't wait until it's too late and you're turning in poor or unfinished work. "Telling leads when you have too much work is another thing that people can be pretty scared of doing," Evan says. "I've been scared of doing this, too, but it's helpful to tell your managers when you're too busy or when you need them to set priorities for you. You have to rely on them in that way because it's a portion of their job." Unfortunately, Evan has gotten pushback from his leads on occasion. "The most common reaction I've gotten is 'I can't believe you're telling me that.' Like initial shock." It's scary to keep pushing after that, but he's "gotten multiple compliments" during his career where managers said, "the best thing about you is that you push back when you have too much work on your plate." Standing up for yourself won't go over well with every manager, so figure out what works in your particular situation. You'll develop an understanding of their requirements, and they'll learn your preferences. If you can't get what you need after several tries, and your work is suffering, go get help. Talk to your team about their strategies. Talk to your lead's lead. If you think it's a personality issue, go to HR. But don't suffer in silence. Actively seek the help you need to do your best work.

Next!

Look at you! You've settled into your life as game writer. You're collaborating, delivering assignments on time, and finding creative fulfillment. Time to kick back and enjoy the fruits of your hard work, right? Nope, not yet. Once you've established a comfortable work routine, you should start planning your next steps. Yes, even if you're perfectly happy where you are. It's important to have a plan and goals for the future. Even if your goal is simply "be the best entry-level writer this studio has ever seen," you want recognition for that, don't you? Maybe you want to get better at your craft. Maybe you want more pay for your extraordinary work or to secure a promotion with your stellar performance. What's next for you?

Know Yourself

There's a corny job interview question that asks "Where do you see yourself in five years?" I always roll my eyes at it, because five years is a long time in game dev years (an entire career for some people, remember?). What will the games industry be like that far off? It's impossible to predict. But know what you want for your future in a general sense. Maybe your goal isn't the specific "I want to be the creative director at Big Name Studios reviving their Legendary IP." But knowing you want to be, say, a narrative director is a good first step toward achieving that goal.

Take a look at the org chart you located on your first day. Where do you want to end up? You might think this is an easy question. You're probably thinking, "Well of course I want to be at the top. I want to be a creative director or narrative director and have control of the story." But do you really want that? Or is that simply what's expected? There's a lot of pressure in the games industry—and society in general—to be on top. Success = career advancement. It's unthinkable to turn down a promotion or suggest that you're happy with your current role. What if you like writing and don't want to take on managerial responsibilities? What if story management sings you a (very efficient) siren song? Now that you can see what these roles look like in practice, in a real working environment, be honest about what interests you. Ask yourself what appeals to you.

Personal motivators

▪ High wages	▪ People management
▪ Bettering my craft	▪ Travel
▪ Setting vision	▪ Organizing

Or perhaps something else motivates you. When I sat down a few years ago and asked myself these questions, I realized I was project motivated.

- I need creative fulfillment and innovation. Once a game ships (or sometimes once the story is locked down), I get restless and want to move on to a fresh project.
- I want to be better at my craft and have some control over the story.
- I like to travel and experience new cultures.
- I like mentoring and teaching (surprise).
- And I want the ability to walk away from toxic environments as quickly as possible.

There are many different roles in the hierarchy that offer some of these elements but add them all up and lead roles are the sweet spot for me. The role is usually a mix of control, craft, team management, and mobility. So that's where I landed. You might decide to be a principal or director—or shoot for the moon as creative director. Perhaps you'll switch career tracks entirely and move over to production or business management. Whatever you decide, make sure all your career choices point toward that goal. Also, make sure you understand what those roles look like *at your studio*. For example, I worked at one studio where the lead role was heavily involved in production work, tasking, line management, and lots of administrative work. And another where the lead writer ... primarily wrote the story. Which one is it at your studio?

The more you know about those roles and what they look like at your studio, the more you might decide they're not actually a fit for you. That happened to me. I was initially excited to become a narrative director on a project, thinking I could finally make the stories of my dreams. But being a director wasn't for me. The role requires diplomacy and political acumen, and it can take Game-of-Thrones levels of maneuvering and alliances to get what you want. You also don't (or shouldn't) write. Your job is to set a vision and guide your team toward it. For those reasons and more, you might decide, like I did, to shoot for a different level on the hierarchy. Or to stay in your current role, if you're happy. The important thing is to *know your goal* so you can actively work toward it.

Set Your Goal

I never met a "me" when I was a journalist. No one ever sat me down in front of someone and said, "this is the writer for our game." Narrative just wasn't talked about in the way it is now. I just looked at the jungle of games development, saw an opening and began hacking my own path through it

—Rhianna Pratchett, Freelance writer

Luckily, the narrative jungle has clearly defined paths now. Which one is right for you? Check out the organization chart in your studio. You're looking for two things: where you are in the hierarchy and where you want to end up. Let's say you're an entry-level writer and you dream of being a narrative director someday. Look at the org chart to see how many steps you'll need to take to get there. For example, let's say a mid-level writer wants to become a Principal.

In the chart shown on the next page, you need to become advanced and senior before sidestepping into Principal, and those roles may have their own requirements and specializations. Now, read the job description for Principal and for the *next role on your path*. Keep your ultimate goal in mind, but focus on the next attainable step. What skills do you need? Are there opportunities in your current role to start doing that work or do you need training? List the skills you need to take that next step up and start planning for that promotion.

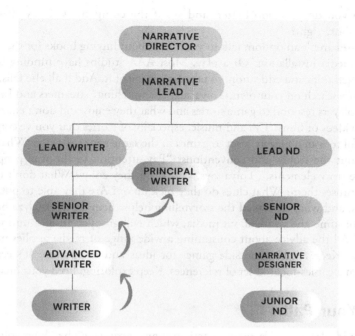

An example AAA narrative org chart.

Keep Growing

One of the best ways to get promoted is to show that you've improved or gained a new skill and can handle harder work. How do you do this? Get training! Many companies have a wide range of training courses. Ubisoft has an entire mini-university of short classes and seminars employees can partake in. Other studios offer external sessions that range from giving better feedback to media training. One studio even requires all new writers to take one of Robert McKee's story seminars! It's to the company's advantage to have an employee willing to keep up with tech advancements or learn more about their craft, so they're usually happy to cover the cost of training or classes. Talk to your lead or chat with HR about opportunities. If you're groaning at the thought of "school," remember that your skill and knowledge travel with you throughout your career. It might be the certification you need for a specialist role or an additional skill you can add to your resume. Maybe it's just the satisfaction of getting better at the work you love doing. I can't stress enough what a fantastic chance this is to "git gud" on the company dime.

If your company doesn't offer training, research public classes that teach the skills you want—within reason. A class in technical writing is easier to sell as a valuable skill than, say, Kpop dancing. (Unless you're working on a romance game about Kpop idols. Then that's legit research.) Find a class, explain how it will help you do your job better, and see if the company will pay. It's at least worth a shot, right?

If classes aren't an option, talk to your lead about buying books for the team. Or seeing a media installation. Or a play. Most AAA studios have funding for team-building activities and education, so take advantage of it. And if all else fails, you can always do research on your own. Toiya suggests watching "streamers and Let's Plays. See how players respond to game stories and what they enjoy and don't enjoy. Watch reaction videos of films, TV, and music, especially of stories that you've consumed." It's helpful to watch players react to games in the same genre of yours. What do they think about the tropes and conventions? "Pay attention to the way people break down the story elements," Toiya says. "What do they enjoy? What don't they like? What confuses them? What clues do they pick up on? Are they able to put together mysteries, and what aspects of the storytelling helps them do it? Analyze how other people consume and think about media, which will give you insight into your own writing." All the advice about consuming a wide range of media applies now more than ever. Keep reaching outside games for ideas and inspiration. It's easy to get trapped in a games-focused set of references. Keep exploring. Feed your imagination.

Map Your Path

You should also keep learning, practicing, and acquiring the skills you need to grow as a writer. When you've set your goal, have a one-on-one meeting with your lead and ask for their help achieving it. A good lead will map out a plan with clear steps for advancement and frequent check-ins, but your progress is up to you. Ask questions about ways to improve, ask for more training to help you gain the necessary skills, and ask for feedback. You should be receiving frequent feedback on your work anyway, but how's your performance? It always surprises me how few reports ask for updates on their initiative, teamwork, or communication skills. Those factors play a key role in any promotion, so make sure you're hitting your goals there too. If your manager is too busy for one-on-ones or hasn't sat down and discussed your career path with you, try to find someone else who can help. My advice is to seek out someone who has the role you want and ask them to mentor you. Document your own progress. Check in with your colleagues about the promotion process, and get a list of role descriptions. Keep updating your lead and remind them of your goal. And get ready for the next phase of your career.

CHALLENGE

■ Make a list of your motivations.
  • What inspires you?
  • What parts of the work do you like best?
  • What *don't* you want to do?

- Read the job descriptions for narrative roles at your studio.
  - You might have to look at public job posts or dig through HR information.
- Locate the role that interests you on your company's org chart
- Talk to the person currently in that role.
- Have a chat about their work and how they got where they are

OR

- See if they'll mentor you.
- Talk to your current lead about your goal. Ask for work or assignments that will help you achieve it.
- Follow up every month by asking for feedback on your performance.
- Document your progress and accomplishments.

Chapter 13

Steps and Obstacles

Remember that you are doing highly skilled work and that you are a professional. Your work is deserving of respect, as are you. There should be adequate time built into the schedule to allow you to do your work well and iterate on it, as well as reasonable feedback and approval loops. Don't get steamrollered. Stand up for your work and yourself.

–Richard Dansky, Narrative Director and
Central Clancy Writer, Red Storm/Ubisoft

Your first year in the industry is flying by. You're developing your abilities and learning new ones. You're connecting and collaborating and learning your studio's unique way of making video games. But don't get so lost in the project that you neglect your own goals.

Keep Up Your Networking

All the networking you did before you got hired should continue. Your career doesn't stop growing just because you have a job. Now, you should shift your focus from meeting industry folks in general to developing your network and deepening your professional friendships. Other writers will have the answers you need when you're struggling and can offer advice. They'll be the people whose shoulders you cry on when you're disappointed or who make you laugh with a funny cat meme when you're down. They're also the people who can help you find work if you decide to leave. One of the biggest mistakes I see people make is to get a job, say "well, that's that then" and let all the hard work they've put into

DOI: 10.1201/9781003282235-14

building their network and brand fall into dust. You'll have to start all over again unless you maintain it. Fortunately, that doesn't require much work, just an occasional check-in with folks.

Promote Yourself

Now that you're a working dev, you'll find social doors opening. People will follow you on social media simply because you work in games. You'll be asked to chat on podcasts or to do interviews for gaming sites. It's gratifying and exciting to talk about your craft to an audience. Just make sure you're not violating your NDA or the studio's media policy. Most companies have an internal permission process and want you to clear opportunities with them first. They have specific marketing and promotion plans, so make sure you're not interfering with them. I've found that as long as you're discussing narrative work in general and not discussing a specific or current project, most studios are happy to let you do podcasts or have your own livestream. It's a way for studios to promote the creativity and knowledge of their devs and to do some light recruiting. With marginalized folks, it's a way for studios to show the industry that women, BIPOC, and LGBTQIA+ devs are a key part of the company and valued for their expertise. Your company should offer promotion opportunities throughout the year, not just during Black History Month or Pride.

If you're forbidden to do any sort of professional promotion—and this is rare—you might still be asked to participate in game marketing. This can be anything from helping out in booths at conventions like PAX or ComicCon to recording "dev diaries" of your work. At ArenaNet, the entire studio held a week-long "slumber party" where we stayed up all night to play our demo with fans at gamescom. It was exhausting and exhilarating and an experience I'll never forget. For interviews, you'll get media "talking points." Those are key statements you'll be asked to repeat so the game's message gets out. See if you can spot my talking points for *CONTROL* in the First Look interview I did with Engadget at E3 2018.[1]

If you want to present at GDC and other cons, get permission before submitting your talk. Some global studios have so many devs volunteering for panels and talks that they hold internal speaker competitions. If you're not selected, you can't go that year. Disappointing, but a minor setback. Suggest a different convention or try again next year. Absolutely get out there and share your professional wisdom, but make sure you know what your studio's policies and rules are first.

---

[1] Some keywords were "metroidvania," "world within a location," and "gameplay-driven." https://www.youtube.com/watch?v=ShSltxoEDlg

Press

I've had extensive media training during my time in gamedev and heard the same refrain: "Reporters are not your friends." That's not technically true, as I'm close friends with several reporters, but I concede the point. It's literally a reporter's job to find and publish news. If you're hanging out with a journalist at a bar and feeling relaxed, your slight slip of the tongue could end up on the front page of Kotaku. Or you could be having a nice chat on a livestream and accidentally reveal a game feature. Don't be that person! If you mess up, there can be significant consequences, and none of them are pleasant. If there's the faintest suggestion that you leaked something on purpose, or if it happens more than once, you can be fired for violating your NDA and contract. Games are a multibillion-dollar business. Do you really want to be the person who helps your competitor succeed by leaking information? Just for clout or a quick dopamine hit? That tiny thrill could cost your entire career. It's not worth it. Don't do it.

Fans

If you become even moderately successful, you'll pick up some fans. Whether they love the games you work on, your witty banter, or they just really connect with a talk you gave, they'll write to you and follow you on social media. Your relationship with your fans is one of the most rewarding parts of gamedev. I mean it. At the end of the day, that's who you're creating stories for. This is interactive media, and they're the ones who bring your work to life. It's gratifying when someone gets—really, deeply gets—what you put into your work. All your creativity and hard work culminates in their experience. We often design characters with cosplay in mind. What's a unique feature that instantly identifies your character? What can cosplayers do with it? Some fans will even create fanfiction or fanart of your story and characters, which can be both touching and, uh… .um … yeah. Let's stick with touching. Interactive work craves that symbiosis. When you and a player walk an open world together, side by side, and actively co-create a story in real time? That's the deep magic.

You'll become friends with fans, and that's okay too! Just be very careful what you say. Remember that you're still under NDA. You can't drop hints or talk about your work in any but the most general ways or you could lose your job. Also, some fans may believe you're closer than you are. They get attached to you through your work or through your public presence. If a fan crosses the line into stalking, let your studio know immediately. They have Community and PR people who can step in when a situation creeps over the line. If worse comes to worst, they can go with you to law enforcement. But even with your studio's help, you'll have to take steps for your own protection, both physical and mental. Here's how one writer handles her aggressive fandom.

Because I'm a woman with a visible public presence, I tend to get blamed for anything players don't like, even in the junior years of my career. The high-level story isn't what they were expecting? It must be that junior writer's fault. Character models not up to par? Let's harass this woman about it even though she's never modeled a character in her life. It can get really exhausting, but I've created rules for myself to limit how much I see of it. I avoid forums at all costs. I block the worst offenders on social media. I remove all ways for strangers to contact me privately. It's awful that I even have to take these steps, but unfortunately that's the reality of being a woman in the spotlight.

Every gamedev sets their own limits for fan relationships, so I won't tell you what to do or what limits to set. But set your boundaries early in your career, long before you have a following. Fan relationships are incredibly rewarding and enduring (shout-out to my amazing *GW2* family who've been with me for a decade), but know your limits and protect yourself.

Obstacles

Guarding your public presence and finding ways to network and promote yourself are only a few of the challenges you'll face in games. You'll encounter obstacles along every step of the path. Keep working and growing, and eventually you'll reach your goal. But what happens when your goal is *right there*, your path is obvious, but there's something—or rather someone—standing in your way?

Imposter Syndrome Part 2

Oh no, here we go again. One of the worst obstacles is yourself. Imposter Syndrome can twist your reality into knots. I've known people in our industry who have done legendary things, worked on games that are jaw-droppingly good and have won every conceivable accolade for their work. Yet they truly believe they're faking their way through the industry and *any minute now*, they'll be exposed as a fraud. Imposter Syndrome is irrational like that. The higher you climb, the more people will try to tear you down and make you doubt yourself. Don't help them. Don't do their work for them. I know it belongs on a poster with a kitten and some flowers but Believe in Yourself. You have to be your own biggest fan. You'll reach low points in your career when you're fighting for something—a role, a raise, a chance—and nobody will think you can do it. Believe in yourself. When you're defending your work in critiques and you have Big Name on the Project scoffing at your vision, you need to know in your heart that you're right, it's good, and fight for it. Nobody's going to believe you if you doubt yourself. Remember how far you've come and all you've accomplished to get here. Then stand up and fight for what you want. If all else fails, then do it for spite. You might think I'm joking, but it's a powerful motivator! Show everyone, including you, that they were wrong to doubt you.

How to Ask for a Promotion

So, you've been at the studio for a while now, and you're feeling confident. You've crushed your Imposter Syndrome, picked up some speaking opportunities, and feel good about your standing with the team. You've mastered your current responsibilities and learned new skills. You've grown as a writer and taken on more work. All your colleagues agree that you're ready for the next big step in your career. It's time to move up.

Asking for a promotion can be scary. I know, because I've done it myself several times. Sometimes, it seems easier to wait and hope the studio promotes you on their own initiative. They've seen all your hard work, right? Unfortunately, it doesn't always happen that way. You have to advocate for yourself. Tara acknowledges that people—especially feminine-presenting folks—are "conditioned to believe that if they do good work, that will naturally be recognized by management and rewarded accordingly. The hard truth is that no one, and I mean NO ONE, cares as much about your career as you do." But don't worry! I've got you. The same tactics you used to negotiate your salary will come in handy here. It's about knowing your worth and standing by it. Document your achievements as you go along. Remember that desktop folder you created to combat Imposter Syndrome? Dig through it for reminders of everything you've done. Tara files her accomplishments as she goes along. "When you get a great email from a coworker thanking you for your contributions, chuck it in your folder. A nice Slack message from your boss about your work on a recent project? Screencap and throw it in there too. Make it a habit, and at the end of the year you'll have a nice little collection of kudos." Not just kudos! It's the proof you need to make your case. So grab your receipts and approach your line manager.

If you and your lead have been communicating well, they'll already know you've hit the agreed-upon targets and this promotion chat will be a formality. Even so, keep formal requests like this performance-based and backed by data.

- **Bad:** "I feel like I should get a promotion because I've been here a while."
- **Good:** "I do the same work as the senior writers so I think I deserve the title too."
- **Best:** "I meet all the requirements for the senior role and have been doing work at that level for a while. The senior role description states that I need to coordinate with other teams. I've done that by doing x, y, and z ... etc."

It's hard to argue with facts, so stick to those and make your case. Send your lead an email outlining your position. The email should contain the following information:

- A reminder of the goal you both agreed on ("As we've long discussed … I've met the criteria for being a senior writer.")
- A summary of the role requirements and how you meet them. ("Looking at the job description for a senior writer, I meet all the criteria. I write quality screenplays, coordinate with other teams, etc.") Use keywords from the desired role's job description.
- Any additional information you think will help your case. ("I wrote the trailer dialog when …")
- A clear statement of what you expect. ("Now that I meet the criteria for the role, I'm ready for my promotion!")
- Next steps. ("What happens next in this process?")

From that point on, it's on your lead to make it happen. Hopefully, they're ready for the request and have laid the groundwork to make it happen. It might take longer than you'd like. "The reality is that a promotion is seldom granted by a single person alone. In any mid to large-scale organization, performance evaluation is a process," Tara says. "One that your manager may need to go to bat for you to achieve." Be patient while your request goes through the approval process; it won't happen overnight. But it's reasonable to expect progress within a week or two of your request. My fingers are crossed for you!

Balancing the Scales

Promotions aren't the only time you'll have to advocate for yourself. What if you do everything right during salary negotiations—if you do your homework, demonstrate your worth, haggle hard, and arrive at a figure you can live with—but you still end up with a lower salary than you should have? It happened to me once. Despite all the help I had from friends in the industry and despite all my research, I learned a year into one job that one of my male reports was earning more than I was. I wasn't happy, to say the least. But I didn't sit and seethe. I approached my lead with my case for a higher salary, and he agreed. I ended up getting bumped to the top of my salary band. A happy ending to an unfortunate situation.

If you ever learn that you're underpaid—or if you'd just like some more money, please—you know what you have to do.

How to Ask for a Raise

The process for this is very similar to asking for a promotion. Find out what the pay bands at your studio are. This can be surprisingly difficult to do. Many studios won't have that information posted anywhere, so you'll have to ask HR or Finance.

If you want to know if your salary is fair, talk to your colleagues. Some variations might exist for experience or expertise, but if you're doing the same work at the same level, your pay should be the same. When you know the wage at your company, look at similar roles at other studios, check Chapter 10 salary sheets for comparison, and then submit your request. Use a similar format to the one for promotions. Here's my current salary. Here's what I think I should make. Here's why I deserve it—backed by many examples of your improvement and stellar performance. There are many articles out there about how to properly do this, so I won't go into more detail. Definitely do your research! But I will add that if you don't get a cost-of-living adjustment every year to account for inflation, you're effectively taking a pay cut. It's absolutely reasonable to request an adjustment for your cost of living, even if you're not requesting one based on merit.

When the Answer Is No

But what if you make a reasonable request for a promotion or raise, bolster it with data, and it still gets rejected? There are a wide variety of reasons why companies might say no, including your performance and the timing of your request. What matters here is your takeaway. Can you live with their decision? Yes or no?

- If yes, then wait, gather more proof of your performance, and ask again when you're able.
- If no, then what are your options?

Here's where I again point you to the internet experts. There are excellent resources out there for pushing back against an unfair decision at work. You can do things like appeal the decision up the approval chain, rework your request and ask again, speak with your guild, labor council, or union representative (if you have one), or if you suspect discrimination, report it to HR. Alternatively, you could leave and find a better situation.

Switching studios is, unfortunately, sometimes the best way to get a raise or promotion. It's better to move and find a place that pays you well than stay and simmer in resentment. Sometimes, the threat of leaving is enough to get your company to come around and give you what you asked for. Sometimes, it's not. If you give an ultimatum or threaten to leave, then be prepared to follow through. Don't make idle threats. Hazel has this advice if you find yourself in this situation, "It's a hard thing to do, and requires a lot of introspection and confidence. But ultimately it is necessary if you feel you aren't being valued. You have to value yourself, and your skills, and recognize that what you bring to the team needs to be adequately appreciated and compensated for." If you've tried everything you can to negotiate with your current studio and you can't reach a mutually satisfactory agreement, then leaving might be your only option. I'll talk about what leaving looks like in Chapter 15, but for now, be reassured that it's fairly common. As Hazel says, you "should never feel beholden to a studio that is not valuing you. Look for other opportunities. Network with other writers elsewhere. Keep advocating for yourself. It is so easy to feel discouraged and stuck, but we have to keep trying to move forward and believe in our abilities and our worth." Knowing your worth, standing up for yourself, and doing what's right for your success and well-being spill over into other aspects of studio life too.

Crunch Part 1

You will inevitably crunch when you're in the games industry. I say this with exhaustion, frustration, and the weary impatience of someone who's been there countless times and doesn't want to go there again. Avoiding crunch is a never-ending battle. One writer says that "It's not just crunch itself, but also the foreboding way it permeates everything. The way people are like, 'You know, at some point in this project, we'll probably have to crunch.' And it kills you. It's this dread that's always kind of there." At this point, the industry knows that crunch is bad. It's not effective, it reduces productivity over time, and it ruins the lives of developers. It destroys personal relationships because devs don't get to spend time with their family and friends. It kills creativity too. Your mind travels along the same well-worn path day after day, and there's no time to feed your imagination with outside influences. Crunch also causes significant, severe health problems, such as burnout, mental illness, heart attacks, and in some cases, death.

There are notorious stories of crunch in games. Some of the biggest game studios in AAA are famous for their so-called death marches to get projects out the door. Devs are asked to work up to sixteen hours a day for months on end, and they're often *paid no overtime* for it. The company will buy dinner for people staying late and there might be bonuses and incentives for hitting goals, but most salaried workers are getting paid the same rate. I once worked 107 hours in one week to do an emergency rewrite of an entire story script. I received nothing for it except my normal wage and "thanks." Let that sink in the next time you hear about crunch.

Crunch is painted as an unforeseen, unavoidable turn of events, but the sad truth is that some companies build it into their schedule. One company I worked for bragged that crunch is "where the magic happens." Mikki told me a story about a scriptwriter who got holes in his memory from working so many hours of overtime. He'd crunched hard, without complaining, but he finally decided to leave the studio. When he was leaving, he confessed that he'd had blackouts. His last memories were of being at work, then he'd suddenly find himself at home, several hours later. He didn't know what he'd done in between. "Presumably, he just did some work and then came home. There's no reason to believe that anything else happened. But for all he knew, he could have been doing anything,"

Mikki said. Crunch literally stole time from his life. He'll never get that back. That's what crunch means to devs. Yet, you'll still very likely be asked to crunch on your project.

When It's Crunch Time

First, find out if you're contractually obligated to work it. QA testers, for example, sometimes sign agreements to work up to 80 hours a week. If they don't agree then they won't get hired. If you refuse to crunch after signing a contract saying you will, you're in a precarious position. The studio can say you're violating your contract and technically you are. You'll have to weigh your options at this point. Crunch can affect your career—in good and bad ways. One writer says he didn't want to crunch, but his studio valued him more when he did. "I don't think it was necessary. I don't think it was productive. It made me reconsider whether I wanted to be in this industry. It also creates this messed-up feedback loop. I very much noticed that feedback on my writing and my performance improved when I started crunching, and that's not a good way to train your workforce." It shouldn't happen. It's terrible that it does. But … it does. Many devs face this dilemma: If I refuse to crunch, how will this affect me later? Another writer said that "When I crunched, if I had said I was too busy, I don't know how that would have gone down, to be honest. Probably not well."

Pressure

I know that it's easy to look at this from the outside and say "On the one hand you might lose your job, on the other you might *die*. Where's the dilemma?" But things look very different in the moment when you have bills to pay or a family to feed or you just desperately need that first game credit to launch your career. A lot of people suck it up hoping that the crunch will be short, not too terrible, and worth it in the end. I wish I had advice to give you, but all I can say is know your options and do what's best for you. Do I think you should crunch? No. I don't think it's worth it. But I don't know your specific circumstances.

The personal decision to not crunch can feel even tougher because of peer pressure. I'm sorry to tell you, but some people like crunch. You'll encounter a "warrior" (I'm rolling my eyes here) mindset in the industry that views crunch as a badge of honor. For some people, work is their life. Therefore, the more work the better. Some managers will compare your dedication to these workers.

There's also the softer pressure of not wanting to let your team down. As I've said before, you'll be very close to your friends and coworkers and want to help. It's hard to leave at the end of the day, even when you know it's the right thing to do, when your coworkers are all still there plugging away. And they might come to resent you, however unfairly, for letting them shoulder the burden alone. The good news is that people are beginning to rethink work-life balance and this happens less often. Increasingly, we understand that crunch is bad and that being asked to do it isn't right. Let the cleansing light in!

Flow State

There's another kind of crunch that the industry still hasn't confronted: self-imposed creative crunch. When you, as a creator who takes pride in your work, want to stay and finish a task you're absorbed in. When you're in "flow state"[2] and know you're doing good work, and you just want to keep riding that wave. Or when you're hyperfocused and don't realize you stayed three extra hours. There's a growing understanding that some places take advantage of creators' perfectionism to encourage crunch-like conditions. Many companies present their crunch as voluntary "People stay and work because they want to. It's their choice." This is tricky because if it's completely voluntary and short, then … I'll be honest, I do it. I'm doing it as I type these words. Nobody's pressuring me except me, but it's still crunch … or is it? Here's a good test:

- Am I staying because I want to, not because it's required?
- Is it a short time span (a few hours or one day)?
- Is it a rare occurrence?
- Am I doing extra work outside of my normal day-to-day responsibilities?

If you can answer yes to all these questions, then it probably is a genuine desire to stay in flow. Even with yeses across the board, it's fine to call it a day. But if you have any nos, then you're crunching and need to make a call about what's best for you. One game writer said that once you're established in your career, "you become more confident saying 'what's a reasonable timeline? What's a reasonable amount of work?' and you can set some boundaries in your workplace. But people have to respect your work first. So, you're vulnerable to crunch in that early-middle phase." Decide on your stand now, before crunch comes knocking. Know your contract, set your own limits, and be careful opening that door.

Burnout

Crunch enough and you'll burn out. That makes sense, right? But it might surprise you to know burnout frequently comes without overwork. It can come from having no control over your work or schedule. Or having so much work that you can't do a good job. If you're a creative person, it might come from having no

---

[2] Flow is when you're immersed so deeply in your work that the world and time fall away. Being "in the zone."

creative outlet or doing unfulfilling work. Burnout can ambush you. You think you're living a healthy life with reasonable hours and *wham*! It drops on you like a Looney Tunes anvil. That's what happened to me in 2014. I ignored the warning signs for years, kept my head down, and persevered through a soul-killing project. I thought I'd be fine when the difficult project ended, so I took on another project soon after. I'd just rolled onto the new game when it hit me: ten years of built-up stress, anxiety, frustration, and grief. I ended up having a complete mental and physical breakdown. It was so bad that I had leave my shiny new job and take time off to recover. It took six months before I felt like myself again, and over a year before I got my writing back. And I'll be honest, I'm not the same person I was before the breakdown. My friends say the experience "knocked some of the fun out" of me, and ... yeah. That feels about right.

The industry is starting to take burnout seriously. Where people used to think it was purely mental exhaustion or a sort of emotional deadening, now we know that burnout is a real, medical problem and can cause serious physical harm to people. It's taken a few high-profile cases of burnout to get us to that realization. Osama Dorias recently went public with his burnout experience, and it's one of the worst (and saddest) I've heard. He agreed to share his story so that other people could learn from it and get help for their burnout before it became a problem.

CASE STUDY: OSAMA DORIAS

Osama is a Senior Partner Relations Manager at Unity Technologies and a career game designer with 15 years of experience in the industry. He's been all over the industry and shipped over 30 games, so he was no stranger to the hard realities of gamedev life. But burnout still hit him hard. Here's his story in his own words:

> *There were a lot of things that contributed to my burnout. My mother was diagnosed with cancer, and so I had to work reduced hours (4 days a week) and take care of her the other 3. My bosses were kind enough to accommodate me, but this took a huge toll on my energy and health as literally everything else took a backseat to my new schedule. I no longer had time to socialize, teach, exercise, even to spend time with my kids.*
>
> *Thankfully my mother recovered, but that happened just in time for COVID to send us all to our homes. My life had been so thoroughly disrupted that I buried myself in work. It didn't take long before I started feeling the effects of burnout.*
>
> *I started dreading activities that once brought me joy. I couldn't find the energy to leave bed, but if I called in sick I'd instantly get a little*

> *bit of a boost. And worst of all … I would get angry. I'd sometimes wake up angry, without anything specific to be angry about. Eventually this led to being physically unable to get myself to do any work at all. I couldn't focus on anything. I couldn't find joy in doing anything, even things that I once loved. I would get SO angry for no particular reason, mostly at myself I suppose.*
>
> *Because I buried myself in work, I also never left the house or did any kind of physical activity. It got so bad that even walking for a couple of minutes gave me intense knee pains. I couldn't sleep. On a good night I maybe got 2 hours of sleep. I had panic attacks. My anxiety was through the roof.*
>
> *I finally told my boss that I couldn't keep going like this, and I went to see a doctor who immediately put me on medical leave and prescribed me meds. I started seeing a physical therapist for my knees and a personal trainer for my general health. I'm still in the process of recovering. It's been a year and a half and I can at least work now. I used to be an overachiever. I'm just an achiever now, but even that realization brings me so much joy! I get waves of fatigue out of nowhere, but I can take naps or go for walks to recharge. I don't know if I'll ever go back to my seemingly endless reserves of energy, but honestly even if I just maintain my current levels, I'll be happy.*

So how do you avoid burnout? Sure, you can say no to crunch, that's an obvious step. But if it's so insidious, how can you make sure you're not nurturing it with your daily routine? Osama points to several factors. Taking care of yourself physically is part of it. But you also need to clear room for enjoyment. His biggest mistake "was cutting the activities that gave my life purpose and gave me joy in order to make room for the work that was burning me out. My career goals have changed. Work-life balance is now more important to me than anything else. Not title, salary, project, team …. nothing else comes close. I simply will not allow myself to burn out again." Protect your time. Protect your happiness. And do whatever it takes to get balance back in your life. Osama offered a final bit of advice for writers. "This may be controversial, but if you're feeling burned out, I strongly feel that a change of context is necessary to recover. You can't heal in the place that hurt you."

Wherever you are and whatever your circumstances, take steps to avoid burnout right now. Talk to your leads and colleagues about what you're feeling. If you're overwhelmed with work, see if another writer can help. If you're making yourself sick to meet a deadline, see if you can get extra time. Maybe the task isn't that important and you can drop it altogether. If it's work overall that is burning you out, then maybe you can step back from it for a while. In Sweden, they have a specific program for "burnout leave." You take off work entirely for a month or two, then gradually ease up to your normal working hours. You start at 25% of your schedule, then 50%, then 75%, until you're well enough to work normal hours again. You could also consider cutting down your hours permanently. Four-day work weeks are increasingly popular now. Here's how Eevi persuaded her studio to reduce her hours: "It was quite easy at my current employer, since they don't just talk the talk when it comes to work-life balance. I went to HR, explaining that I was experiencing burnout and laid out reasons why a four-day workweek would help me get back to a healthier space both physically and mentally." She also agreed to a pay cut for the reduced hours but says it was worth the exchange. She's even had a promotion and pay raises since then, so it didn't affect her career. Eevi says she'd tried reducing her hours at a previous studio but "was met with a lot of hemming and hawing and 'needing to check project needs'" so don't assume it'll be easy. If you decide to try for it, Eevi recommends negotiating it into your contract from the start or taking advantage of moments when your work is critical to the project and "you have the upper hand."

Whatever steps you take to improve your work-life balance, start right now. Use your vacation days. Fight for creative control of your work. Find a schedule you can live with. You have a long, fulfilling career ahead of you if you take care of yourself.

CHALLENGE

This one is simple. Take three steps today to improve the quality of your work life. Here are some suggested actions:

- Talk to your lead about your workload and deadlines.
- Find time for activities you love or pick up a new hobby that is unrelated to your professional work.
- Set your personal boundaries for crunch and know ahead of time where you'll draw that line. Stick to it!
- If your work is unfulfilling, start a side project as a creative outlet. Don't monetize it or let it become a second job. Be creative for the joy of it.

Chapter 14

Leadership

The real problems are hardly ever creative or artistic or tonal, they're organizational.

—Ed Stern, Lead Writer, Splash Damage

Hey! You made it! You worked hard for your goals, made your case, and got promoted. Now, you're stepping into your new role with a heady mix of excitement and fear. Where do you even start? And how can you maintain your healthy habits when there's an entire team of people looking to you for answers?

When You're Senior

Before you run amok with newfound power—or panic—take a moment to look back at where you came from. Remember when I had to explain what a "golden line" was? Now, you're a seasoned professional with shipped titles to your credit. You've earned this spot. What you don't already know, you can figure out. Learn your job description inside and out so you understand what's expected from you. Look to other seniors as advisors and role models. If your studio offers management training seminars, sign up for them right away. Know what the studio thinks good leadership looks like.

If you're a line manager, a whole new world of documentation will open up for you. You'll need to know the procedures for reviews and raises, hiring and firing, supplies and opportunities. You're now the go-to font of wisdom for your team, so make sure you have the information they need—or at least know how to get it. You'll discover a fervid new interest in internet articles about How to Be a Good Manager. There are many resources out there for general management advice;

that's not what you need from me. Let's focus on the game-writing-specific tasks you'll have in your senior roles:

- **As a mid-level:** The best thing you can do is show entry-level writers and NDs what the industry is all about. They might know almost nothing about writing games professionally, so show them the ropes. Any new knowledge is useful at this stage. Be supportive, try not to dim the stars in their eyes, and help them navigate this strange new industry. Educate!
- **As a senior or principal:** Help juniors with their craft. Teach them what you know about interactive narrative, realizing a vision, creating characters, writing within systems, etc. You're their role models when it comes to craft so help them shine. Feedback!
- **As a lead or manager:** Help juniors with their journey. Keep them invested in their work. Don't let folks slip out of that leaky pipeline. Support team members with special needs. Help your team learn specialized skills: How to collaborate with other teams for holistic work. How to estimate a line count.[1] How to map a character arc against the story. How to plan a narrative that works within existing systems and features. How to work with actors in a mocap studio. Mentor!
- **As a narrative director:** Provide a story vision and help the team understand it. Show off their work and present the team in the best light. Be Narrative's liaison to the publisher and public. Inspire!

Fight for What You Need

Steering the story ship means you're responsible for providing a clear vision for the team to follow. Narrative drift is inevitable, so you'll have to adjust your course to account for surprise cuts and changes. (I refuse to let this maritime metaphor take over.) Directors and leads must negotiate with other disciplines to achieve their own agenda and get the time and resources the team needs. This often means evangelizing your story to people with no interest—or too much interest—in game narrative. This is when you'll often encounter Rhianna's "story by committee" situation. She warns that you'll have to work with "numerous people who have no narrative experience, big titles and even BIGGER thoughts about story. You must be extremely flexible and try to leave your ego at the door. But at the same time, you have to work out what's worth fighting for, which hills are worth dying on. Because you're going to find out that there are A LOT of hills." I learned this the hard way. When I first became a lead, I used to snarl at every little story change like war was declared.

---

[1] Exactly what it says on the box. An estimated number of all the voiced and unvoiced lines of text in the game.

I thought of every cut as retreat. I worried that I'd be forced to fall back and fall back until there was only a tiny strip of story left to stand on, so I wouldn't give an inch. Ed Stern understands the need to defend your work. He says that much of game writing is "trying to use words to fix tonal or thematic problems that lots of the team might not see as problems." Ed has great advice for moments when you're fighting to keep parts of your story. As always, it comes down to good communication. He advocates for clear phrasing of the problem and its consequences.

- "You want X changed? OK, but you realise that means that Y isn't going to get done, right? Here's an email from me, so ... . "

Ed stresses the importance of a clear chain of command. Know who owns each part of the game and who has a stake in it. Know who actually has the power to cut or change your work. If someone demands a change to your team's work and they don't have the authority to override your ownership, then he suggests you say, "Sorry you don't like this, but the deadline for feedback was a week ago and also we agreed that you don't actually have veto, so ... " The language of these responses is blunt but effective. Being clear and direct can cut through to the heart of the problem. And to avoid any nasty surprises in the future, try Ed's technique for spelling things out clearly:

Brief and Back-Brief to double-check you're aligned (and to get it all down in an email paper trail):

- **Why:** general context/summary of current situation
- **What:** what specific problem will this solve?
- **Who:** Who's doing the work, who's Responsible and Accountable, Consulted or Informed, who does feedback and final approval? Also, Who's the audience for this thing? Team? Management? Publisher? Public?
- **How:** format, tech specs, wordcount, level of detail (Game Bible? Bullet points?)
- **When:** deadlines for initial back-brief, initial delivery, feedback, next iteration delivery, and final deliverable.

And then get them to reply in their own words so you can tell if you're all on the same page.

Even when you're being straightforward like this, don't forget to use the language of the discipline you're talking to. Sketch a diagram if that helps Concept Art. Toss some figures into a spreadsheet if that's what Production needs. Make a short slide presentation for your publisher. You'll quickly learn that nobody on the team wants to read a wall of text from Narrative. That's how we communicate, but it's not the best way to get your ideas across to other disciplines.

However, sometimes friction can force you to see an outside perspective. "Perversely, I think miscommunication is a greater risk with teams where everyone gets on really well," Ed says, "because when you're personally and socially aligned it's easy to assume everyone's on the same page with the same information. If you're all a bit more cautious, you check." However you communicate, the important thing is to listen as much as you talk. That's how you get the information you need. Don't fight to the last ditch like I used to do. Game development isn't a battle; it's a dance. If you step back in one area, step forward in another. If you lose fifty lines from this feature, add them to another. If a key character gets cut, give their lines and traits to another. It's a ballet of give and take, wins and losses. At the end of the day, you're all working together to make a game, and you all want the game to be good. If you're smart, everyone wins this dance battle.

Sharing Your Vision

The best way to win people over is to tell them a story. Advertisers know it. Politicians know it. It's clear throughout human history. And lucky for you, you're a storyteller. I don't mean "tell a story" in the literal sense. Don't go into a meeting and recite *The Odyssey* at stakeholders. I'm talking about engaging their imaginations. Get people excited about the work you're doing. Actively involve them in solving your narrative problems. And, okay, yeah, that does sometimes mean sitting down and telling them your game story. But there are other ways to share your vision.

- **Wikis:** An obvious way is to make a searchable wiki out of your team's work. The story bible especially makes for engaging reading and helps other teams understand how your work meshes with theirs. Make your documentation interesting and inviting. Share links to it often.
- **Newsletters:** Monthly updates are usually enough to show off your team's latest work. Borrow some concept art and stuff your updates with puns, and people might actually read them.
- **Presentations and Talks:** If colleagues are having trouble understanding a particular aspect of your story or game world, give a short presentation about it to the whole team. Eevi Korhonen and I gave a tentacular presentation about New Weird because it's a tough concept to grasp. The slides on the next page show how helpful even a simple presentation can be.

  The important thing is to speak your collaborators' language and always bring your talk back to why they should care. Get their buy-in!
- **Open Office Hours:** At one studio, I set aside a half-hour every week for Story Time. Anyone could stop by with questions about any aspect of the narrative and get an immediate answer. Shy people who "didn't want to bother" us would come by because they knew they were welcome at that time. And busy leads poked their heads in with "just a quick question." That dedicated half-hour can end up saving you hours of time otherwise lost to emails.

Mystery! Tentacles!

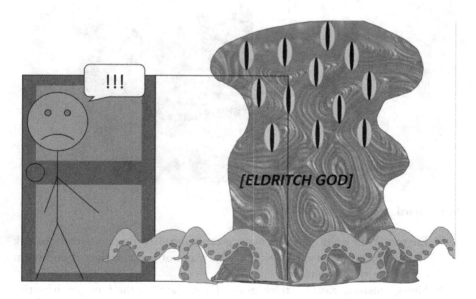

Horror.

Sci-fi and Fantasy.

New Weird.

- **Envoys:** Your team members make great evangelists. Empower them to talk about their work on the story and what parts of it excite them. Send them out to the wider team!
- **Signs, posters, ravens, telekinesis:** I'll try any method to get narrative information to the wider team. The more they know, the better aligned we are and the greater our chance for that coveted synergy. This sometimes means resorting to devious tactics.

THE HERO'S JOURNEY SIGN

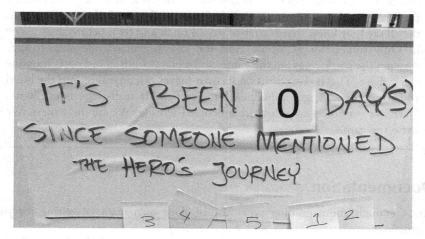

The Infamous Sign.

Here it is. The infamous sign. It's become a running gag in game-writing circles. Sometimes I hear groans, and sometimes I hear chants of "RESET THE SIGN!" with me. What few people realize, however, is that the sign has a serious purpose. I alluded to it back in Chapter 2 when I poured salt on unqualified narrative teachers. The truth is that most people don't understand writing or story. They think they do. They've been writing their entire lives after all, right? How hard can it be? Maybe they've read a book about Story. They now know everything there is to know about game writing and want to explain to you, an industry veteran, what you're doing wrong. Invariably, they reference the Hero's Journey or *Star Wars* or *Save the Cat*. There is nothing you can do for those folks except smile, nod, and reset the sign.

However, the ritual of resetting the sign gets attention. People get curious. They ask why it's bad. They ask about Joseph Campbell. They want to hear alternatives. And it kicks off casual-but-critical discussions. Beyond that, The Sign becomes a *shared* joke. It unites the team and raises awareness of your work as a craft in its own right. Other disciplines learn to understand and respect your team's expertise, and that's the goal of it. Building respect for the work we do.

Some disciplines think of writers as a service department, instead of an equally skilled part of the team. They think you're there to make their work "sound pretty" or provide a "narrative wrapper" for the essential game elements—their work, of course. Give this attitude no air. Kill it on sight. If you don't, you'll see non-writers slip their own work into the game because they have writing aspirations. Or add "just a little joke." If you discover it, they'll say they knew that Narrative would catch and fix it before anyone saw it. Only sometimes we don't. And the joke is bad or offensive. It slips through the cracks, stays in the game, and a player finds it and posts it online somewhere. This is dangerous on its own (never put anything into the build you wouldn't want going public), but also because it disrespects our work. Narrative isn't there to polish other people's writing. We are the writers. We write the game.

Documentation

That's enough about guiding other teams! Your own team is waiting for your instructions.

Your writers and NDs need extensive documentation to help them with their tasks. Don't make them chase you around the studio for answers to basic questions. Stuff your wiki or Confluence page with templates, style guides, references, and examples. If you don't have time to scribble out all this documentation—and you won't have time—delegate the work and answer questions along the way. Your team is more likely to remember a template if they create it themselves anyway.

Priorities

You'll soon discover that you're not just short of time for documentation; you're short of time *period*. It took Ed "too long to learn that you can only Take Time, not Make Time. Everyone's busy all the time. If you try to fit something in as well as everything else, you're not being honest about the fact that it's not going to get done. It's 'Instead Of,' not 'As Well As.'" This is another hard reality of leadership. You will spend an absurd amount of time in meetings, a problem that has only been exacerbated by the pandemic and work from home, and your tasks will languish untouched at your desk. Eventually, they pile up, your team demands your attention, you feel overwhelmed, and you start to hear this weird, loud ticking-clock sound in your mind. That's the road to burnout, my friends. To head that off, learn how to do three things:

- **Prioritize:** What's on fire? What has to be done for an imminent deadline or because it's blocking other work? Who is waiting on it? How much work is it? My readers with Executive Dysfunction are trembling, but this is easier than it seems. Enlist a producer to help you triage your tasks and come up with a plan of attack. They love this stuff!

- **Assess and Adapt:** If this is important, does it have to be done this exact way? Can we simplify it? What's the MVP[2] version of this task? Can it be moved? *Do we even still need this?*
- **Delegate:** Do you need to do this task or can one of the writers do it? Is this something your team needs to do? Can another discipline do it? Can a codev[3] team do it? Can it be outsourced? (Careful with those last two. You want to maintain oversight of your work.)

Above all, you have to get comfortable with letting things go. You can't do it all, and some things will fall off. It's unavoidable, but you know what? It's okay. If you did a good job prioritizing, it won't be anything important. But if you're an overachiever, you'll find this part of leadership hard.

Finding Balance

Another challenge of leadership is finding time for creativity. You became a game writer to write games, not sit in a conference room and talk about them. Ed finds that "one of the perennial struggles in more senior positions is making sure you do the stuff that's long-term vital but not immediately urgent. Reading. Writing. Mentoring. Acquiring and practicing new skills. Being bad at something first, then doing it again and again until you suck less at it." I have the same struggle as Ed. In fact, when I talk to writing leads around the world, I hear pretty much the same story: it's a constant balancing act between managerial work and creative work. The happiest leads have made time for creative work in their schedules. Their manage/create ratio is uniformly about 60/40. If less than 40% of your job is creative work, it can start to feel like drudgery. I'm sorry to say that some writing leads have ratios of almost 9:1—and they've fought to maintain even that sliver of creative expression. To be fair, some leads prefer the management side of things. Mentoring and oversight are their north stars. But other leads looked at me with naked despair when I asked about their writing or creative output. What can those leads do? How can they stay creative when there's so much administrative work weighing down their schedules? Samantha splits her time between her duties as a lead and her individual contributions.

---

[2] MVP = Minimum Viable Product. The simplest version of something. The baseline version.

[3] Codev = co-development team. Another studio that is working on the same project with you. Ubisoft has several studios that exclusively do codev work.

On any given day I can be maintaining the high-level outline of the story, attending brainstorming and planning meetings with other leads and directors, and providing guidance to my writing team, but then I also need to make time to complete my portion of the actual scriptwriting for the game. It's fun to be able to float back and forth between lead work and writing work, but it is a game of balance. I need to constantly assert my boundaries, even to myself, and not let the work overtake my life and become two employees in one. I think that's a danger every lead faces.

It's tempting to let the administrative work slide, to cancel all your meetings and sit down and write the game yourself. But if that's what you want, then you should be a Principal. That role requires no mentoring or people management. Perhaps you'll realize that your goal has changed. Perhaps a different path suits you better now that you've achieved this goal. That's not uncommon! Set a new goal and start working to achieve it. But right now, your first responsibility is in your title. Your team needs a good lead.

Leading with Empathy

The good news is that by the time you become a line manager, you'll have seen the role of lead practiced countless times. I hope you'll have many examples of wonderful leadership to model yourself after, but odds are you've also got some bad examples. Sometimes people become managers when they have no interest in or aptitude for the role. Maybe it's a necessary step on the way to a role they really want, or a promotion's the only way they can earn a raise. If you survived your bad managers, then you have perfect examples of what not to do. Some of my best and most inventive leadership comes from remembering a terrible manager. When faced with a tough decision, I've stopped and asked myself, "What would that Bad Lead do?" And then I've done the exact opposite. This is the secret to being a good line manager: remember what it was like when you were more junior. That insight is invaluable. Ann Lemay believes that "being a good leader means constantly exercising empathy." There's a lot of stress involved in making games and it takes a toll. "Practicing empathy means that when something goes wrong or someone does something that upsets you, there's a reason for it that's not malicious. It's easy to assume the worst of people." That's especially important when you're busy. Stepping outside your whirl of responsibilities and trying to see tasks from your team's perspective can be tough. A producer once explained to me that time flows very differently for leads and their teams. A writer or ND might spend days researching, taking notes, brainstorming with other teams, and crafting work they're proud of. Then they go to pitch their idea, which is always a nerve-racking experience, and their lead whips through it all in a half-hour, giving fast, verbal feedback. The writer is devastated. It seems like the lead didn't care. But the lead might think they were being efficient. Or they might have fought to clear that half-hour in their schedule and knew they had to give feedback then or never. It's important to stop and see those moments through your team's eyes. Ann says you should "Establish relationships with the people you work with, learn how to work with your peers, and when it comes to your team, always, always spend the time to listen to them, pay attention to how people treat them and how they react, understand what drives them." Some writers will meet you halfway, or learn to manage you like Evan does his leads. But ultimately, it's up to you to give your team what they need and to help them grow.

One of the greatest temptations you'll face as a lead is to do the work yourself. Sometimes you'll watch an ND struggle with a flowchart or a find that a writer's character bio is way off base. Instead of writing up feedback and instructions, you might think, "I could finish this task myself and get it done in half the time." Yes, you could. But then you'll *always* have to do that work because your team learns nothing. Ann says she's tried to fix that impulse in a conscious way. If "someone on my team is not doing something the way I would have done it, that doesn't mean it's bad. My job isn't to rewrite or edit scenes to the way I myself would have chosen to do it—my job is to take my team's work and make it the best possible version of what it can be. And make sure my team gets to shine." While doing that, leads also have to manage "the expectations and needs of the game as a whole, the IP holder as relevant, the Creative Director's vision, etc." Piece of cake, right? But to be serious, maintaining empathy for your team and yourself is the hardest part of leading a writing team. It's also the most rewarding. Because if you're lucky, you'll handpick the writers and NDs for your team and can choose people with talents you're excited to nurture. The hiring process can be a frustrating churn for everyone involved, so here's another place where empathy serves you well.

Building a Narrative Team

Remember how it felt to interview for a job when you were first starting out? How intimidating the whole process feels? Yes? Then don't be a jerk in interviews. Don't create monstrous writing or design tests that waste candidates' time. Give applicants a fair chance when you're reading writing tests. You might only have a few stolen moments between meetings to look at resumes and read through tests, I get that. But remember what it felt like to pour your heart into a test for a job you really wanted and give each test your full attention and fair consideration.

Step 1: Assess Your Needs

The first thing you should do when you start putting together your narrative team is assess the project needs. This means breaking it down by scope, schedule, and skills.

- **Scope:** How big is the project? How many tasks have a "long tail" that includes passes by other teams like Cinematics, VFX, Audio, or Design? How much is voiced and how much is text only? If you haven't already estimated your line count for the game, do some napkin math to assess the total amount of work remaining. Output: A workload estimate in the form of specific tasks and features.
- **Schedule:** Look at the project road map.[4] How much time do you have to complete the work for each task or feature? (For example, recording dates are usually set in stone because you have to book studio time, work with actors' schedules, and process VO.) How fast does your current team produce work? At that writing rate, how many people would you need to get all the work done on time? (Again, get a producer to help you. They're amazing at these kinds of assessments.) Output: A staffing estimate, like "four writers and an ND."
- **Skills:** What abilities does the work require? Is it mostly screenwriting or barks? Do you need someone to structure the story or create narrative systems and features? What skills does your team already have? What abilities are missing, if any? Output: A list of skills and requirements, like the one in job posts.

Step 2: Make a Hiring Plan

- Assemble the information you've gathered into a hiring plan. "To do X amount of work in Y time, I'll need Z number of people who have the following skills ... "
- Meet with your lead and producer to review the plan and figure out a hiring schedule. Your lead can help you determine what you should hire for. "We'd need two mid-level writers and a narrative designer to do that amount of work that fast." Production will help you figure out when to bring the writers on and will cross reference your needs with the budget. They might suggest alternatives to hiring, such as codev or outsourced work. Output: A hiring schedule. "We'll hire a senior ND in the spring, a mid-level writer next summer," etc.
- Meet with Recruitment to review your needs and discuss the job requirements. Output: A job posting.

---

[4] This is the Big Picture schedule for (ideally) the entire duration of the project, with deadlines and publisher check-ins.

Note: I sometimes hear applicants complain that companies "don't know what they want" when they're hiring, and I understand that it seems that way. But needs are constantly shifting because the project scope has changed, features got cut and new ones added, or internal priorities got revised. Hiring managers sometimes have to adjust midstream when their "perfect" candidate no longer matches the project needs. It's tough on everybody, especially the writers applying.

Step 3: Alternatives to Hiring

After coming up with a hiring plan and reviewing your budget, you might decide there's no need to hire FTEs. If the work is for a short period of time or for a specific task like writing a story treatment, then you're better off spending your budget on short-term solutions. Hire a freelance writer for a limited contract. Many talented writers prefer to set their schedules and rates and do "mercenary work" on AAA projects. Some of the top talent in game dev works this way, so it's worth exploring your options. Kim Belair suggests rethinking the entire idea of permanent hires or fixed contracts. If a studio says "'Listen, we have only $10,000. We can't hire another writer.' I think, 'No, but you have $10,000 of a writer's time. How do you want to use that?'" Instead of a permanent role where writers might spend half their time waiting for tasks to come available, leads can break the work into focused, concrete tasks. "Do extra prep on your side to make sure that $10,000 is fair to a worker who comes in for a little bit of time, makes changes that you need, who gets credited, and who gets compensated," Kim says. "If you can't hire full-on, make a contract, figure out what you need and scope it." Another solution is to hire writers for brief, onsite workshops. One AAA lead said their studio had experimented with this solution and achieved great results.

> We knew we wanted to bring some writers from outside the project early on, since the concept was more ambitious than our previous project. It involved several ideas that were outside our usual wheelhouse and required respect and care in their handling. We wanted to mimic the writers' room concept from TV to quickly generate and validate ideas, but we couldn't sustain that big of a writer headcount so early in the project.

The studio found workshop writers by digging through the existing stack of applications from previous narrative hiring rounds. They chose their top candidates, contracted them for a few weeks of brainstorming, and got the material they needed quickly and efficiently.

Step 4: Hiring

If there's enough work for full-time writers, and there usually is on AAA projects, you'll likely hire several writers for your team. Every team will be different because every project is different. When I'm putting together a narrative team, I'm looking for completion. I hire to fill in missing abilities and round out the skill set of the entire team. So let's say you're hiring for a fairly linear, narrative-driven game like TLOU. You'll need to hire strong cinematic writers, sure. But you'll also need to hire people good at narrative design and barks and coordination with other teams. Someone has to write all the weapon and inventory text, and all the objectives and menus. That's lot of different types of writing, requiring different skills. Most game writers I know are versatile and can write all in sorts of genres, styles, and formats. But that versatility comes with experience. Most younger writers get in more time writing thousands of barks and UI text and might not know how to craft an emotional cinematic where every word is carved from gold. Think of the project holistically when you're hiring.

Points to Consider When Hiring

- Every manager and writer will have different taste when it comes to writing. Try to get many different eyes on candidates' work and make decisions based on consensus, not personal preferences.
- Check with your studio for training to avoid unconscious bias in hiring and interviewing. I use a point system to assess each candidate. It helps me judge them on their own merits rather than comparing them to each other. I give 0 or 1 point for every stage of the hiring process. Great samples? 1 point. Solid writing test? 1 point. Terrible interview? 0 points. I sometimes give a final bonus point for extraordinary work, effort, or knowledge. At the end of the process, if you're torn between several candidates, you have numbers to help you make your choice. Of course, you'll encounter dealbreakers along the way. I once had a candidate say he didn't "really care for video games." Shockingly, he didn't get the job.
- I also recuse myself from the process when a friend is applying. I let a director or a senior writer assess candidates in my stead. That way, I know I'm not playing favorites or only hiring my cronies.

An All-Purpose Team

Whatever your specific staffing needs, most AAA narrative teams have some of the following people:

- Strong, skilled seniors who can bang out glorious, polished work quickly and mentor the younger writers.

- Mid-level writers to do the meat-and-potatoes work of bringing writing from pitch to polished and attend meetings as team envoys.
- Juniors to write a bajillion barks and UI text and process VO strings and coordinate with localization. They should be drafting scenes and getting feedback from the seniors so they can move up.
- Contractors to swoop in and flesh out your world with vivid writing and minimal oversight.
- Narrative designers to plan and integrate your work.
- You might need to outsource some work to other studios, so somebody will have to oversee and coordinate that entire process.
- You'll need an editor to put that final gloss on everyone's work because it's an endless sea of typos without them.
- And everybody needs to evangelize the game and work with other teams.

Writing Tests

If you're a senior or lead on a AAA project, you're no doubt familiar with writing tests. I discussed these at length back in Chapter 9, so I'll only remind you to design a test that you'd want to take. What that looks like will vary according to your project's needs. But keep it short. Respect the applicants' time—and your own. Ann says, "A good writing test will specifically focus on what was lacking from a candidate's portfolio, or will seek to be specific to your project as a last check. Making a round of feedback and second submission part of the interview process can help get a sense of a candidate's personality and reactivity to feedback."

You might decide that you don't need to offer a writing test. If the writer or designer has experience and you know their work is good, why put them through that process just to tick a box? Alternatively, you could treat the test as a short contract. James Phinney did exactly that when he was hiring writers for an unannounced project. He didn't have "infinite money" or a "guarantee of success" so he had to be careful about who came on board permanently. He ended up "treating these as small contracts rather than, hey, write a bunch of stuff for me for free so that I can maybe get back to you and tell you no." Phinney went with the best structure for his project and studio, but it also allowed him take a chance on less experienced writers. The writers got paid and they got real-world AAA experience and a credit. Phinney got a small bit of work done for a reasonable cost and a chance to see what the writers would do with an actual assignment. Everybody won!

Once you've hired your amazing team, you'll need to onboard them and get them set up for success. Follow your company's standard processes, but make sure they also have the Narrative-specific info they need. Give them a buddy to shadow for training in the day-to-day. Do all the things you wanted done for you when you started. That will always be your touchstone: remembering how it was for you and fixing the problems you had back then.

Running the Writers' Room

Once your team is up and running, you'll start holding writing summits to figure out the story. Hopefully, you've had the chance to run a writers' room before so you're prepared. If you're not, and you don't know what that process looks like, here's what to do:

Safety First: To have an effective writers' room—heck, to have an effective team—your writers need safety. They need to feel comfortable suggesting ideas without fear of being laughed at. They need emotional safety to talk about difficult subjects like rape and suicide without fear of disrespect or re-traumatization. And they need room to talk out ideas without being dismissed, discounted, or talked over. In a good writers' room, amazing ideas come from anyone and everyone. Ed agrees. "The best meetings are the ones where at the end of it you have a solution so bloody obvious it looks stupidly simple once written down, but nobody knew it at the start of the meeting, and everybody contributed towards it and it's no one person's idea." He told a story about spending all day trying to fix a cinematic scene with designers, "racking our brains, trying to remember if this problem had been solved in any other story in any other medium at any point in human history." Finally, one of them said, "'Wait … why doesn't the character with the gun just … shoot it?' The most obvious, basic, game-ish action you could think of, and we thought of it last."

Share the Fun: As lead, you'll usually run the show. You'll drive the discussion, bring up points to debate, keep conversation focused, ask questions to push ideas along, and walk people through story logic to ensure it works. It's an exhausting role! But it's also incredibly rewarding. Make sure you step aside occasionally and give your team a shot at leading discussion, especially your seniors. Help them grow and flourish. And not just in their work. You're responsible for every aspect of their work experience.

Crunch Part 2: Protecting Your Team

Crunch is hard on managers too. It's tough to keep team spirits up when everyone is physically exhausted and emotionally worn down. And while you might be personally opposed to crunch, you could be asked to make your team crunch. If that happens, you can become the focal point of their frustration and aggression, whether or not that's fair.

The number one thing you can do as a manager to help with crunch is to avoid it. Schedule your work in such a way that you've built in massive time and resource buffers against it. This requires working with your leads and producers to come up with a plan, a fallback plan, a Plan C, and an emergency contingency plan to protect against the issues that lead to crunch. Be loud about wanting to avoid it. If you work at a pro-crunch studio, share articles and studies that show how ineffective crunch is and propose strategies like harder downscoping or out-sourcing. However, despite all your best efforts, the entire project might end up in crunch and your team will be asked to work overtime. What can you do in that situation?

- Talk honestly to your team about what it means. If you've built a good relationship with them, they should be comfortable sharing their concerns.
- Even if the project is in crunch, you might be able to find solutions or shortcuts to lessen your team's load. Put everyone's heads together and strategize.
- Find solutions that fit your team. Maybe there are writers who can't work extra hours. Maybe some can work long hours only twice a week or on weekends. There's no one size fits all for crunch. See if you can tailor the extra time to people's needs as much as possible. Be flexible.
- Take no for an answer. You have to be okay with someone on your team not wanting to crunch. What if they have young children at home? Or they're taking night classes? Or they understand the health risks and just don't want to do it? *Be okay with a no* and defend your team.

An especially tricky part of being on Narrative is that our crunch comes before everyone else's. We often enter Production while other teams are enjoying the relative freedom and languor of Prepro. By the time other teams start crunching, we're talking to loc, dealing with bug fixes, and planning for DLC and sequels. Or, worst case scenario, we're still crunching and are already worn out. It can look like writers are leaving early when the rest of the team is staying late, or that Narrative is being sour about a "few weeks" of overtime. Here are some tips to raise the visibility of your team's hard work:

- Be ostentatious about your team's deliverables and deadlines. I get up in people's faces about the fact that my team is crunching when nobody else is. Keep it funny, keep it light, and don't point any fingers, but make your point.
- Call out the fact that Narrative is the canary in the coalmine. If we're crunching now, they'll be crunching later. Not only does this spotlight your team's extra efforts, it can bring scoping problems into focus early and (ideally!) help the project to change course so nobody else has to go through what you are.
- Propose cuts. You'll have to make some hard choices about what your team can and cannot do. If you're looking at crunch, revisit your narrative plan and see what work you can cut. Take the revised plan to your lead, or Production, or anyone who has the power to enact change. Explain the situation and propose alternatives to working more. Maybe now's the time to suggest outsourcing or contract work.

Whatever solutions you arrive at from these steps, you've made leadership aware of the problems and fought for your team's well-being.

Work-Life Balance

It's super easy to burn out as an ambitious lead, so maintaining balance is critical. For your own health, of course, but also because you're modeling work habits for your team. Trust me, they notice when you tell them not to work overtime, and then you send emails all weekend. Or when you tell your writers to leave on time, but you stay until 8:00 PM every night. Make it easy for them to advocate for themselves by practicing what you preach.

CHALLENGE

Create a hiring plan for a AAA project. Pick an existing game to plan for. For this exercise, I recommend a smaller title like *Stardew Valley's* core game. Follow the steps I outlined in this chapter.

- Break the game down into its various features: NPCs, conversation systems, seasonal content, etc. Give yourself two years to make the game.
- Assess your needs with scope, schedule, and skills. Your goal is to determine how many writers and NDs you'd need to do all that work. (Yes, I know Barone did all the work himself. He says it was hard, lonely work, so let's not be him.)
- Put together a dream team based on your assessment. How many senior writers would you need? How many narrative system designers? How long would you need them for?
- Write job ads for each of your dream team members. Make sure you're covering every skill set you'll need.

Now do that for your own project. Enjoy meeting all the wonderful, talented folks who will apply for the roles.

Chapter 15

Moving On

Successful companies are not always stable and stable companies are not always successful. If you're lucky, you might get to work for one that's both.

—Josh Scherr, Narrative Director, Crop Circle Games

What happens when you're stuck in a role that's losing its zest? Maybe there's no promotion on the horizon, or perhaps you got one and the role isn't what you hoped. What if you're working on a project that doesn't interest you? Or what if you're bored and long for something new? There are countless reasons people decide to move on. During the pandemic, record numbers of people moved jobs. They had time to sit and think about their lives, or they realized their current workplace didn't value them, or they simply got a better offer somewhere else. Whatever the reason, there was a Great Exodus by the workforce in recent years as people left to find more rewarding work. The games industry experienced it too. Almost every day, I'd see someone announce a new job or a new role. But taking that risk can be scary. You don't want to quit your job in a fit of frustration or exuberance and not have something lined up. Always try to have a new gig lined up before leaving your old job. I understand that sometimes you're in a toxic situation and have to get out immediately. That's understandable. In emergencies like that, your health and safety come first, so do what you gotta do. But in situations where it's a matter of being bored or ambitious or simply eager to see what else is out there, don't leap without a safety net. It can take a while to get your next gig, so start planning ahead. But how do you know if leaving is the best choice? And how do you know when it's the right time to move on?

DOI: 10.1201/9781003282235-16

The Right Time

Every few months, check in with yourself. Remember why you got into games? Your north star? See if it's still burning bright. Are you still motivated by the same things as before, or have you found a new aspect of the game dev universe to love? It's okay if you have! It means you're growing and learning new skills. That's a wonderful thing. If that's the case, ask if your current job feeds your new interest. Are you doing work you care about? Are you being paid the wage you want? Do you have opportunities to grow? Whatever you desire, are you getting it? If the answer is yes, then you're good. Possibly chat with your lead about ways to get more of what you enjoy. But if the answer is no, then it might be time to move on.

Just Looking

I joke that I'm *always* looking for my next gig because I keep an eye on what's out there, even when I'm happy where I am. There's no harm in looking, and it's healthy to see a tempting job and do a temperature check on your situation. If nothing else, it will reaffirm that you're where you want to be right now. As long as you're discreet about it, there's no problem. You'll meet some new people, poke your head out of your project bubble long enough to see what else is out there, and come back to your work with a fresh sense of commitment. Or you might see your dream job and be grateful that you were alert and didn't miss the opportunity to go for it because your head was buried in a project you were only so-so about. Reading job ads also lets me glimpse what other studios are working on, even if I don't apply there. It's a good way to keep up with how Narrative roles are evolving. There are some writing roles I'd never heard of until I started snooping around for this book. Story manager was a new one for me, but it makes sense when I read the job description.

If you're considering a change, go back and follow the steps in Chapter 3 to start your job hunt. Research the possibilities available to you now that you have experience. Maybe nothing will catch your eye. In that case, try to fix whatever's making you dissatisfied with your current situation. But maybe you'll see a project or role that lights you up and makes you feel the excitement that's withered on your current project. Maybe you'll find an easier commute, or a higher salary, or a chance to switch your specialization. When something piques your interest and lights you up inside, you'll know it's time.

Working While Applying

Before you rush in and apply to a studio, go back and look at your contract again. Now's the time to thank Past You for negotiating so hard. Good job, you! Refresh your memory on the different binding clauses. You're looking for two things: your notice period and the noncompete clause.

- **Noncompete Clause:** Look for language about not working for competitors in certain geographical regions or for any corporate affiliates. When I was a freelancer, one company tried to limit the work I could do for other studios by genre, mechanics, and themes until their game shipped. Obviously, I pushed back because it would've ended my career. If the game I was working on had never been released, then technically that clause would have kept from me from legally working on a project again. We know from Pete's advice that clauses like that are often unenforceable, but still. Scary stuff! Most noncompete clauses are regional. They're meant to keep you from leaving one studio with top-secret info and walking across the street to work for another studio. Those clauses are very rarely enforced. Writers ping-pong from studio to studio within major game hubs without retribution from studios. It seems like every writer in Montreal has worked for every studio in the city at some point. Even so, you're technically violating your contract and that always makes you vulnerable.
- **Notice Period:** This one's straightforward. How far in advance do you have to submit your notice? In the United States, with at-will contracts, it's usually 2–6 weeks. In Europe, it's usually much longer. It's not unusual to see notice periods of 3–6 months, especially for hard-to-fill senior roles. Look carefully at the language around the notice period to make sure you understand the process. Do you have to give notice in writing? Do they need to sign off before it's official? Are there any penalties incurred by your leaving? For example, the company might require you to repay a percentage of your relocation costs if you leave within the first year. Make sure you understand *exactly* what your leaving means and decide if it's still worth it.

Make a New Plan

Once you know the fine print of leaving your studio, you can start to plan. First, look for a new gig. Remember that it can take a while to go through a studio's hiring process. Get started early. Send in your resume or application, and then figure out your timeline.

- **Timeline:** When I'm planning, I give myself six months from the time I start looking to the time I start working. The equation is "however long you think it will take to get to the contract-signing point" *plus* the time of your notice. Add extra time for relocation. So, let's say three months to find a job, two months of notice, and a month to pack and relocate. That's six months if everything goes right and you find a job right away. It might happen much faster. You could tell a friend you're looking and get a job offer from their studio within dayss. Or you could have trouble finding a project you want to work on and spend six months just waiting for the right project to come along. Make sure you plan for the worst-case scenario and budget your time carefully.

A NOTE ON ANGER

Sometimes you're looking for a job because you're angry about your current situation and you want to let work know that you don't need them, screw you, boss, I'm outta here! I get it. If you've been mistreated at a studio, it's especially tempting as a means to take back some power and even the score a bit. But it's not going to help your situation to act out like that. Save it for your letter of resignation.

Be Discreet

If you're applying for a job while you're working, I advise discretion. Most employers aren't going to be thrilled that you're out talking to other studios. It's perfectly legal—and I would argue normal and healthy—to explore opportunities, but many employers view it as risky behavior or a lack of commitment on your part. My advice is to wait until you're serious about an opportunity. If you have to take off work for an interview, you don't need to announce it to the team or tell your lead. An appointment is an appointment and that's all anyone needs to know.

References and Samples

References are especially tricky when you're looking for work and you're not telling your current employer. You can't show your current NDAed work as samples, and you don't want your potential employer to contact your studio and reveal that you're exploring your options—especially if you haven't landed the job yet. So, what should you do?

For samples, fill your portfolio with work from other projects and possibly write a custom piece or two in a similar style to the work you're currently doing. Do not *do not* DO NOT violate your NDA at this stage. I cannot stress it enough. Showing current work while you're under NDA is extremely dangerous—especially if the game hasn't shipped or been announced. Leaks happen that way. Be careful how you handle anything that could be construed as a breach of contract. You won't impress either company that way and could sabotage both your current gig and any future work. I interviewed a writer once who desperately wanted off a bad project. He wanted to work somewhere that would treat him "like he was human." We were very sympathetic to his plight, but during the interview he broke his NDA over and over. He revealed so much about the (unreleased) game that I came out of the interview knowing the entire plot. The producer on our call vetoed him as soon as we hung up. "Poor guy," he said. "But absolutely not." So don't do it. Better to show older samples or personal work than to risk it. If you explain that you're under NDA, hiring managers will understand.

If you need references, either confide in your lead or a senior team member. Anyone you trust to keep your secrets. But it's also okay to just acknowledge that your current company isn't aware you're looking. It happens all the time, trust me.

The Big Decision

So you interviewed for another job and reached an understanding with the new studio. They like you; you like them; everyone's excited about you joining the project. They send you an offer letter and it looks great. What do you do? This is the big moment. It's real, now. You have to choose. I hope you've been checking your options and emotions all along to know that you're taking the right steps. But now, check your feelings one last time. Just to be safe. Do you feel overwhelming joy and relief? Then sign that offer letter and get things rolling! If you're not happy, then ask yourself why. Maybe you're not as ready to leave as you think you are? If so, that's okay! For most people, leaving a job is bittersweet. It's especially hard if you've been at the company for a long time or if you're leaving from frustration. It's perfectly fine to ask for time to think things over.

Leverage

If you decide you're not ready to leave after all, don't just chuck that job offer in the bin. Use the opportunity as leverage. Maybe you want a promotion? Maybe you want more ownership? One writer used their leverage to secure a four-day work week, remember? It's a well-known industry truth that the fastest way to increase your salary is by hopping studios—use that fact to your advantage. Decide what you want, then go to your current company and let them know you have another offer. See if they're willing to make the changes you need. Maybe they can fix the problem that made you want to leave in the first place. Most studios, if they're happy with your work, will try to match the offer. If they can't or won't, then it's decision time again. You can still stay, but you've lost this negotiation if you come out empty-handed. And they might not take future threats to leave seriously. If they say they can't offer you anything now, but promise you a raise at a future point: get it in writing. Negotiate hard. However, be prepared to walk away if you can't get the changes you want and it's unbearable to stay. Hopefully, you're moving toward a better situation. One ND asked for a raise so that their salary would be the same as a new ND who'd just been hired. The studio told them to be patient. Instead, they applied to a studio in the United States and took the job. They're happier and more fulfilled in their new role—a role the old studio said they weren't ready for. "They did give me a raise, just before I left, to about 500 USD a year higher than the new narrative designer. I found that really pitiful. I make 1.5x more now than my salary at my old studio, even including the raise."

At the Crossroads—Two Perspectives

Careers are made or broken in that electric moment when an offer letter arrives. Should I stay or should I go? Both options have their pros and cons. Personally, I'm very much a "devil you don't know" kind of writer. I'll always take the new job because if it's hell, at least it's a fresh hell. And it might be a dream job! But I'm a risktaker, and I have more freedom to move around than most people do. It's common for devs to stay at studios for 5, 10, even 20 years. They make deep friendships, ride the ups and down with the company. and it's the right choice for them. Both paths are valid, so how do you choose? I chatted to some Lifers and Leavers about their decisions.

Lifers

What makes someone stay at a studio year after year? Sometimes it's hard to leave, even when you know it's the best thing for you. Mikki was at Remedy for ten years before making the big leap to another studio. "There was a lot of emotional attachment for me," he said. "And, to be honest, a really fulfilling attachment. Something really worthwhile. Something that I still miss quite a bit sometimes." He was aware that "this can be an industry that's kind of crappy to storytelling and writers," so he wasn't confident leaving would land him in a better place. So, is it fear and inertia that make people stay? Not so, says Ed. For him, it's the challenge. "The projects kept getting bigger and more challenging and I wanted to know if and how I could do it. The studio (Splash Damage) and the games have grown enormously over that time, so it hasn't felt like standing still." Josh said much the same thing. He worked at Naughty Dog for over 21 years because he had "a consistent progression of new and interesting challenges. Plus compared to my jobs in feature animation, I had a ton of creative freedom." At previous jobs, he felt "like the proverbial cog in the machine" but then, all of a sudden, he was at a studio where "you were encouraged to put your own stamp on the project, express yourself, and grow beyond your job description, so long as you were helping and not hindering." When a studio gives you the support and resources to experiment and try new techniques, it's mind-blowing to creators. Both writers appreciated the opportunity to develop their skills and, as Ed said, "develop deep institutional knowledge and muscle memory. Whether you realize it or not, newer hires will regard you as the custodian of the studio's Special Sauce."

On the downside, one veteran writer says the experience you gain might not be good or useful in the wider industry. It's easy to fall behind the latest innovations in our craft—and game narrative evolves fast these days. "Stay too long you get taken for granted. Always think: 'If they had to replace me and my skills and experience with a new hire, what would it cost them?'" they added. Josh advises anyone who feels like they're stagnating to move on. "The goal in your early career should be to get a good broad range of experiences. I was lucky and managed to do that at one studio for two decades. If you feel like you're stuck in a rut and there's an opportunity for you to grow somewhere else, so long as your circumstances allow for it, then that's what you should be aiming for."

Leavers

I've already explained several reasons why writers get the itch to move on, but are boredom or ambition the only motivations? One writer says they felt they had no choice.

> To be completely honest, I've found it absolutely necessary to move on from a job when you hit a ceiling. At each studio I've been at, there's been a moment—whether it's been a stagnation of raises to the point of bringing me below industry standard, or the reluctance to give me a promotion or more responsibility, or even just the feeling that I can't grow as a writer anymore in the current environment—when I've said, "Okay, it's time to move on." I think we're conditioned to think that loyalty to a single company for many years will always reward us in the end, but I've seen so many talented writers who are underpaid and underpromoted because they stay with a studio that doesn't value them

Leaving a studio comes at a cost, as Mikki said. It's a gamble for the writer and a loss for the studio. As a contractor, Kim has to leave over and over again. "I'll work with someone as a contractor on a team, and we have an incredible rapport. We made something really good. Okay, bye now. They're going to stay there because the project was successful. They're going to stay where I can no longer collaborate with them because I'm going on to other stuff." She says the industry can't "value collaboration and creativity in any way because these structures are in place." But until those structures change and there's greater inter-studio collaboration, leaving a studio means leaving behind your friends and work you've poured your heart into, perhaps for years. Either path you choose, it's not easy.

How to Leave

If you make the call to leave, you'll have to submit a resignation letter. Or rather, email. My advice is to keep it crisp and professional. A short paragraph explaining that you've accepted another role and will be leaving on whatever date you've specified with the other company. I like to very clearly state that I'm giving my three-months' notice to invoke the terms of my contract. I'm ashamed to say that I have written some passive-aggressive resignation letters in the past, filled with unhelpful complaints and grievances as explanations for why I was leaving. I cringe to think of them now. Don't do it. Your studio will likely have an exit interview with you. You can provide feedback or vent or air your grievances in that forum. The recruiters expect it and it's the appropriate forum for it. If you prefer to have your complaints in writing as you leave, you can email them a written document of your feedback. But again, keep it professional. Think about how you'd feel if the letter was read out loud in a court of law. That should guide your wording. However, this doesn't apply if you're leaving because of abuse or harassment. Say whatever you want because that ain't right. I'd still advise you to apply the court-of-law standard and stick to the facts, but hey. I understand if you can't.

Your resignation is also the appropriate stage to lock down permissions for samples. Have discussions with your studio about what work you can and absolutely cannot share. If they say you can't share anything, then try to pry some concessions from them. What if you share work after the game releases? Can you share it if you scrub the serial numbers off? Work with them to reach an agreement. And get it in writing. It's easier to secure this now and in person than it will be three years down the road when the current team is gone and nobody remembers your contributions. Also, be careful if you're downloading documents for your own records. Do that, for certain, but make sure you understand what your NDA covers and what you're free to take with you. You don't want to accidentally abscond with company secrets.

That brings me to another critical point: credits. Hopefully, you secured an agreement during contract negotiations. If you didn't, lock that down now. Again, in writing. When it comes time to submit names for the credits, you'll be long gone and the memory of your contributions will have faded. Even places with the best intentions might not correctly recall all you accomplished. And, to be blunt, there are cases when someone left because of harassment or bullying, and their harasser was in charge of compiling the credits. Bullies can and do retaliate by diminishing your credit or changing it altogether. In many cases, a game's history gets rewritten to erase people a manager doesn't like. Sometimes out of a personal grudge and sometimes out of a desire to take credit for their work. What I'm trying to say is that once you're gone, all bets are off for credits. There are a million things that could happen to deprive you of the credit you earned. Don't leave until you've reached an understanding. Don't leave it to chance. Know in advance what you'll be credited for. Regardless of how you're credited—or if you're left out of the credits—you can still list the job in your resume. The work you did there is valid.

Paperwork

Once you've resigned, you'll have to fill out a metric crapton of paperwork to leave. Danger danger danger! Be very careful what you're signing. If you negotiated hard with your contract, don't ruin everything by signing away any rights now. If you're not leaving on good terms, *especially* don't sign anything that binds you to arbitration, puts a gag order on you, or any other limiting factor you don't want. Remember, you're already leaving. There's no reason to sign anything like this! Most companies only ask you to confirm that you're leaving on a specific date and have returned any company property. That's the sort of final paperwork you should feel comfortable signing.

Don't Burn Bridges

I've given a lot of worst-case scenarios in this chapter, but most of the time you're going to leave a studio amicably. Game devs come and go from the same studio many times in their career. You night work at one company, leave for another project, then come back when you're done. I've worked at Ubisoft twice, on two different continents. And there are several studios from my past that I'd happily work for again. Keep that door open if you can. It wasn't the right project or role for you now, but it might be in the future.

Take a Break

What if you're not happy where you are, but you're not ready to leave yet? You're not a Lifer or Leaver, you're a … Lifever? Leafer? You're someone who just wants a break. In that case, chat with your lead and see if your studio offers any sort of sabbatical program. Maybe they're happy to let you take off for three months to study or travel or take on a short contract. Academia is a popular side gig for narrative folks and the path that many of us choose when we're ready to leave the industry for good. Mary taught some game-writing classes while working at Insomniac. She had to teach on top of her regular responsibilities, but it was "a great chance to reconnect with best practices in narrative design outside of my own studio and team." But don't go into teaching thinking it's an escape. Academia has its own set of problems and politics. Hazel says that she "left academia because, believe it or not, it is more precarious and exploitative than the game industry." She's "eternally thankful I managed to build a fulfilling career outside of academia."

When I was burned out, I took a break and worked outside AAA for a bit. I contributed to art installations, ghostwrote a memoir, designed a serious game, and wrote two (abysmal) novels. It was exactly what I needed. I went from feeling dead inside and thinking I didn't have another major game in me, to exploding with creative energy. I came back to AAA and did some of the best work of my life. If it's a possibility for you, I highly recommend it.

On Repeat

So there you are! One way or another you shouldn't come out of this chapter unchanged. Maybe you moved on to a new studio or negotiated a better situation where you are. Or perhaps you simply stepped back and found new avenues for fulfillment. You will find yourself at this crossroads time and time again in your career. You should make it a habit to question your comfort every year. Lift your head and scent the air. See if new adventures are right for you. The decisions you make—stay or go, here or there—link together over time to form the golden line of a long career. I wish you joy in your choices.

CHALLENGE

- Follow the steps for finding work in Chapter 3. Apply for any role that interests you.
- Do the initial phone screen with the recruiter.
- If it seems like what you want, continue through the hiring process.
- If you get an offer, weigh your pros and cons. What are you giving up if you leave? What can you get there that you don't have now?
- If you're unsure of what to do, talk to your current lead about your offer. See if they're willing to sweeten the pot.
- Make your decision to stay or leave. READ YOUR CONTRACT before you resign.
- Enjoy your farewell party OR your improved work situation.

Chapter 16

International Work

> You should go on a trip of some kind. Might be good for you.
>
> –Joseph Campbell, probably

When you're thinking of writing work in the games industry, especially AAA, you probably think of the big studios in the United States: Naughty Dog, Sony Santa Monica, Insomniac, Blizzard, Riot, Crystal Dynamics, and places like that. There are a few key game hubs in the United States—Los Angeles, San Francisco, Seattle, and Austin are the biggest ones. And there are plenty of smaller studios scattered around the country. These studios seem to dominate the headlines and get outsize attention because of their big blockbuster games. Living in one of these regions is a distinct advantage because there's a gaming network built up in these areas. If you're unhappy at Blizzard you can hop over to Riot. If you're tired of working at Bioware, you can talk to Arkane. There's a high demand for games industry folks and being local gives greater access to opportunities. Or maybe you live in the US and dream of working in a European studio with their legendary healthcare and vacation benefits—or maybe studios in China, Japan, or Korea are more your dream. Maybe you live in a country with no video game companies or opportunities at all and dream of moving *anywhere* that has a vibrant gaming hub—like the cluster of studios in Montreal. Whatever your circumstance, relocating to a tech hub gives you an advantage in finding work. Heck, I once found a games job through the Seattle Craigslist. It was that easy.

Of course, not everyone can pick up and move their entire life for work. Older writers especially, who might have partners or kids in school, can't simply sell their homes and relocate to an expensive tech hub halfway around the world on a whim. Relocation disrupts their kids' lives, costs a fortune, and often means leaving your support groups behind. And what about your partner? Maybe they like their

DOI: 10.1201/9781003282235-17

current job. Maybe they don't want to move. Relocating for a job comes with big changes and many unknowns. Even when you're fairly fancy-free, like myself, it means leaving behind the friends, connections, and familiar routine to start a new life in an unfamiliar culture. This can be a real hassle for reasons ranging from the logistical to personal. At the time of this writing, I have bank accounts in three countries and have to shuffle money between them for various bills and obligations.

Remote Work

One of the only good things to come out of the pandemic is that we proved remote work is viable long term. AAA studios that were once sticklers for in-studio work have loosened their requirements for working offsite. That makes working at these big US studios possible in a way it hasn't been before. When you're applying for a job and you know you can only work remotely, have that conversation with the studio at the start of the hiring process. I've heard people say to wait for an offer and then see if the studio will let you work remotely. Maybe they'll be so blown away by your brilliance that they'll let you work from *wherever*. While it's possible this could happen on (extremely) rare occasions, most companies are unlikely to change the working arrangement on a case-by-case basis. That's because hiring—especially international hiring—involves numerous political and legal considerations. For example, some governments offer tax breaks to incentivize game studios to set up base there.[1] Tara warns that "these benefits sometimes come with hiring requirements, so the company might be legally obligated to search for candidates locally first." Make sure you know the restrictions for a gig before you enter the lengthy AAA hiring process. Companies like Bungie can only hire remote workers from certain US states. Other companies can only offer remote roles to independent contractors. And contract work means you lose all the benefits that come with full-time AAA roles. Maybe that's fine with you! But go into the process with all of those issues resolved so you don't waste time applying for a job you can't take.

Applying for International Work

Global job aggregators like GrackleHQ have made it easy to find international work. If there's a specific country you want to move to then GameDevMap helps

[1] The Kerryman. "Tax breaks for video game firms can open a door for Kerry." Kerry Newsletter/Independent.i.e. 18 May 2022. https://www.independent.ie/regionals/kerryman/business/tax-breaks-for-video-game-firms-can-open-a-door-for-kerry-41663305.html

you find studios there. But before you start applying for an international job, it's good to know what the country's visa requirements are. Some countries require that studios prove your expertise to justify hiring you over local candidates. That proof usually comes in the form of your education and employment history. If you're applying for a Special Expert visa, common for work in the EU and Nordics, you'll need to submit diplomas and contracts representing years of work. The application process for international work can take a long time and cost a lot of money, so definitely find out upfront what you're in for. Talk to the recruiter about this stuff before you get too far into the process. Here are some good questions to ask:

- Is remote work an option for this job?
- Who qualifies for remote work?
- Does the studio pay for relocation?
- What does the typical relocation package include?
- If I relocate, what type of visa does this job require?
- How long does a typical relocation take?
- Does the studio have any requirements outside of the standard application process?

This last point is particularly important because some companies require a background check that can double the length of your relocation time. It's good to know your timeline so you can plan accordingly. For example, I usually give myself three months to find another job (a standard notice period), but I add another three months on top of that for international relocation. That means I might start looking for work six months (or more!) before I actually leave the studio. A gap this long means planning way ahead.

Relocation

> When I started at Ubi, the guy who hired me was a creative director who knew he was a bad fit for his job. He hired me to replace him. He had offers from a bunch of companies. He told me, "I'm not that great, I'm just willing to relocate." I think about that conversation a lot.
>
> –Palle Hoffstein, Producer at Ubisoft Massive

Let's say you've talked to the studio, you're excited to relocate, and you're ready to get that process started. What do you do now? No clue, right? Luckily, most AAA companies are familiar with the process and have trained professionals who can walk you through the paperwork. Some studios offer more support before you move; some offer more support after the move. There are advantages to both approaches—and tons of paperwork you'll have to figure out—regardless of what help you get. Let's go through this step by step.

Relocation Package: Usually, your relocation package is written into your offer letter or contract. Some companies offer a lump sum that you can spend however you want and some companies have preferred moving services that will move up to a set cubic amount of your belongings for you. Some companies pay for the whole shebang and all you have to do is get yourself and your family/pets there. But for lead roles and down, you'll usually have to make arrangements yourself. Find out what your studio covers and what you have to sort out on your own. Tara says it's easier to negotiate "a better moving package than a higher salary, so if they won't budge on the latter, push for more on the former. Moving internationally is expensive, and you will end up eating into your own funds quicker than you anticipate." Research your travel costs and the local cost of living for your studio to get an estimate for your move, and use those figures to make the case for more money. Unless you travel light, most packages don't cover enough. I'm happy if I break even on costs for an international move.

Passports: you will need a valid passport to travel. This is a long, multistep process that you should start immediately if you don't already have one. Apply through your country's state department (or equivalent) and follow their instructions carefully. The passport industry is rife with scams, so be very wary of fake document services. Make sure you're going through a reliable, accredited service before you hand over sensitive documents like your birth certificate or identification card.

Visas: As I mentioned above, you'll need a visa to work in another country. They come in all flavors and types, but they're basically permission to live and (importantly!) work in that country. You'll have to supply documentation ranging from diplomas to travel history to proof of sponsorship from your company. Sometimes you'll get a temporary visa that will allow you to enter the country and pick up your final visa once you arrive. Sometimes you'll get stuck in limbo between two countries while they issue your permanent visa before entering. There are also tricky timing issues associated with the visa—when you can enter the country, how long in advance you can apply for one, and how recently you've visited the region. It's a bureaucratic labyrinth, but most companies help you navigate it. If not, ask for professional relocation assistance as part of your reloc package. Trust me, you don't want to mess this up. One US game writer moved to Australia to work for a small studio there. The studio was new and unfamiliar with the visa process and flubbed his paperwork. The writer's visa expired, unbeknownst to him, and he got thrown into a detention center (jail!) for several weeks while they decided his fate. He ended up being deported to the United States and barred from returning to Australia. Needless to say, the experience was incredibly traumatizing. Don't let this happen to you. Don't risk getting any detail wrong. Have a professional walk you through the process step by step.

A SIDE NOTE ON VISAS AND IMMIGRATION

If you've only lived in your home country, you have no idea how hard most countries make it to emigrate. Visas are one way to weed out applicants. If you don't have an advanced degree, you'll have to compensate for it with work experience. Tara says Germany required two years of work experience for every year of a degree she lacked. The United States has even stricter requirements. If you want an O-visa for "individuals with extraordinary ability"[2] or H-1B visa, which is the kind they give to skilled tech workers and game designers, then for every year of college, you need to have three years of experience.[3] Clara notes, "Here's where that diploma comes in handy, because without it you'll need the equivalent of sixteen years of work history." That's a significant obstacle. It's not like you can suddenly come up with a degree or experience, so international relocation might be closed to some writers.

Evan says that "government bureaucracy is way scarier" when you're working in a foreign country. "As a native citizen of a country, the government has an implied obligation to you. They almost owe you a certain level of protection, as a member of their state. But those relationship dynamics are completely different for migrants. They don't owe you that same protection, and both sides know it." This was brought home to him when he lost his UK visa and had to get a replacement. All his travel plans got canceled when he was forbidden to leave the country. "It was a bureaucratic nightmare for a long time. And I was lucky enough to actually get the replacement in the end. But if I lost my equivalent in the US, which would be a driver's license, it would be replaced in a week." He says it's not just the red tape. "You get treated differently in different parts of the world. In some ways that can be better, but in some ways it's unexpected and worse."

Tara recommends that you "get multiple certified copies of every single important document you could possibly ever want" before moving. If you can, "get all of these certified with a notary or apostille. Stick the documents in a giant expandable folder" and tote it everywhere you go for the first year of living abroad. "You never know when you are going to need a specific document, and sometimes they absolutely will not tell you ahead of the

---

2 US Citizenship and Immigration Services. "O-1 Visa: Individuals with Extraordinary Ability or Achievement." Accessed 20 August 2022. O-1 Visa: Individuals with Extraordinary Ability or Achievement | USCIS.

3 Shihab & Associates. "Degree Equivalency & Work Experience." Accessed 20 August 2022. https://www.shihabimmigrationfirm.com/employment-based-immigration/h-1b-visas/degree-equivalency-work-experience/

appointment that it is critical that you have it with you for the appointment. Don't have the document and you may end up with costly delays in setting up essential services." Be prepared for any type of bureaucratic demand. In fact, be overprepared.

Biometrics: In this digital age, you'll be asked to provide biometric information as part of the visa application. That's a fancy word for fingerprint and facial scans. You can only get these done at specific, limited locations. This can be a dicey part of your relocation process. You must go to an embassy or consulate of the country you're moving to, which might be located quite far from where you live. Appointments must be made in advance (no walk-ins) and they're usually booked solid for weeks (or months) in advance. I lucked out when I moved to Finland from the United States because I lived in Washington, DC. I was able to stroll downtown, get my biometrics done, and return home a few hours later. In Sweden, I had to take a train and stay overnight in Stockholm for a next-day appointment at the British visa agency there. And in Canada, I was stuck in airport limbo with two scared cats while authorities quickly threw together a temporary visa for me. My advice is to triple-check your documentation before going. If you're missing anything, they can't process your application. Then you'll have to rebook your appointment and do the whole process all over again. Don't take chances!

Hidden Fees: All that paperwork I just mentioned costs money. You'll need to pay for passport pictures, processing, and delivery. Visa applications can be enormously expensive. The United Kingdom requires that certain applicants pay for five years of NHS services in advance, on top of standard application and processing fees. And if you go for biometrics, you're potentially paying for flights, hotels, and meals on top of the processing fees. Add all of this up and you can be looking at fees ranging from 5000 to 10,000 USD upfront. Many agencies don't accept credit cards, so you'll need cash in the bank. This might be a deal-breaker for many writers, who rarely have stacks of gold piled in a vault. Talk to your company about including these costs in your relocation package. They absolutely should. A standard arrangement is for writers to pay all the costs and then get reimbursed for expenses on arrival. But if you don't have enough money to cover the costs until then, ask for a prepaid credit card to cover the costs. Explain your situation and talk through options with them. Be clear that you can't move without their help, and they'll find a way.

Household Moving: Now comes the hard part: what to take with you. Once again, check your package to make sure you understand what the company does and does not cover. If they're paying for movers, what's the limit on what you can pack? If you're paying for movers, what's your budget? Depending on where you're moving to, you'll have a wide range of options from packing it all yourself, to pods and shipping containers that you load and they move, to full-service movers who wrap and pack everything for you. Just remember that if a price seems too good to be true, it probably is. Look for hidden costs like harbor fees, ship-to-door costs, and insurance. Price isn't your only concern, as international shipping is unsurprisingly riddled with scams and shady companies. It might cost a bit more to ship with reputable movers, but at least you know your stuff will arrive intact.

As for packing itself, keep in mind that countries have voltage differences. Unless it's an unusual electrical item (a beloved antique lamp, for example), you're better off ditching your appliances and buying all new ones there. I know it's hard to part with belongings, but embrace the spirit of adventure and replace your household items with products from your new country. If you got rid of everything you could bear to part with and you're still over your shipping budget, consider putting some items in storage or leaving them with a friend to send later. Ask the studio to put you in touch with someone who made a similar move to yours. They'll be a goldmine of tips about good movers and what difficulties to expect on the other end.

Pets: Of course you don't want to leave your darlings behind! But traveling with pets is one of the trickiest parts of international moves—especially if you're relocating to another continent. The moment you even *think* you're moving to another country, look up their requirements for importing pets. You'll need a specific type of microchip, proof of negative rabies and titer tests, and a verified health certificate stamped within a few days of your trip. If you're flying, airlines have strict rules about pets flying in cabins or in cargo, and they require crates that meet rigid standards. The entire process gets much easier if you get your pets a passport, but getting one of those is a process all by itself. Plan ahead and make sure you know exactly what you need to do to get your pet legal and able to enter the new country smoothly. The last thing you want is to arrive, discover you're missing critical documentation, and have your pet put into quarantine for months. Some quarantine periods, like Japan's, can be up to six months! Don't risk it. Pet relocation is also unbelievably expensive. It will eat up a huge part of your relocation package, so budget wisely.

Arrival

I love to travel, so arriving in a new country is always exciting for me. If you know people in the new country, see if they can recommend good local restaurants or stores for your first few nights in town. If you're traveling with pets, you'll also have to make arrangements for their arrival. They will likely be stressed by the travel, so anticipate their needs. They'll want food and water, and cats will need a litterbox right away when you arrive. See if a friend can bring pet supplies by. For my last move, one of my coworkers lived next door to my company apartment, and she kindly let me order supplies to her house. But I have also been that haggard, haunt-eyed woman roaming the streets at 10 PM on a Tuesday to find an open pet store. Don't be me. Plan ahead for your pets and your sanity.

Housing

Most studios will offer some kind of temporary housing for relocated devs. This can range from a nice hotel or extended-stay housing to actual dormitories where devs from your studio live. The quality of these accommodations varies widely. I've generally had good experiences, but some housing situations are … less than ideal. Company quarters are meant to be short term and provide a landing spot while you get on your feet. You'll have a lot to do in your first few weeks, so not having to worry about immediately finding a place to stay is nice.

If the studio has no accommodations for you and no plan to help find them, that's a huge red flag. It's incredibly rare. I only know of one instance where that happened and it was an accident—it was a new studio and they were hiring internationally for the first time. But make sure you have everything lined up, especially for that first night in the new town. You'll want a place to crash facedown after your long travels. When I moved to Finland, I was so exhausted after a 24-hour day of moving and travel, that I drank an entire can of juice I was allergic to rather than get up and go buy another. Make sure everything is in place.

Settling In

If you're lucky, your studio will hire an agent to get you settled in. You'll need to register with the new government, set up a bank account, get a local phone plan, learn how to get around the new city—and a million other little intricacies of life that we don't think about until we have to start over. This can be difficult and frustrating when you don't speak the language, so try to negotiate for a helper on that end. Google translate is an incredibly valuable tool and you should lean on it as much as you need to. The best advice I can give you for getting set up in a new town is "ask for help." Being independent is great, but there's a limit. How else are you going to find out which restaurants the locals like and which ones are tourist traps? Where are the hidden secrets in town? One town I moved to had tiny little finger monkeys you could pet at a local zoo and mysterious little mouse houses that appeared in random spots. Another town had a local tradition of burning a straw goat every year in the fall during a pagan ceremony. This is the kind of stuff you need to know! Don't be afraid to ask for help and advice on every network you have access to. You're going to have a hard enough time adjusting to life in a foreign culture without trying to do it on hard mode.

Culture Shock

Tara had this to say about culture shock:

> You are walking into a fundamentally different culture. That sounds obvious on the surface, but don't underestimate the impact that will have on your day-to-day life. Culture is what happens when no one is looking, and it's in those smaller moments that cultural frictions sometimes come to a head. What is considered rude in one country is being polite in another, and it is easy for tempers to flare. There are absolutely going to be things that utterly confuse, frustrate, and try your patience. And so many times it will be something utterly ridiculous in retrospect.

Even if you love new experiences and view your move as an exciting adventure, you'll likely experience culture shock. It can strike at the strangest times. I almost broke down in tears when I tried to find American pancake mix at a Finnish supermarket. I felt overwhelmed by all the flour choices—none of which I could understand. Every society has a host of unspoken rules and behaviors that we know so well they've become invisible. When you're in a new country, you'll bump up against those all the time without realizing it. If you're lucky, people will think you're charming or helpless and understand. In Finland, if I asked for directions, the person I asked would invariably walk me in the direction I needed to go. They took one look at me and realized I was hopeless, so they helped me even when it *clearly* ruined their day to do so. Tara tells a story of trying to buy aspirin in Germany "and you need to tell the pharmacist why, so they can ensure they are giving you the right medication." Her headache was so bad that she couldn't remember the right words. "I was frustrated and tired, and in a not small amount of pain. I could have gotten flustered and left the Apotheke in a fit of frustration and shame, but instead mimed head pain to the best of my ability. The baffled clerk suddenly lit up and laughed, 'Ah! Kopfschmerzen!'" and Tara finally got her aspirin. She says that "learning to just lean into the awkwardness with a cheerful attitude has helped diffuse many situations and gotten me what I needed in the end."

Do your best to learn the language and local customs. Your studio might offer language classes or offer to pay for tutoring. Absolutely take them up on it. The best cure for culture shock is to understand the culture. And that means engaging with it. Explore your city. Learn the language. Make friends. Put down roots. It'll be tempting to live out of suitcases and not decorate your apartment much at first, but I strongly advise against that. Unpack. Put up pictures. Make your rooms comfortable. Give yourself a safe space that feels like a home. And make an effort to build a new life. If you don't find ways to connect with daily life there, you won't last. Evan says that having his partner travel with him made things a lot easier. He has someone to get out into the new culture and share his experiences with. And that's important. "I think it's specifically useful for a writer to better understand the world around you, but also culturally how things are different. To realize the background of the world that you take for granted." You won't realize how much your perspective has changed until you go home and look at your old, familiar world with fresh eyes. It's illuminating to see how many aspects of day-to-day life became invisible to you through sheer familiarity. Being able to see them clearly again is the great gift of traveling and living abroad.

Isolation and Friendships

Another reality of moving around for writing work is that friendships fade. You'll meet all sorts of wonderful new people and make new friends, but maintaining those friendships is hard when you keep moving around. You might drift away from people you've been close to for years, and that increases your feelings of culture shock and isolation. You *have* to keep reaching out. Social media has been my lifeline as I've moved around. I've made five international moves in the last nine years. That means that I was moving on as soon as I established a comfortable life. It felt like I was always starting over from the ground floor again. Even for someone as adventurous as I am, it's been tough to keep rebuilding. You'll have to work at keeping your friendships going—especially when time zones mean your best friend is on the exact opposite sleep schedule as you are. But having those connections is what makes it all possible. It can take anywhere from six months to a year before you really get settled into a new country and it feels like "home," so be patient with yourself.

Sometimes, despite everything you've done, you'll feel isolated. I remember walking through the busiest mall in central Helsinki, surrounded by dozens of people speaking five different languages, and feeling completely alone. Loneliness, isolation, culture shock—they strike when you least expect it. The pandemic has made meeting new people harder too. The United Kingdom was in lockdown when I arrived, and we didn't return to the office until about a year after I moved here. It's tough to make friends with those obstacles. But somehow you do. And you will. You'll pick up a board-game night here. A running partner there. A chat with your neighbor on bin collection day. And before you know it, you've woven these fragile threads of connection into a rich new life.

When It All Goes Wrong

Sometimes, despite all your best efforts, a move to another country just doesn't work out. It can be a mess-up with paperwork like the writer who landed in an

Australian jail, or it can be a role that turns out to be a bad fit. I moved to the UK right when Brexit hit and the country went into lockdown. Flights were canceled, imports stopped, services went on hiatus. I'd make moving arrangements, cross that item off my list, only to have the arrangements canceled the next week. To get my cats there, I constructed a four-country Rube Goldberg machine of flights, taxis, hired cars, and ferries. It worked out, but it took twenty-two hours for a journey that usually takes three.

Studios think globally.

Sometimes, even with all your efforts, everything can go wrong in a perfect storm of literal crap.

Amazon Studios Game Designer Jennifer Klasing told a story[4] about relocating that shows exactly how bad it can get. She says, "I moved overseas in late 2020 for an opportunity at a game company that will remain unnamed. This is the story of how I came and went in only 5 weeks." Here's a condensed version of Jennifer's horror story:

- She responded to an opportunity on Twitter. "'Come make content for our new game! It's set in [cool franchise that I like]!' I got excited. I inquired."
- She interviewed and got an offer which included a "relocation package which amounted to about 4k USD … to move internationally. I made it clear that this would only cover part of my expenses, but they didn't budge."
- They asked her to move earlier than she wanted to, which she explained "would trigger a non-negotiable lease break fee." The company insisted, so she began making preparations.

- The relocation package barely covered her lease break fees, so she tried to move as cheaply as possible. "I ended up giving away or selling all but one piece of furniture and about ~10 boxes of belongings." It ended up being about 75% of what she owned. "I sold my car, rather than ship it over. I also rehomed my dog, since it was going to cost me 7k to relocate him with me and his health was suffering from the stress of moving already."
- Once she'd stripped her belongings down to "3 suitcases," she booked her flights.
- She didn't worry about her visa because the studio said, "they had relocated dozens of Americans and that this was standard procedure for them."
- A month before her flight, she still hadn't heard anything about her visa. Her relocation coordinator said they would start the process. She trusted them to handle everything.
- She kept working at her job "until 2 weeks before I'm supposed to ship out. I wanted to make sure I didn't leave my team hanging, and frankly I needed the income right up until the move. Still no word on the VISA."
- The relocation coordinator said she should have her visa by then, but it apparently got lost in the mail. She frantically tried to hunt it down, but then four days before she was supposed to move, her home was threatened by the California wildfires. She had to evacuate to a hotel room with her suitcases and the rest of her stuff in storage—a half mile from the fires.
- Still no sign of her visa. "Crickets from the relocation coordinator. You'll notice that I'm still trying to make this work at this point. All I can say is that I truly assumed it was going to make my life better, and escaping a literal fiery hellscape, both physically and politically, was SUPER appealing in that moment."
- She spoke to the Swedish Embassy at 4 AM, to see if she was ever granted a visa but they couldn't answer over the phone. She was finally able to get a rush copy of it from an East Coast consulate.
- The fire "evacuation was lifted. I now have 48 hours to get ready to leave the country. It was tight. I was MAX stressed."
- She gets to the airport, goes to the gate and shows her passport, itinerary, and other documents. But "they asked if I had a negative COVID test. 4 days ago, a test was not required. I checked." Her coordinator hadn't mentioned it. She scrambled to meet the new requirements and fly out that day but had to change the second leg of her flight. "I was supposed to fly into Denmark. Instead, I fly into Stockholm, 5 hours north. I was supposed to arrive at 2 PM on a Saturday and start work on Monday. Instead, I arrive at 1 AM Sunday."
- She was told to pick up her keys at a hotel near the train station, so she walked there with her suitcases. "No one mentioned the cobblestones. So here I am, trucking three suitcases over cobblestones at midnight, past a few nightclubs, getting all sorts of strange looks. I am also on the verge

of crapping myself because I'd eaten nothing but grab-and-go meals in the past 48 hours."

- When she finally arrived ("exhausted") at the company-sponsored apartment, she couldn't get in the front door. "I'm fried. I'm staring at this keypad without a code. The note with the keys mentions nothing about a keypad or a code." In a stroke of luck, one of the other residents was out walking their dog "at 12:30 AM. On a Saturday night." He showed her the trick for entering with a key fob and helped carry her suitcases up the stairs.
- "I quite literally crap myself on the threshold of my new home, shower, collapse into bed, and pass the **** out for 18 consecutive hours."

Jennifer's temporary housing was small and dank, and she had problems with local food. She also had problems at work.[5] It won't surprise you to hear that she decided to move back home a few weeks after she arrived. I share this story because it demonstrates how many moving parts there are to international relocation and how many disparate elements need to line up perfectly for a successful trip. Jennifer did everything right, but she still had problems with negotiations, budget, paperwork, communication, logistics, natural disasters, health regulations, travel, dietary requirements, time differences, culture shock, and, well, even bodily functions. Hers isn't the worst story I've heard either. She made it to her studio. Some people don't get that far. I'm not trying to scare you off the idea of relocation, but I won't conceal the darker side of it. It's complicated and requires enormous amounts of meticulous planning. Don't enter into the process lightly. Make sure it's right for you.

Communication

Your saving grace through all these adventures will be language. If you speak English, you can go almost anywhere in the world and make yourself understood. English is the new French (a little joke for you language buffs out there.) English has been the common language on the floors of most AAA game studios, so you'll be able to make yourself understood. And you'll usually write the game in English. It's very easy to not learn the local language, but that's a huge mistake. There are many practical reasons to speak the language. It'll help at tax time, for sure. But also, as writers, as storytellers, we know how much culture lives inside the words people use. Learning to speak the native language will not only help you understand your new culture better, it will expand your intellectual horizons. Make the effort. Take some classes with friends or colleagues.

---

[5] There's a Swedish Adventure Part Two thread, if you can stomach more horror.

Pry back the surface of conversations and learn the nuance and history that lies underneath. Learn the local myths and legends in their original tongue. It's an incredible opportunity for wordsmiths like us to have, so don't throw it away just because English is easy. You could stay home, if that's how you feel. You're in a new land. Embrace every part of it.

One of the joys of travel.

Final Thoughts

I'm a big fan of living abroad, but I sincerely understand it's not for everyone. If you can't pick up and move, or you simply prefer not to, there's no judgment here. For those who remain at home, I encourage you to reach out to game studios around the globe and see if you can work for them remotely. That way you can enjoy some of the glamour of travel from your desktop.

CHALLENGE

I have no challenge for you because the move is challenging enough. My only advice is to know the visa process and immigration requirements of your new country inside and out. Don't leave a single detail to chance. The consequences could be dire in this current political climate.

Chapter 17

Strategies for Marginalized Communities

> Find your people. Find your communities. Try to get involved where you can give as much as you take.
>
> –Kim Belair, CEO, Sweet Baby Inc.

It's time to talk about problems in the games industry. I struggled to write this chapter. Not because I had nothing to say, but because the flood of words over-whelmed me.[1] I've touched on a few industry problems throughout this book: crunch, burnout, difficulties getting the promotions and pay you want, and the leaky pipeline among others. I haven't sugarcoated things, but I also haven't ad-dressed one of the industry's biggest problems: the playing field isn't level. Being a game writer is harder for some people than it is for others. Breaking in is harder. Staying in is harder. If you look at the highest levels of leadership in most Western AAA game companies, it is overwhelmingly white and male. Yet, studies by groups like the Entertainment Software Association (ESA) and United Kingdom Interactive Entertainment (UKIE) routinely demonstrate that the player base[2] and development communities[3] are far more diverse. I'm not going to jazz-hand this

---

[1] The current chapter is 1/3rd its original length. Yeah.

[2] Entertainment Software Association. "2022 Essential Facts About the Video Games Industry."

[3] Taylor, Mark. "UK Games Industry Census Report 2022." United Kingdom Interactive Entertainment.

DOI: 10.1201/9781003282235-18

question and ask "Why do you think that is? What do you think is happening?" because we know. We've all read the headlines and followed the lawsuits. We've seen the studies. We know what's happening, and I won't play that disingenuous game. That's not what this chapter is about. While interviewing people for this book, I heard some shocking and heartbreaking stories—enough for a whole, separate book, to be honest. I've included a couple here as examples, but that's not what this chapter is about either. This chapter is for honest talk about what to do when bad things happen.

Even When It's Good, It's Bad

Everything you know is a problem out in the wider world is also a problem in the video games industry. These issues are exacerbated by industry demographics, which lean whiter and more male than its player base.[4] In games, as in society, you'll find the usual lineup of suspects: sexism, racism, homophobia, ableism, ageism, and a bunch of other discriminatory practices. There are glass cliffs and glass elevators, misogynoir, and unconscious bias toward every marginalized group you can imagine. I can't begin to cover every issue you'll encounter in this one little chapter, but let's hear from your mentor collective about some of the problems they face.

All the -isms

- **Racism:** BIPOC face hurdles everywhere they turn in games. It's harder to break in. Their ideas aren't valued or understood. They're held to a different standard than their White peers. Intersectionality can make it worse. Son M says she "can't tell you if it's because I'm femme presenting or because I'm Algerian and Muslim or because I'm pretty outspoken on my goals. I can tell you that these factors, their percentage of involvement varying based on who I am talking to, is weighed." Kim got called to work on an Afrofuturism project at a AAA studio. When she met the writing team, "it was three white dudes from Canada, and I was like, 'Oh no, that's probably not going to get you where you need to go.' And they responded, 'We'd agree, but these ones had the experience and the writers who were Black and had the skills, didn't have the experience.'" It's rare to see the industry's problem with race so clearly illustrated, but you'll encounter more subtle variations of this same problem all over. Son M says it's not just AAA; it affects the pitch system for indie games too.

---

[4] 61% male and 67% White/Caucasian, according to the IGDA's 2021 Developer Satisfaction Survey Report.

We have this joke, called the strike rule. When talking to a publisher or a funder, there's a secret strike rule to gauge how risky your project is. Marginalized identities often fall into this "high risk" factor, and can lead to difficulty securing funding partners. Your main character is a woman and she's brown and your studio is led by people of color? That's three strikes of risk. Why is that risky?

That same sort of risk affects BIPOC on individual levels. Kim says it's hard "when somebody comes to you with a portfolio, that is great, right?" But they're having trouble breaking in "and you see that blocker of the industry. Because you see it's not a meritocracy."

- **Transphobia:** Race isn't the only vector of discrimination. While the games industry has a reputation for being more open and accepting toward LGBTQIA+ folks, Willow still feels the need to limit her presentation in the office. She avoids it partly to avoid making colleagues uncomfortable, but "the biggest part is not knowing how a change in apparent appearance might impact how I am treated or perceived by colleagues." She grants that "studios of all flags and sizes are steadily getting better at supporting gender diverse people as an increasing percentage of developers find themselves working with trans and/or non-binary colleagues." But homophobia and transphobia are significant prejudices—as recent headlines reveal. It's already tough to get a foot in the industry, but biases make it harder for transgender people. "Nowhere is going to simply tell you they are discounting you based on your gender, but it can and does happen. Cultural fit can be important but when it devalues diversity it's a problem."
- **Sexism:** "I've been talked over in meetings or had my experience as a woman and/or bisexual person explained to me by someone who was neither of those things more times than I can count," Mary says. It's not unusual. Talked over. Passed over for promotions. Glass-ceilinged. Glass-cliffed. Gaslit when they complain. The problems women in games face are well-known. Many writers have trouble proposing ideas for female characters. Pitches about menstruation or female friendship often garner a baffled reaction from leadership. "Why would anyone be interested in that?" The answer is "because half the human race has those experiences," but it doesn't always go over well. One lead said a writer's female-focused work was "too political." Female-presenting writers can get a lot of push-back when they fight for their ideas. Sachka says that people "listen to women as long as those women have suggestions that fit predefined models of a 'good idea.' So for a long time I tried to fit in and to guess what those people wanted to hear." She didn't feel confident pushing the issue. When she was finally ready to pitch ideas that reflected her "true personality and experience, then these ideas were generally regarded as weird, or silly. Because many people still haven't understood that inclusion and diversity aren't just about who you hire but also about what new ideas you're ready to consider worthy of interest."

- **Neurodivergence:** "Open offices are hell." That sums up many of the problems I heard from neurodivergent game writers. They also mentioned that clear communication is an issue and they often feel misjudged or misunderstood. Considering communication of all sorts is the baseline work for writers, it can be a significant obstacle for neurodivergent game writers and NDs.

- **Disability and Ableism:** Imagine you're a disabled writer and you can't get to your job. The elevator at the studio is broken that day, and you physically cannot get up the three flights of stairs to your desk. Situations like this are commonplace for disabled game devs. Writers with invisible disabilities or mental health problems have trouble accessing healthcare or have to justify their absences. While companies have a legal obligation to make reasonable accommodations, disabled folks can still face daily challenges that non-disabled folks never have to consider. As writers, we're also becoming aware of how insidious ableism is in our everyday language. We see how often we use words like "crazy" or "lame" as pejoratives and try to replace those terms with more neutral language like "wild" and "dull." It can be a challenge. When I was working on *Dishonored: Death of the Outsider*, I spoke with a disability consultant about how to write disabled characters like Billie Lurk. The consultant explained the ambivalent relationship that many disabled people have with their prosthetic devices and cautioned us against depicting disabilities as "inspiration porn" that only serves to make non-disabled people feel better.

- **Ageism:** When I first saw the trailer for Housemarque's *Returnal*, I gasped. There, as the central protagonist in a major AAA title, was an older woman. A woman with visible lines and nasolabial folds. A woman who looked like her model had been designed with care and wasn't just a poorly and artificially aged younger model. And her age wasn't presented as a stigma. It's shocking to say this as if it's revolutionary, but in video games, it *is*. Men fare only slightly better. Game companies are still coming to terms with the fact that their market—and their developers—are getting older. I've been in hiring discussions where a veteran writer asked for a high salary—not extraordinarily high, but commensurate with his experience—and one of the managers joked that the studio could hire two mid-level writers for the same price. And don't get me started on those "Thirty Under Thirty" lists. That's what you're up against.

- **Healthcare:** You might be wondering why I put healthcare in this chapter. It's not a contentious issue, is it? If you think that, you're probably not in a marginalized community. You're not a trans man wondering if HRT treatment is covered. You're not a woman in the United States wondering how much longer birth control will be available or if the company health tracker is going to report you to the police if you miscarry a pregnancy. You're not neurodivergent and struggling to get diagnosed for the first time in your life. You're not a Black woman discovering that the company-provided doctors don't listen when you try to get treatment for chronic pain. Healthcare is less of a concern in some countries with socialized medicine that guarantees some kind of treatment, however long you might have to wait. But in places like the United States, healthcare is simply out of reach. For most of my career, and this is true for many USians in games, any sort of preventative healthcare was simply unattainable. The problem is worse for contractors, who might work full time and not have any healthcare at all. As a contractor, I chopped up my finger to the bone in a blender (accidentally) and almost didn't go to the ER. I stared at the bone protruding from my mangled finger and wondered if I could fix it with duct tape. (I didn't. I went to the hospital.) But I hesitated because I had no health insurance and very little money. As a full-time writer on a AAA project! For people who have healthcare, the fear of losing it can keep them in an unsatisfying job.

Even if your employer offers health insurance, your plan might have huge deductibles or low coverage so healthcare is prohibitively expensive. If your wages are low on top of that, then you might not be able to afford it. Even with coverage. When stats show that marginalized folks earn less, this is another area where the -isms can hurt.

- **Maternity and Parenting:** "I need a wife." That's the joke many women crack when they're juggling careers and domestic responsibilities. Add kids to that equation and it becomes more difficult. As we know, the games industry doesn't always provide a good work–life balance under the best circumstances. If your entire studio is crunching until 9:00 every night and you have to leave at 4:30 to pick up your kids, it can look like you're not committed to the project or pulling your weight. Even if you jump online to finish up at home, the optics can be bad. As women are generally the primary caretakers, it can have serious consequences for their careers

I'm going to stop here, but this is a thin slice of the problems people face. I think we all know I could write an encyclopedia of examples and anecdotes related to these prejudices and the others I haven't listed. It's a lot to take in. As some of my examples show, these problems seep into the fabric of your work as a writer.

When Biases Affect Your Work

When game devs transition, they worry it will impact their perceived performance. Willow describes a potential shift in attitude from some studios and the fear of "previously positive assessments suddenly turning negative, missing out on advancements, feeling excluded from social events, or having your feedback ignored or sidelined as you transition." Dealing with bias on top of your usual work is the reality of every marginalized game dev. It can hugely impact the daily creative work of game writers. For Evan, it's meant that his leads sometimes don't value his ideas. They get "shot down as not interesting or not worthy of exploration because they don't resonate with my superiors. I'll pitch something, and it will be centered on a specific experience of a marginalized person or a minority or a Black person. And it will either get changed or taken as not interesting." He believes the judgment is "a subconscious thing" that comes from the industry being "so white and so homogenous, people aren't picking up on the experience that you're trying explain or tell a story about."

Unconscious Bias

The hardest part of being a marginalized writer is often unconscious bias. You have options for battling outright discrimination, but unconscious bias is insidious and tricky and hard to document. It can make you doubt yourself and feel gaslit. After all, your lead respects you! There's no way they wouldn't treat you fairly when it came time for annual reviews … right? The problem with unconscious bias is that it's unconscious. Nobody's doing it on purpose. It's not the overt racism or homophobia of calling someone a slur. It's the rock-solid belief that you hired that guy who's just like you because he's "the best one for the job," not because you unconsciously associate certain traits he has with greater competence. You just don't want to "lower your standards" by hiring for diversity. It's the way your lead prefers your male colleague's pitches because "he's more persuasive" or has meetings with your White report instead of you because "he's easier to talk to." It's most painful when you hear statements like this from people who are generally nice and well-intentioned. They'd be shocked if you told them their behavior was an -ism. The only way to combat this kind of bias is to acknowledge it exists, stop being precious about it, and actively work to counteract it. (Here's another time where I direct you to the internet for advice.) My advice is to gently educate the people around you and ask your studio for unconscious bias training. That should ease the unintentional issues.

"Allies"

Sometimes the people who should help you are the ones you cause the most harm. Rhianna has experienced this with other women writers. She calls it "Highlander Syndrome."

> When I started out, there were very few women working in narrative which meant that we didn't often come across each other to compare notes and offer support. That's definitely changed for the better. However, although the number of women in the industry has increased so too has the culture which seeks to set them up against each other. It pits women against each other and gives them the impression "There can be only one!" and they must vie to be the queen bee on a team. It's nonsense, of course, but I've seen it actively encouraged by male developers and been on the receiving end. In fact, the worst behaviour I've experienced in the industry – which included gaslighting, abusing contacts and trying to block me speaking at conferences - came from another woman who perceived me as a threat. It was heartbreaking.

But this syndrome doesn't just affect women, it affects any writer who feels they have to compete with other marginalized folks for a spot in the industry. Sometimes the people you count on to defend you against problems—leads, advisors, support groups, and allies—actually *are* the problem. People are individuals with ambitions, schemes, and traumas of their own. Give people the benefit of the doubt, but don't assume that someone will help you just because you're both marginalized.

On a final note, be wary of any self-identified ally. There is a special place in Hell for a certain type of progressive dev who is outwardly sympathetic to marginalized communities, but who reaps the benefits of discrimination against them. These are the people who ask what it's like working at Studio X, hear that marginalized folks won't work there because it's terrible, and say, "Well, I should be okay then" and take the job. They enable the entire toxic system.

Enemies

> I live my life such that my very existence pisses off those that would oppress others. Making no enemies means never standing up for what's right.
>
> – Calvin Wong Tze Loon

I have a feeling this might be the line that haunts me most from this book, but here it is: don't be afraid to make enemies. If you stand for anything, if you stand up for yourself or others, you're going to make enemies. Nobody with integrity and a spine is going to be liked by everyone at every studio. It's impossible. The sooner you accept it, the better. This isn't an excuse for bad behavior because "Oh, Anna said it's okay to be mean." That's not what I'm saying at all. What I'm saying is that everyone comes into the workplace with their own set of beliefs and values and you might find yours in direct opposition to someone else. There's a reason that many studios have a "no politics, no religion, no sex" rule for discussions on internal chat. These are all heated, polarizing issues (especially these days) and it's better not to discuss them on the floor. You can try to find common ground with people who don't share your views, but sometimes it's impossible when you believe fundamentally different things. Sometimes their beliefs challenge who you are. I worked with a man who thought women didn't belong in tech. Flat-out thought that women should stay at home and raise kids. How was I, a woman whose mere existence at the studio violated his core belief, supposed to find common ground with him? I couldn't. And, frankly, it wasn't on me to do so. But there's no way you can be collegial with somebody who thinks you don't belong in your job and undermines your work and your career with contemptuous behavior. In situations like that, it's perfectly fine to say, "This person is actively harming me and is therefore my enemy."

Sometimes it's less personal, and you'll see someone doing something that violates the studio's values. Or the law.

Sexual Assault and Physical Abuse

My only advice here is to do what you have to do to protect yourself. I encourage you to tell someone you trust *outside of work* first, whoever that may be, and go from there. I'm not going to pretend that some career advice from me will fix this problem. But if you want justice, or help, or comfort, *please* reach out for it.

Inappropriate Conduct

In theory, inappropriate conduct at work is illegal. Yet, it seems no studio on earth is free of it. It can take many forms, the worst of which are sexual harassment and extreme bullying. What if your lead is sexually harassing someone on your team? Or you. What do you do? If you report them to HR, they might get reprimanded but remain in their role. And they might be aware that you're the one who reported them. They're legally forbidden to retaliate against you or their victim, but guess what? Sometimes they still do. Legally, these are the protected classes:

Protected classes

Sex/Gender	Religion
Age	Pregnancy
Race	Marital status
Disability	Veteran status
National Origin	Genetic information

If you're being discriminated against in any of these categories, don't try to handle the situation on your own. You have legal recourse. Document the hell out of every incident and report it to HR right away. They have legal obligations here and generally take these issues quite seriously. Keep records of the discrimination outside of work. You need to be able to access all your documentation even if you leave suddenly. Also, make sure you're keeping colleagues and friends outside of work informed about your situation. They can both support you and verify your story later on. But the proper legal channel to start with is HR.

A NOTE ABOUT HUMAN RESOURCES

"HR is not your friend." If you've been in the industry for any length of time, you've heard this saying. You see it in articles about abuses and you hear it in whisper networks. For the record, I know a lot of people who work in HR who are lovely people with great intentions. HR does a lot of unsung good in people's daily lives. I've seen it as a hiring manager and been grateful for the support they gave my team during crises. But sometimes HR's mandate conflicts with your individual best interests. In those cases, it's sadly true that HR is not your friend. I'm not talking about edge cases where there's a conflict of interest, such as the head of HR covering up misbehavior because they're dating the abuser. That's a shameful abdication of responsibility regardless of department. Or perhaps the person abusing or harassing you is the CEO or the game director or someone directly tied to studio leadership. Then there's not much HR can do to help. At the end of the day, they've been hired to manage people as a resource for the good of the company. And they might decide that the best thing for the company isn't what's best for you. In those extreme situations, I'm sorry, but you'll have to go outside the studio for help.

I can't emphasize enough that you should give HR a chance to do right by you. Don't assume they won't help you or won't take your problem seriously. Give them a chance. Document everything and hope for the best. If they aren't taking your case seriously and you have no recourse to any internal support group like a union or labor council, then do whatever's best for your well-being and look to outside support groups instead.

Here's where you lean on your friends and allies. Stick together. Document together. Report together. And if things don't get better, leave together. There's power in a united front. I was part of a group of women who exposed a longtime harasser at one company. HR did the right thing and got rid of him, but it was a harrowing experience—being harassed and going through the awful procedure of documenting and describing the mistreatment. Perversely, it brought us all closer. Our shared trauma created a sisterhood of survivors. I'm still friends with those awesome ladies today.

The Answer

Whew, enough of the bad stuff about the industry. I'll bet you're ready to hear solutions to these problems. Well, guess what? I don't have them. Or, rather,

I don't have The Answer that will fix all the problems in the games industry. What I have is advice from your mentor collective. We've all dealt with these problems in the past and have developed strategies for handling them.

Be Heard

What if you find yourself in Evan's spot and your work is being dismissed or judged harshly? What if nobody appreciates your ideas? He recommends "getting a network or a group of people who can validate your work." When you doubt your work or have questions about feedback, then you can "turn to them and say, 'Do you think this was an interesting idea or do you think it wasn't?' It's gaining a system of people that you can trust with your work and show your work to. They'll help you be more confident." Evan says that his confidence grew with time and seniority and he felt more comfortable fighting for his ideas and saying, "no this is worth exploring." But you don't have to wait until you're a senior to defend your ideas. Here are some strategies:

- Frame challenges as questions. For example, if your client thinks the lead character should be White, but you wrote her as Black. Calmly ask questions like, "That's an interesting direction! Can you walk me through why we need the change? What are the character requirements?" Make them justify their choices but in a pleasant way. Your attitude should be open and curious, not combative. Even if you have to grit your teeth into a smile, it's important that you appear relaxed and friendly so they don't start arguing with you.
- Talk it through. Hear what they have to say. Sometimes there's a good reason for what they want. Sometimes not. Find out which one it is.
- Back it up. Make sure you're bringing data to discussions so it's not a matter of differing opinions. If they're saying "Well, I think the character should be a guy" and you're saying "Studies indicate that player bases like ours prefer female protagonists by a ratio of 3:1 and are more likely to spend money on cosmetic items for a woman ..." Then you're arguing from a professional, informed place and not defending your opinion. It's not about you anymore; it's them vs. the data.
- Yes them to death. I learned this skill as a bartender! Say yes even when you're saying no. If they want you to change something, never say no. If your client says, "I don't like dark hair. Make her a blonde." Then you respond with something like "Changing her hair is a great idea! I'll talk to the artists about a different look for her." It sounds like you agreed to what they want, but you've actually bought yourself a chance to repitch the dark hair in another look. Worth a shot, right?

I realize these are very granular examples, but you can apply them to the big stuff too. The main thing is to not let Imposter Syndrome drag you down. You're an experienced professional with good ideas and a body of work behind you. Stay pleasant and reasonable during heated arguments and keep the focus on the issues, not you or your abilities. It can feel deeply personal at times, I know, but force yourself to step back and stay calm. It's okay to say, "I need some time to consider this issue. I'll get back to you," and pick up the discussion again when you've cooled off.

Know When to Stop

For me, the hardest part is learning when to let go. Sometimes, the client or your boss or colleague is right and they're making the call based on data you don't have access to. Fair enough. Sometimes they're wrong, but you're not going to win. You have to learn to recognize when to stop arguing. That's been the hardest part of game dev for me. When I know my idea is good, but I have to settle for someone's less-good idea. It happens. Know when you're beating your head against a wall and walk away. You'll be less frustrated. Try to find a compromise with them so you can get the important part of what you want in the game. That ballet of give and take, remember? It's very easy to get labeled "difficult" as a marginalized person in games, so you have to learn to walk the line between compromise and making work you believe in. People's confidence in you will come from a series of interactions where you demonstrate your knowledge and skill. And even then, some people aren't going to respect you. They never will. It's not fair. It's horrifically unfair, in fact. But that's the world we're working in.

Real Allies

From WIT organizations to groups like Black Girl Gamers to Pride discords, there is growing support for marginalized groups in the games industry. They'll understand what resources are available to you and what legal recourse you have. In some cases, they can provide legal aid or advice. Rather than sit here and list all the help they can give, I'd rather point you to them and encourage you to reach out. But please remember that orgs like these have their own problems and limitations too. Problematic people can find their way into these orgs under the guise of being allies or members, and then take advantage of the people there. It's not the norm by any means, but it happens. I'm not saying this to discourage you, but rather to advise you to go in with caution. Be wary, but give them chance. Hopefully, you can get the help you need.

Organized Labor Groups

Increasingly, game developers are forming unions to secure better benefits and treatment at AAA studios. If you're unable to find the resources you need through your studio or support groups, then reach out to a labor group. Some studios have formed their own unions, like Activision-Blizzard's ABK, while places like Sweden have national organizations like Unionen. Game writers have had mixed success with our trade guilds. WGGB invited game writers and NDs into the guild with open arms, while WGAW in the United States has been less welcoming. There are too many developments happening on the labor front to list here. I suspect the information in this section will be woefully out of date by the time this book gets to you.

Mentoring

Of course, I have to mention mentoring! I hope this book has shown you the value of having an experienced writer to guide you. But my book wouldn't exist if finding a mentor was easy. There are groups that offer limited mentorships, like Limit Break, and there are some spreadsheets for mentoring volunteers floating around out there. Nobody has vetted the list, so dig out your saltshaker one last time. Apply the credentials test to mentors same as you would any instructor. It's also worth setting up a mentorship program at your studio. See if you can get management to support the idea and throw some money at it. Barring that, set up a monthly sync with someone at your studio, maybe someone who's doing the job you want. And don't be afraid to approach people you admire for advice! Nobody's going to get upset if you message them and respectfully ask a few questions. They might not have time to help you, but they won't mind if you ask. So ask!

Be a Mentor

> It's not on already-marginalised people to make things better, it's up to privileged non-marginalised individuals and organisations not to pull the ladder up after them.
>
> —Ed Stern, Lead Writer, Splash Damage

You don't have to wait until you've been in games for decades to be a mentor. You can reach out and support juniors at any stage of your career. Once you've learned how to navigate any part of the games industry, pass that knowledge along! However, it's especially important for non-marginalized writers to reach out and lift up their juniors. Eevi lists some simple ways you can help.

> Seek out and lift up marginalized voices whenever you have the power to do so. Take time to diversify your media consumption – read, listen and watch media produced by marginalized people. But when you inevitably get inspired by them, don't just steal their ideas and culture. Pay them actual money for their time, their talks, their consultancy. Hire them, preferably! And not just as juniors, get them into positions of leadership and seniority in your company.

She acknowledges that this work entails looking hard at yourself and your company culture to find problems and the courage to fix them. Ann's advice is simpler: "My god, just – fight like hell" to make games a better place for everyone.

Whisper Networks

Sometimes when big revelations about abuse hit the headlines, marginalized people in your life shrug and say that they already knew. Sexual predators, "broken stairs"[5] and abusive leaders are all notorious in their communities before they hit the news. Talking to people is your best way to protect yourself. Asking around in SIGs and support groups can help you tap into whisper networks. These network groups aren't infallible, but sometimes they can confirm your gut feeling about someone. Which brings me to …

Trust Your Gut

If you think something is wrong, it probably is. Mary wishes she'd trusted herself more "when it comes to sensing and responding to abusive or disrespectful behavior." Early in her career she'd convince herself that she was overreacting to toxic behavior or not giving others a chance. "That led to me ignoring very real warnings about the way certain people and studios treated me, and it took much longer for me to break free of toxic relationships." Don't stay somewhere that makes you miserable. Trust yourself and get out.

---

[5] That predator in your friend group or at your studio that everyone knows about, but nobody does anything about.

Open Up

As time passes, the friends you made while trying to break into the industry will get jobs at other game companies—or perhaps your own studio. Your current colleagues will move on to rival companies. Or you'll move on to another studio and leave them behind. You'll encounter the same faces time and time again. The games industry is a kaleidoscope of shifting pieces, their patterns forming, breaking, and assembling in new configurations. Through all the rotations and permutations, you'll still be friends—albeit friends who are on different sides of an NDA. One thing I wish people understood was how silly studio rivalries are for working devs. Most devs will switch studios several times in their career. As you can see from this book, I have colleagues in every corner of the industry; companies and consoles don't matter to our friendships. Do I speak openly to them about release dates, project details, or studio plans? Abso-fracking-lutely not. Do I confide in them about a difficult coworker or how much I hate spreadsheets or ask for advice on creating better casting materials? You better believe it. Be smart and don't blow your NDA, but feel free to enjoy some of the most rewarding friendships you'll ever have.

Break the Rules

Kim wants you to worry less about NDAs and more about practices around them. Not violating your NDA doesn't mean "protecting a company that's working poorly. For me, it's never going to cover like, 'Hey, this person's racist to me on the daily' or 'Hey, this person is talking down to me in meetings.'" The important thing to remember is that "the rules don't exist for you. The reason you're having problems is because of the rules that exist, so you cannot listen to them."

Refusing to play by the rules helped her do better work and actively fix problems on the project. You know the narrative hierarchy, but you have to understand that there are unspoken rules about who can talk to whom in that system. It's unusual for, say, a junior writer to routinely email the creative director. But Kim consciously broke that rule.

> It took breaking my view of the system in order to work within it and to understand where I could actually move. To say, "Hey, creative director, this isn't working. I see a problem." And obviously that's not always going to be received well. Only do it if you feel safe. But if it's an avenue that you can pursue, always try to find ways to advocate for yourself in those spaces. Or try to break the chain of command if that command is being unkind or oppressive to you. It's worth finding ways to work collectively.

Don't Get Pigeonholed

I remember the first time I was asked to talk about game writing instead of what it's like being a woman in games. It sounds strange, but that's when I knew I'd made it. I was successful enough as a writer that people saw that instead of my gender. Toiya says being pigeonholed by your marginalization is common—and it's a trap.

> If you get invited to speak somewhere, it's to talk about being marginalized in the industry or how to write marginalized characters. Your team members want you to give a monolithic perspective about marginalization to make the game's representation better. There's nothing wrong with discussing these issues, but it should be because you're wanting to address them, not because you're the token in the room.

She managed to avoid this trap and carve out her own niche, by moderating panels about writing and by teaching game narrative workshops. "The other thing that helped was being around a narrative community that wasn't labeling me as a marginalized writer. I was just a writer."

Even When It's Bad, It's Good

Finding a group of people to be open with makes all the difference for marginalized writers. It's the greatest gift you can give yourself. I spent the first eight years of my career feeling alone as a game writer. I didn't really know any other successful game writers or have friendships with the few I did know outside work. Then one day I went to ECGC. It's a smaller con in North Carolina with a Narrative track run by Richard Dansky. That was the first time I sat in a room completely surrounded by people who understood the work I do and what it means to me. There were 20 other game writers, with varying levels of experience, and they all *got* me in a way nobody ever had before. I was just coming out of bad burnout, and I was still pretty sick. My self-esteem was circling the drain, and I was creatively broken. I wondered if there was a place for me in video games or if I should find a different career entirely. Talking to those writers made me remember why I was in games. It made me remember why I love interactive writing. Their kindness, their acceptance of me as a fellow writer, made me feel welcome. For the first time in my career as a game writer, I felt like I belonged to a community. I saw a place for myself in the industry and a path forward. That convention, that community, changed my life. It saved my career. I stayed in games because I found it. I'm in games now because of it. That's what it means to have friendships with your fellow writers. That's finding your community. It's that important. And it helps every problem in this book.

CHALLENGE

This one's simple: Go out into the world, find someone doing the exact work you want to do, and ask them to mentor you.

Conclusion

So here we are, at the end of my advice. Twenty years of industry experience condensed into a few hundred pages. I said so much, but barely scratched the surface of what you need to know. Perhaps you read this book in a few hours or days, but for me, it's been many long months of steady writing. I began this literary venture in December 2021 and I submitted the manuscript in August 2022. Those months are a blur of words and interviews, yet a few memories stand out: The mystery of Speaker 3 haunting my transcripts. That night Word got possessed and sent me a cryptic message (That's it. That's all recruiters need. That's it. That's all recruiters need. That's it. That's all recruiters need). And all the times I despaired of finishing this work and the writing community rose up to support me through my doubt.

If you remember nothing else from this book, I hope you remember my final lesson: even when it's bad, it's good. Your experience in games will have its ups and downs like any career would. You'll work at studios that support you and studios that don't. Some of your games will win awards, and some games will flop. Your passion for games and game writing will wax and wane. Sometimes you'll question why you're in the industry at all, and some days you won't want to be anywhere else. You'll share your adventure with friends and colleagues. You'll swap resume tips as new writers and shout "congratulations!" for each new job. You'll brainstorm story ideas together in the giddy early days of Prepro, and console each other through the hard cuts and reworks of Production. You'll speak on panels together, and do interviews, and craft a trailer for a game you all love. You'll hold your breath together when the game is announced and pop champagne at the release party. And above all else, you'll grow together as writers. You'll watch your colleagues' skills improve over time, and you'll see your own work grow stronger, deeper, and better. You'll learn, as your mentors promised, to trust your writing and yourself.

The quotes that begin each chapter are answers to a single question: "What one thing does every game writer need to know?" The responses, many from writers I admire intensely, illuminate every aspect of game writing: our craft, our careers, our ambitions, and our creative struggles. I hope you're as fascinated as I am to see what writers value and consider significant. The heartbreaking part of writing this book was reducing hours of interviews and insights into, in many cases, a single pithy pull quote. (Oh, the knowledge lost to the cutting room floor!) But there's one answer that encompasses the message of this entire book, and I want to share it in full. So here, now, at the end, are Sam Lake's words of wisdom:

> In my experience, in practical terms, writing for games is iterative teamwork. This, for someone dreaming to be a game writer, is the one thing you should know. This one thing then translates into several things.
>
> It's vital to understand what the game is to write a story for it. Your story can be the best story ever, but if it doesn't fit into the game, create a dialogue with the game, it will not turn out good. You should work hard to understand the storytelling methods and tools available for this game to tell the story. And the budget and the cost of these methods, the scope. The better you understand this, the better you can tailor the story to fit the scope. Once again, the story can be brilliant, but if the tools you have are not the right tools to tell it properly it will not turn out good.
>
> You need the team to turn your writing into a game. You need to sell the story to them, make them as excited about it as you are. But you also need to understand that when they get excited about it, they will feel it's their story as well, and they will have opinions about the story. You should be willing to take their feedback and find ways to use it when you write new drafts of the story, or if some of their ideas don't work, take the time to make them see why they don't work, why something else works better.
>
> You will need to change the story. There are a million reasons. There are many good reasons, and then there are reasons that are not that great, but they are still there. Technical reasons, creative reasons, schedule reasons, budget and resource reasons. You should always talk this through with the team to make sure the reason is valid. If it is, you should not fight it. You should make sure the cost of the change is understood, but beyond that you should be willing to make changes. You should embrace this, you should be excited about it, you should see it as an opportunity to make the story, and the game, better. Every change is an opportunity to find ways to make the story better. Sometimes this is not possible, but you should try, take it as a challenge. You should roll with the punches and hit the ground running. You should learn to love the change.

Some of the reasons to change the story are commercial reasons. Unless you are making a small indie game, you are making a product that is expected to make profit. It's business. Some of the notes might be that it needs to be simpler, safer, to make sure it doesn't offend anyone, that it's not too difficult. Or that it needs to be done faster, that quality doesn't matter that much. My screenwriting teacher, Pentti Halonen, once told me that our job is to find ways to hide art into our work. I think it's our duty. If you don't need to hide it, then great, congratulations, you are in a writer's paradise. But often, its value might not be understood, and with that you need to hide it to be able to keep it. Because we should always strive to make art. And if art is not wanted, we should disguise it, but still, always, always, we should put it there. Go the extra mile, find ways to elevate it. It's important for your own sake, for all of us, for the audience, even if they don't know it. How do you know what's art in this case? Art is subjective, and this art is your art. You will know. You will feel it. It's the sharper edges. It's what thrills you. It's what makes you feel proud. It's passion and it's what makes this work worth it.

My teacher also told me another thing, and this is a thing of mercy. Sometimes the work can be stressful. Yes, you should always aim to do your best and you should always be ambitious. But you should never fall into the trap of thinking that your best effort today can or needs to be your all-time best work, that you should only be satisfied with your all-time best. It very rarely is, because of, well, life. You should aim to create the best work you can today, given whatever the current circumstances are, and then be happy and satisfied with that. To me, this has been a very comforting thought through many years of working as a writer.

If I could presume to offer advice on top of Sam's, it would be to enjoy your collaborations. We make some of the most extraordinary stories the world has ever known. We dream new worlds into being and then convince a team of brilliant people to help us craft them into reality. It's magical work, but it's *hard*. Don't do it alone.

Don't get worried or panicked because you're not moving up as fast as you think you should or because you're comparing your career to someone else's. Remember why you're here in the industry, and find the right path to satisfy your goals. Those 30 Under 30 lists are poison and ageism is a terrible problem in the games industry. Go at your own pace, measure your progress against where you've been and how far you've come, and take the path that makes you happiest. Be kind to yourself.

Writing this book has been a journey (don't say it), but it's brought me a measure of peace in this burning world. I found reassurance in the wisdom of the people I interviewed. We commiserated over broken systems, and they inspired me with their brilliance and compassion. I found comrades striving to create a better world. I found deep generosity and kindness and eagerness to lend a helping hand. Above all, I found a new love for the games industry. I thought I knew it all after twenty years, but I learned so much while writing this book. I found corners of the gaming world I'd never seen before and met people making games with fresh voices and visions for the future. I want to stay in this industry and make games with them. I want you to join us. I hope you will. I hope I help you make it here. And I hope to work with you soon.

Printed in the United States
by Baker & Taylor Publisher Services

Printed in the United States
by Baker & Taylor Publisher Services